NATO and the European Union:
Confronting the Challenges of European Security and Enlargement

Conference Papers I

ISBN 1-882160-04-5

CONTENTS

PREFACE AND ACKNOWLEDGMENTS

This volume is the product of a significant cooperative venture involving a number of organizations. Originally conceived as a workshop sponsored by Kent State University's Lemnitzer Center for NATO and European Union Studies and the European Community Studies Association (ECSA), the project progressively assumed larger proportions with the inclusion of other parties. Ultimately, an international conference, "NATO and the European Union: Confronting the Challenges of European Security Cooperation," convened on October 16-18, 1997, in Thessaloniki Greece during that city's tenure as "Cultural Capital of Europe."

The Hellenic Foundation for European and Foreign Policy (ELIAMEP) in Athens, Greece and the American College of Thessaloniki (ACT) joined as cosponsors of the conference. Dr. William McGrew, president of ACT, graciously offered the fine facilities of his campus and members of his skilled staff to oversee local arrangements. We are most grateful for their efforts and also for the special roles of Dr. Spyros Philippas, head of academic affairs in the NATO Office of Information and Press, who supplied important advice on the conference's organization, and of Spyros Pappas, director general of information, communication, culture, and audiovisual in the European Commission, who provided encouragement and guidance at a critical juncture. Holger Pfeiffer, NATO's deputy assistant secretary general for defense planning and policy, supplied insights into NATO's positions with his presentation, "NATO Enlargement, Partnership for Peace, European Security and Defense Identity."

Apart from the contributions of the Lemnitzer Center, ECSA, and ACT toward meeting the conference's costs, vital funding came from the NATO Office of Information and Press in Brussels. The office of the European Commission in Athens also granted assistance. Additionally, the Greek Ministry of Macedonia-Thrace hosted an evening reception for participants. We extend our thanks and appreciation to these organizations.

S. Victor Papacosma
Lemnitzer Center for NATO
   and European Union Studies
Kent State University

Pierre-Henri Laurent
European Community Studies
   Association
Tufts University

About the Contributors

GIANCARLO CHEVELLARD is head of security issues in the Commission of the European Union in Brussels. Formerly, he served as director of foreign policy planning in the Commission and as director of press and public affairs in the European Community delegation in Washington, D.C.

THEODORE COULOUMBIS is professor of international relations at the University of Athens and general secretary of the Hellenic Foundation for European and Foreign Policy. He received his Ph.D. from the American University and taught there from 1965 to 1982, after which he returned to Greece for a position at the University of Thessaloniki before moving to the University in Athens in 1989. Among his many publications are *Greek Political Reaction to American and NATO Influences* (1966), *The United States, Greece, and Turkey: The Troubled Triangle* (1983), and *International Relations: Power and Justice* (1990), coauthored with James Wolfe.

ANTHONY FORSTER has his M.A. and Ph.D. in European politics from Oxford University and is lecturer in politics at the University of Nottingham. He has published widely on European security issues and British foreign policy, including articles in *Survival* and *Journal of Theoretical Politics*. He is currently completing a book manuscript, "Britain and the Negotiation of the Maastricht Treaty," to be published by Macmillan/St. Martin's Press in 1999.

LAWRENCE S. KAPLAN is university professor emeritus of history and director emeritus of the Lemnitzer Center for NATO and European Union Studies at Kent State University. He is now a contract historian at the Department of Defense, adjunct professor at Georgetown University, and visiting lecturer at the University of Maryland. His long list of publications includes *A Community of Interests: NATO and the Military Assistance Program, 1948-1951* (1980), *The United States and NATO: The Formative Years* (1984), and *NATO and the United States: An Enduring Alliance* (1988). He has also edited six volumes based on the proceedings of Lemnitzer conferences or projects.

RICHARD L. KUGLER received his Ph.D. in political science from the Massachusetts Institute of Technology and is distinguished research professor in the Institute for National Strategic Studies of the National Defense University. His many publications include *The Future U.S. Military Presence in Europe: Forces and Requirements for the Post-Cold War Era* (1992), *Commitment to Pursue: How Alliance Partnership Won the Cold War* (1993), *Toward a Dangerous World: U.S. National Security Strategy for the Coming Turbulence* (1995), and *Enlarging NATO: The Russian Factor* (1996) with Marianna V. Koziatseva.

PIERRE-HENRI LAURENT is professor of history at Tufts University, acquired his Ph.D. from Boston University, and has specialized interests in the origins of European integration and institutions and U.S.-European Union relations. He has written extensively on these and related fields, also editing *The European Community: To Maastricht and Beyond* (1994) and coediting *The State of the European Union: Widening and Deepening* (1997).

IGOR F. MAXIMYTCHEV is a department head in the Institute of Europe of the Russian Academy of Sciences in Moscow. Earlier, he had a distinguished career as a Soviet diplomat, specializing in European affairs and retiring at the rank of minister extraordinary and plenipotentiary. He has published numerous articles and several books in Russian.

S. VICTOR PAPACOSMA, professor of history and director of the Lemnitzer Center for NATO and European Union Studies at Kent State University, received his Ph.D. from Indiana University. He has written extensively on Balkan issues and particularly on twentieth-century Greek politics. Among his publications are *The Military in Greek Politics: The 1909 Coup d'État* (1977), *Politics and Culture in Greece* (1988), and coedited volumes of Lemnitzer Center conference proceedings, *Europe's Neutral and Nonaligned States: Between NATO and the Warsaw Pact* (1988), *NATO after Forty Years* (1990), and *NATO in the Post-Cold War Era: Does It Have a Future?* (1995).

STEPHEN L. REARDEN received his Ph.D. from Harvard University and is now with the History Office of the Joint Chiefs of Staff. His publications include *The Evolution of American Strategic Doctrine: Paul H. Nitze and the Soviet Challenge* (1984), *History of the Office of the Secretary of Defense: The Formative Years, 1947-1950* (1984), and *The Origins of the U.S. Nuclear Strategy: 1945-1953* (1993).

PETER SCHMIDT is a specialist in security studies with the Stiftung Wissenschaft und Politik in Ebenhausen and has coedited *Security and Arms Control: Integration and Security in Western Europe* (1992).

STANLEY R. SLOAN acquired a M.I.A. at Columbia University and is now the senior specialist in international security policy at the Congressional Research Service of the Library of Congress. Among his extensive publications are *Conventional Arms Control and Europe's Future* (1989), *NATO in the 1990s* (edited, 1989), *NATO's Future: Beyond Collective Defense* (1995), and *The U.S. Role in the 21st Century World* (1997).

MICHAEL E. SMITH is completing his Ph.D. requirements at the University of California, Irvine, in political science. He has served as MacArthur Fellow at the University of California Institute of Global Conflict and Cooperation, as Fulbright Fellow in Brussels, and as visiting researcher in the Centre for European Policy in Brussels. His publications have appeared in *German Politics and Society* and volumes 3 and 4 of *The State of the European Union.*

THANOS VEREMIS acquired his Ph.D. in history at Oxford University, is professor of political history at the University of Athens, and serves as president of the Hellenic Foundation for European and Foreign Policy. Included among his many publications are *Greece's Balkan Entanglement* (1995) and *The Greek Military in Politics: From Independence to Democracy* (1997).

VLADIMIR VERES was educated in Belgrade and Moscow and is now deputy director of the Center for Strategic Studies in Belgrade. His research and writing focus on Yugoslav and Balkan strategic issues.

INTRODUCTION

S. Victor Papacosma
Pierre-Henri Laurent

Although their headquarters stand in rather close proximity to each other in Brussels and eleven of their member-states belong to both organizations, NATO and the European Union (EU) have not experienced trouble-free paths in developing policies–either independently or bilaterally–for security, political, and economic challenges in the evolving post-Cold War era. When one reflects on Europe immediately after World War II and the origins of NATO, one might question why the two organizations would have to discuss security issues with each other. After all, Western European leaders supported the formation of NATO in 1949 as a means to draw the United States out of its traditional peacetime isolation and to involve it actively in Europe in the campaign to contain Communist expansion, objectives shared by the Truman administration. Washington also fostered strongly the development of this transatlantic security relationship to encourage Western Europe's reorganization as a more integrated economic and political entity that could eventually assume an equal partnership with the United States.

Success followed in both endeavors, albeit with intermittent difficulties. Without firing a shot in combat, the Atlantic Alliance persevered, the Warsaw Pact disbanded, the Soviet Union collapsed, and the Cold War ended. NATO had offered requisite military security, allowing Western Europe to embark on its integrative program with the European Coal and Steel Community (1951) and then the European Economic Community (1957). The original six nations have now evolved into the fifteen-member European Union, the world's largest trading bloc with a population approaching 400 million and a combined GDP of more than eight trillion dollars. Of considerable significance, Europeans who had been at war with each other in previous decades, such as the French and Germans, have reaped the greater benefits of working together militarily and economically in a half century of peace.

NATO and Western European integration had worked well in tandem to forge military, political, and economic security for millions of people. But the Cold War's end generated new uncertainties in the world, particularly in Europe, with reordered geostrategic, political, and economic realities. The former Communist states of Eastern Europe and the former Soviet Union, especially Russia, had to be evaluated with different criteria. NATO, which had succeeded so well in another era and has heard so few calls for its dissolution in the present, is now seeking to reorient its mission as a collective defense organization to accommodate new conditions. The European Union, on its long road to enhanced political integration and monetary union, is working, among other objectives, for the development of a common foreign and security policy (CFSP). Concurrently, both organizations have launched enlargement programs that constitute their highest priority projects and the most critical components of emerging policy. Establishing clear-cut objectives and appropriate implementation of strategy in both institutions, however, has been difficult and encumbered by many considerations, some of which are historical in their origins.

1

America's role in Europe after 1945, initially domineering in political and economic areas, has waned over the decades. Economic integration served Western Europe well in generating economic strength and greater self-confidence. Militarily, however, the United States stands unchallenged as the planet's lone superpower and obviously as the most powerful member of NATO. Attempts to contest Washington's predominant role in NATO surfaced prior to 1989, most notably with France's Charles de Gaulle in the 1960s, but all failed generally to alter the distribution of influence within the alliance. Indeed, European efforts, such as the revival under French instigation of the Western European Union (WEU) in 1984 after a long period of dormancy, proved halfhearted. Nonetheless, the altered political and strategic environment following communism's demise in conjunction with the "deepening" policy of European Community leaders importantly added some momentum to efforts at forging greater European autonomy in defense and security matters.

Exclusively European solutions for European problems, such as the crisis in the former Yugoslavia that erupted in the early summer of 1991, were not easily available, in part because of the intra-European Community's primary attention to establishing and then meeting the political and monetary requirements in the Treaty of European Union signed at Maastricht in December 1991. This momentous document also committed the member-states to pursue the institutionalization of a common foreign and security policy and confirmed a mission for the WEU as the defense component of the EC and European pillar of NATO. One month before Maastricht's signing, NATO approved at Rome a new strategic concept and call for associated force structures that could assume a greater role for multinational formations in support of the UN or the then CSCE (Conference on Security and Cooperation in Europe) peace missions. In December 1992, NATO confirmed its readiness to support on a case-by-case basis peacekeeping operations under the authority of the UN Security Council, which had the primary responsibility for international peace and security.

The widening conflict in Southeastern Europe provided a backdrop for a number of NATO's decisions. The European Community had been the first international organization that attempted to broker peace in the former Yugoslavia shortly after Slovenia and Croatia declared their secessions on 25 June 1991. Subsequently, the United Nations, CSCE, and WEU involved themselves, and the main fighting front shifted to Bosnia and Herzegovina in the early spring of 1992. The multipronged international involvement failed to bring peace to the region and reflected the consequences of a new-style crisis situation (at least for the post-1945 era) on the European continent and the dearth of crisis management capabilities. Ultimately, after some delay the active military roles of NATO and the United States, following a tortuous path, forced an end to the fighting and influenced the signing of the Dayton Agreements in November 1995. NATO oversaw the organization of the multinational Implementation Force (IFOR) for securing the peace in Bosnia that also included Russia and other former Warsaw Pact states within its ranks.

The transatlantic connection within NATO had asserted itself in the 1990s. There was tacit acknowledgment by Europeans that a truly European organization mirroring common and exclusively European policy decisions was premature and that the indispensable role of U.S. involvement in extending European security was a fundamental factor. In the interim there had been some activity to bolster the European pillar, such as the formation in 1992 of the Eurocorps, initially composed of French and German forces, and the adoption of the European Security and Defense Identity (ESDI) by NATO members at their Brussels summit in January 1994. The latter is a deliberate venture by European members of NATO, approved by the United States, to develop a collective identity in security and defense matters both within NATO and separable from it. Additionally, NATO also approved the concept of the Combined Joint Task Force (CJTF) for use primarily in out-of-area operations by NATO or the WEU with the potential involvement of non-NATO forces.

On the EU side, the summit in June 1997 approved the Treaty of Amsterdam, which included statements favoring the future integration of the WEU into the EU but also emphasizing that the CFSP must not prejudice the specific character of existing security and defense policies of member-states and must respect NATO obligations. These modest, compromise positions reflected the continued existence of divisions within the EU inhibiting more bold initiatives for the establishment of a truly viable CFSP.

The situation of the Central and East European countries (CEEC) and Russia raised a full range of concerns for NATO and the EU member-states as they formed policies to draw these recast states into the Western European sphere. Instead of containing these states militarily, as in the Cold War, Western policy now sought to integrate them. An important step in this direction came with the NATO Brussels summit in January 1994 that accepted the American-inspired Partnership for Peace (PFP). This initiative was designed to incorporate all European states respecting democratic institutions within a framework for operational military cooperation and multinational security efforts that would have NATO at its core. CEEC responded quickly and positively to this opportunity, but many also saw the PFP as an insufficient halfway house on the route toward the greatly desired full membership. After considerable debate and disarray, NATO's July 1997 Madrid summit sanctioned limited enlargement to three states: the Czech Republic, Hungary, and Poland. The prospect of NATO's further "widening" is not excluded as other CEEC queue up in anticipation of joining their former adversary. Concern about the possible alienation and isolation of Russia influenced strategic assessments and resulted in the NATO Russian Founding Act in May 1997 that provided the Russians a minimal comfort level about NATO perched at their doorstep.

The EU began its own "widening" efforts in the late 1980s with the PHARE (Poland-Hungary Assistance for Economic Reconstruction) program, and then the European Agreements of 1991 extended EC ties with other CEEC. Based on Article 238 of the EC Treaty, these first agreements had an association formula. At Copenhagen in 1993, however, internal EC and external pressures resulted in the approval of an accession policy for new Eastern applicants as soon as they could assume some basic obligatory economic and political criteria. Between late 1993 and June 1996, ten Eastern states applied, and in Luxembourg in December 1997, the

European Council endorsed the Commission recommendation to open negotiations for full membership. It did so by slating a larger list of candidates for later entry as well as a short list of five CEEC (the Czech Republic, Estonia, Hungary, Poland, Slovenia) plus Cyprus, which, it was said, could expect a more rapid admission. There turned out to be less certainty about a timetable for this process because of EU attention to satisfying commitments to "deepening" policies and monetary union first and also because of the potential of these transforming economies to meet the minimum economic performance threshold for full membership.

Political conditions in and military threats from the former Soviet Union and Eastern Europe more than five decades ago had inspired the formation of NATO and, tangentially, of Western European economic integration. Now NATO and the European Union were attempting to respond to the altered environment to the east and to the other security-related issues associated with the post-Communist era. The essays in this volume are designed to shed detailed light on and analyze the complex institutional, regional, and national dimensions of European security problems and the evolving roles of NATO and the European Union in confronting them.

Lawrence S. Kaplan provides important background commentary for evaluating the critical relationship of the United States with Western Europe. Basic to the history of NATO is the existence of Atlanticists and Europeanists within its ranks with their fundamental debate that centers on the role of the organization's superpower and the relations of European member-states with it. As the European Community increased its membership to twelve by the mid-1980s and the Cold War closed, the prospect of a Europe without the United States seemed less farfetched than it had twenty years earlier when de Gaulle preached this course of action, particularly since the Soviet threat no longer loomed on the horizon and economic competition increased in the world marketplace. Kaplan posits whether Americans might have created a Frankenstein in their earlier efforts "to rebuild and remold Europe along American lines after World War II." Currently, in a period of policy transition, the transatlantic relationship is experiencing challenges, but the author concludes that attainment of a federated Europe depends on the continued existence and supporting role of the Atlantic Alliance.

In the absence of the East-West rivalry that lasted more than four decades, policymakers have experienced difficulties in formulating strategy to contend with dangers such as terrorism, ethnic rivalries, and resurgent nationalism. Steven L. Rearden relates that the strategic reorientation has not been totally smooth and is made more complicated by NATO's program for enlargement and the organizational problems associated with the development of new force and command structures. Moreover, that NATO no longer is the sole institution for provision of European security constitutes a new reality. Europe's attempts at providing viable alternatives, such as the WEU, EU, and OSCE (Organization for Security and Cooperation in Europe), albeit with diminished capabilities, pose organizational challenges for NATO, which must accommodate the concerns of the United States and European states, particularly France. Rearden maintains that American influence in NATO policy making is less than in earlier decades, notwithstanding European claims to the contrary, and that the focus of U.S. foreign and defense policy is shifting to regions other than Europe, such as Asia and the Pacific.

According to Stanley R. Sloan, NATO remains the prime institutional and ideological bridge between the United States and Europe. Despite the existence of other institutions, such as the European Union, WEU, and OSCE, it is NATO that provides the allies with the integrated structure and capabilities for daily interaction, acting together "in a principled defense of their common interests" and espousing a community of values. But the enlargement and burdensharing debates on both sides of the Atlantic and the perception of European states–and not just of France–that the United States assumes a hegemonic posture toward its allies have complicated policy making in the alliance. Indeed, the role of the United States, as the world's superpower, is a difficult one and requires a more sensitive execution of policy objectives so as not to antagonize allies. If the European Union proceeds only slowly and marginally toward greater political integration, the supreme position of the United States in the Atlantic Alliance will be assured. Sloan asserts that the United States and Europe have no practical alternatives and that they must continue their defense cooperation within the NATO structure.

Departing from the generally Americanocentric approach of the above essays, Michael E. Smith details European positions. Initiatives to develop more regionally oriented European security policy as a counter to the domineering role of Atlantic multilateral security cooperation have tested the ingenuity and resolve of European leaders since the end of the Cold War. Smith contends that the EU has sought to increase its military capabilities at the expense of existing strengths in foreign policy (e.g., its formidable economic power and emerging social welfare structure). Alternatively, Smith acknowledges that EU limitations in the defense area are numerous and that it may be a stronger force for long-term security by using socioeconomic tools rather than military ones.

Expanding on official EU positions, Giancarlo Chevellard forwards that EU enlargement is largely dictated by security considerations akin to those that had originally spawned the movement toward European integration after World War II–that is, integration and mutual dependence among erstwhile enemy countries provides the best protection against new European civil wars. In a new spillover policy, the EU is committed to extending the stability solidified in the West to the East and in return will receive political and economic benefits. In order for enlargement to succeed, the EU must concurrently implement widespread internal reforms. Thus, the EU and NATO are following different paths toward enlargement in terms of "who," "when," and "how," but these divergences should not contribute to tension. In turn, the transatlantic relationship is critical for both enlargement processes, and the enlarged EU and the United States and Canada "should develop a full partnership between equals within the enlarged Atlantic Alliance."

A member of the RAND Corporation team that contributed significantly to the drafting of the enlargement policy and strategy adopted by NATO and the United States, Richard Kugler evaluates opposing positions to this program. Prior to the

Madrid summit of July 1997, the loudest criticism of enlargement came from liberal quarters that had focused on concern over potentially damaged relations with Russia. As these apprehensions diminished, more conservatively inclined critics–mostly Americans and only a small number of Europeans–raised their voices, fearful that enlargement would be enacted in a weak, unwise manner that would damage NATO and Europe. Rather than opposing outright the goal of enlargement, they aspire to influence the process with policy objectives that stress the need for firmness and requisite willpower. In presenting the conservative agenda, Kugler does not dismiss all parts of it but is critical of the tendency to promote fears that seem overstated.

Basic to the development of policy in NATO and the EU are the positions of individual member-states. Two are treated here to illustrate complex aspects of the decision-making process in multinational organizations. Anthony Forster underscores the differing stances assumed by Britain on NATO and EU enlargements. British governments have publicly maintained that there is no linkage between the two programs, reluctantly supporting expanding membership for NATO and heartily backing it for the EU. Concurrently, Britain, consistently averse to the formation of a strictly European defense organization, considers the WEU to be a useful organization to thwart EU moves to develop increased security responsibilities. Forster concludes that London's position on enlargement is presented in such a way as not to alter the essential character of NATO and the EU–to do contrariwise would jeopardize Britain's strategic interests in both.

As Peter Schmidt points out, Germany has advocated policies in the EU and NATO of "deepening" before "widening" as the best approach to avoiding any potentially adverse effects of German unification on the European political order. Germany became the principal exponent of EU enlargement but faltered in its efforts to oversee a significant "deepening first," thereby presaging future difficulties. Within NATO, Germany, cultivating close ties with both France and the United States, assumes an intermediary position in the intra-alliance disputes of the two. Because Germany's foreign and security policy in Europe embraces a primarily institutional orientation, the strong backing of deepening and enlargement has and will continue to confront difficulties.

The status and policy of Russia should not be evaluated with the norms of the Cold War, according to Igor F. Maximytchev. He categorically states that there will never be a place for Russia in NATO in large part because, for many in the West, Russia's entry would purge NATO of its mission. Moscow supports a European security architecture that includes Russia and proposes a collective security system based on an institutionalized OSCE, with NATO, the WEU, and Commonwealth of Independent States as its associated bodies. A growing priority of Russian policymakers aims at augmenting Moscow's associations with the European Union for a number of positive benefits, including the strengthening of Russia's international status.

An important European role in the Balkans is deemed critical by Vladimir Veres. Conflicting nationalisms, an old phenomenon in the Balkans, resurfaced with the fall of communism, but never before had they been in such decided contrast to the democratic and integrative processes in the rest of Europe. All Balkan states should emulate these latter patterns. In Veres's estimation, striving toward the same goal of joining European institutions and organizations by all Balkan states can help undercut the virulent presence of nationalism in the region. The EU should exert more influence in the expectation that contributing to the greater social and economic security among the Balkan peoples will undercut longstanding geostrategic and military orientations. The Yugoslav crisis influenced the redefinition of NATO's strategic mission; without a continued U.S.-backed NATO presence in the former Yugoslavia, the fragile peace will surely crumble. Since Yugoslavia is the only Balkan state without some sort of affiliation with NATO, and since its links with the EU are marginal, Belgrade must oversee extensive domestic reforms and revamp its foreign policy if it is to avoid even graver consequences for its errant ways.

Southeastern Europe offers a different source of regional tension, which Thanos Veremis covers in his analysis of Greek-Turkish problems. Ongoing difficulties between Greece and Turkey over Cyprus heightened after the summer 1974 invasion of Cyprus by Turkey and with disputes over the delimitation of the Aegean continental shelf. Perceived challenges to Greek sovereignty rights in the Aegean area by Turkey added to the chilly relations between two NATO allies and between one member of the EU and another with extensive ties and aspirations for full membership. The ability of both organizations to defuse tensions has been tested and found lacking, offering disquieting insights into potential problems as NATO and the EU pursue enlargement with CEEC, many of which historically have had troubled relations with each other.

Theodore Couloumbis offers a global perspective to security challenges. The end of the Cold War terminated the East-West conflict, but the North-South divide with its great economic disparity has become sharper and the seedbed of future conflicts. There is the need for great power consensus on institutions and practices that can be presented as successful models for sharing and development by weaker states. Couloumbis contends that NATO must reorient itself and concurrently ensure that the partnership between its North American and European pillars is maintained. In doing so, it will be providing an example for emulation by other regions. The European Union is destined to play a similar role. The richer North must, however, systematically contribute to the economic development of the South; a failure in that area will contribute to the undermining of peace, stability, and prosperity in their own societies. The great transnational experiments in the North have to become operable elsewhere.

If the recent past offers any indicators, one cannot foresee a sudden or complete bridging of the divisions between the United States and Europe or NATO and the European Union. As the beneficiaries of longstanding relationships that have brought many positive returns, the involved parties–individual nations and multinational organizations–generally agree on the need for a continued transatlantic relationship and for NATO and the EU to respond to the challenges of changing conditions in Europe and the world. The years since 1945 provided the successful application of an important idea that germinated from the ashes of war–that economic integration can lead to the development of prosperity and a security that is not exclusively reliant on military might for the maintenance of regional peace. NATO and the European Union have complemented each other well. In the altered strategic environment of the now decade-old post-Cold War era, it remains to be seen if the EU's CFSP will assume a more substantive form so as to overlap more with and even complement NATO's mission. Or should the EU focus on promoting security for more Europeans with the tested strength of its social, economic, and related integrative policies? NATO and the European Union, in this latter instance, can provide differentiated security missions, as they in actuality have for their members for many years. And, as has been proposed above, they can also pursue greater global outreach ventures for promoting peace and stability through positive example and action.

ATLANTICISTS VS. EUROPEANISTS IN NATO: A HISTORICAL PERSPECTIVE

Lawrence S. Kaplan

At first glance–and perhaps after reflection as well–it seems that there should be no genuine contest between Atlanticists and Europeanists in NATO. The alliance was formed, after all, to sustain European resistance to Soviet-led communist expansion. The Marshall Plan's massive economic aid would have been insufficient of itself to rebuild Europe's society as long as Western Europeans were politically and militarily insecure. NATO under American leadership would be a counterpart to the European Cooperation Administration (ECA), and both NATO and the ECA rested on the assumption that their common function was to break down the divisions of Europe and build ultimately a United States of Europe. The "Atlantic" component of NATO, therefore, might be called a somewhat shady device to win the support of a formerly isolationist America for a European cause.

Western Europeans were well aware of the American tradition of nonentanglement, a tradition that could be traced back to 1800 when the young republic terminated the Franco-American alliance of 1778. World War I had reinforced suspicions that the Old World would always take advantage of the New. So for the Congress to pass the European Cooperation Act implementing the Marshall Plan–and this was not assured in the winter of 1948–Europeans would have to meet two major American demands: (1) that they demonstrate a willingness to engage in self-help to the maximal degree possible, and (2) that they establish instruments of cooperation among the beneficiaries ensuring efficient use of economic aid. The ultimate American objective was best expressed in Carl Van Doren's influential history of the origins of the Federal Union, The Great Rehearsal (1948), in which he cited the Constitutional Convention of 1787 as a model for other countries to adopt.[1] If thirteen separate sovereignties could merge into a federated union, why could not Western Europeans do the same?

In recognition of American sensibilities and of their own vulnerabilities in the wake of a devastating war, the intended beneficiaries of the Marshall Plan banded together in the Organization of European Economic Cooperation (OEEC) to convince the United States that a new order was arising in Europe. It was one thing to demonstrate that Europe would not abuse or misuse economic assistance; it was quite another to ask that the United States make a binding military alliance with Europe.

To facilitate this transition, Britain's Ernest Bevin opened a path to an American alliance in a major speech in Parliament in January 1948 that envisioned a political union of Europe in which Britain would participate. Three months later Britain, France, and the Low Countries contracted the Brussels Treaty (17 March 1948), a military alliance linking their destinies and reflecting the willingness of Western Europe to apply Marshall Plan principles to political as well as economic collaboration. The result, they hoped, would be an American membership in the new Western Union and massive military as well as economic aid to stop the march of communism. Soviet pressures in the form of the February 1948 coup d'état in Prague and demand for a nonaggression pact from Norway in the winter of 1948 made it likely that the United States would respond to Europe's needs. But it required more than a year before a transatlantic alliance could be put into place.

A major factor in delaying American participation in a European alliance was the conjunction of "Europe" with "alliance." Girding for a presidential election in the fall, the Truman administration had difficulty in coping with the abandonment of a 150-year-old tradition of nonentanglement with the very same European powers represented by Britain's Bevin and France's Georges Bidault. If it was hard enough to win congressional approval of the ECA, which did not become law until April 1948, how much more difficult would it be to convince the Congress to make a political and military commitment to Western Europe? Even the American military leadership, which recognized the weakness of Europe, shied away from commitment, partly out of apprehension that military aid would drain the meager Pentagon budget and partly because they feared commitments the United States was unprepared to fulfill. The European image in the eyes of many Americans was still that of a predator seeking to entrap the United States into its traditional conflicts and eager to tap into the wealth of America to build up its armies. Memories of betrayal in World War I were still alive and of concern to the administration.

It was for this reason that the "North Atlantic" was a vital label to be attached to the European alliance. It made Canada and Iceland more central to the treaty than they might have been otherwise. Over the objections of the Western Union partners, Norway, Denmark, and Portugal were included in the alliance. At best, the Brussels Treaty core nations would have wanted them as "associate members," with a lesser claim to the military aid that would follow from the alliance. While the United States argument was based on the importance of bases that Denmark would provide in Greenland, Norway in Spitzbergen, and Portugal in the Azores, these bases offered an Atlantic orientation as well as necessary American links to the European allies.

Granted that the North Atlantic Treaty was also at pains to conceal potential conflict with the United Nations Charter, the primary concern of the Truman administration and its bipartisan supporters in the Senate was that the treaty would minimize its break with tradition. The Atlantic name would permit Secretary of State Dean Acheson to proclaim that NATO was essentially an updating of the Monroe Doctrine, with the Iron Curtain separating the Old from New World. In the shrunken globe of the twentieth century, the Western European countries were located on the eastern shores and the United States and Canada on the western shores of a shared ocean. The Atlantic now connected democracies rather than separated republics from monarchies.

Once the treaty became operative, the disguise could be abandoned. Actually, NATO as an Atlantic entity was never convincing. The adversary was always the Soviet Union, the potential victims were Western Europe, and the object was to build resistance through some form of unification among Europeans to contain Communist aggression. The surprising aspect in the seemingly devious schemes to support Europe was that genuine Atlanticists did exist, even if they seemed unable to cope with the more numerous and more influential Europeanists.

Canada had a particular interest in the careful calibration of an Atlantic alliance. On the one hand, it needed a European component to keep from being suffocated by the weight of the United States. An arrangement that promised a counterweight in the form of a united Europe would serve Canadian interests. Not only would it provide a check on Communist advances, an objective Canada's leadership shared with the Americans, but it would also leave some room for Canada to maneuver between Europe and America, a role that Canada has tried to play with varying success over the years. At the same time Canada had some concerns about an American embrace of Europe that would leave Canada on the outside as Americans and Europeans molded policies without reference to the other North American ally. These concerns were never better expressed than in the authoritative *Time of Fear and Hope: The Making of the North Atlantic Treaty, 1947-1949*, the work of Canadian diplomat and scholar Escott Reid. An alliance totally focused on the unification of Europe created discomfort in Canadian circles. Reid made this point clearly when he observed that in a "two-pillar concept," one pillar would be the United States and the other Europe; "Canada would be the odd-man-out in the alliance."[2]

The history of NATO reflects a Canadian impact, most notably in the formative years through the "Canadian" Article 2, seeking stability in the area through economic collaboration among the allies. Given the military thrust of the alliance and the existence of other forums for economic relations, Dean Acheson's skepticism about the utility of this article seems justified. But though it has played a minor role in NATO's history, it reflects a longstanding Canadian concern for an Atlantic community broader than a military organization. Canada's leadership among the smaller nations of the alliance was displayed in the report of the "Three Wise Men" in 1956, which urged broadening the nonmilitary aspects of NATO and strengthening consultation among the allies in every area. But there was also a display of disillusionment in Canada's attitudes toward the alliance in Prime Minister Pierre Trudeau's efforts to reduce its commitments to NATO in the 1960s because of unhappiness over American leadership. In a less blatant form, Canada's announcement in 1992, that it would pull its combat forces out of Europe by the end of 1994 because of its troop commitments to peace missions elsewhere, was a signal the Cold War had ended. It was also a signal that the Atlantic community envisioned by Prime Minister Louis St. Laurent as early as 1947 was not to be realized.

Canada was not the only ally to value the Atlantic character of NATO. The United Kingdom and Norway for differing reasons had difficulty in identifying themselves as Europeanists. Facing out toward the Atlantic, Norway looked to British and American connections rather than continental for its security. Although Norway hosted Allied Forces Northern Europe (AFNORTH), and as such was an integral part of the apparatus for Supreme Headquarters Allied Powers Europe (SHAPE), it was uncomfortable over the direction the European Economic Community (EEC) was taking in the 1950s and remained outside the Treaty of Rome. The European Free Trade Association (EFTA) under British leadership was preferable.

Britain was even more troubled about its identification with Europe. Bevin's dramatic speech before Parliament implied abandonment of that nation's traditional isolationism and a willingness to be part of a new unified Europe. This affirmation may have been a device to break down America's own isolationism, but it was also a serious venture into a new relationship, as its membership in the Western Union connoted. During World War II there was considerable sentiment on behalf of a federated European Union composed of leading intellectuals and politicians, as Walter Lipgens pointed out in his monumental *History of European Integration: The Formation of the European Unity Movement*.[3] While Labour and Liberal party figures seemed to predominate, the European Union movement appeared to have won over Winston Churchill when he served as presiding officer and keynote speaker at a major gathering of supporters in The Hague two months after the signing of the Brussels Treaty.

This bipartisan enthusiasm did not endure, in large part out of Britain's concern that its status as head of the Commonwealth was compromised by too close an association with the Continent in 1949. Beyond this consideration loomed an expectation that a "special connection" with the United States would also be compromised if Britain were to become simply another European nation. British leaders nourished a hope, as Harold Macmillan later put it, of becoming the Greek teachers to the more powerful but less astute Romans. This notion persisted throughout much of the first generation of NATO's history, to be shattered in the 1960s when the United States seemed to value West Germany over Britain and to offer little compensation for Charles de Gaulle's dismissive treatment of the British ally. Britain's position as a reluctant European persisted even after it joined the European Community. Despite articulate Europeanist voices in all the political parties, Britain has remained an ambivalent European power, particularly as the Franco-German hegemony moved the European Community into a European Union with the ultimate promise of a United States of Europe.

The positions of Canada, Norway, and Britain–and Portugal as well–with respect to Atlanticism were based on national interests. So, obviously, were those of the continental members of the alliance. Yet, all of them at one time or another spoke of their devotion to the ideal of a United States of Europe, an integrated community superior in population and economic potential to those of either superpower. This was the language that appealed to their American patrons. In each European nation there was a minority dedicated to European integration, which regarded the Atlantic connection as the means of achieving this objective. But for most of the allied leaders, particularly in France, the main purpose of the alliance was to build their defenses against Communist pressures, internal and external, and to supply the confidence for economic recovery that the Marshall Plan alone could not do. Not only was the creation of a federated Europe secondary to these aims, but for the larger powers, again France in particular, its achievement would subvert the nation's pride in its history.

Arguably, it was the United States that harbored the most dedicated Atlanticists and Europeanists who were infused with the idealism that had characterized the European unity groups in Nazi-occupied Europe. That America would benefit from the results of their activities was of less importance to them than the emergence of a new entity on the world scene that took its inspiration from the American example. This was an American tradition that had inspired Thomas Jefferson during the French Revolution and Woodrow Wilson in the aftermath of World War I.

The Atlanticists were a small minority with some influential members. They originated in the vision of journalist Clarence Streit, who created a movement for Union Now with Britain on the eve of World War II, an Anglo-American federation that would ensure the survival of Britain. The concept, extended to include democracies along the littorals of the Atlantic, became the Atlantic Union Committee by the time the war had ended. The committee attracted leading officials, including Secretary of War Robert P. Patterson and Undersecretary of State William L. Clayton in the Truman administration. For them the North Atlantic Treaty would be a way station en route to an Atlantic federation along the lines of the American federal union. Its goal was closer to the European Union's federated Europe than to the framers' vision of the Atlantic alliance. As such, it received nominal support from Senate resolutions in subsequent years, but little more.

Streit did win over one follower, Theodore C. Achilles, director of Western European Affairs in the State Department at the time of NATO's birth, who devoted much of his life to serving the goal of an Atlantic community. Serving in London and Paris as well as in Washington, Achilles sought to separate an Atlantic union from a European union. He saw the Atlantic community endangered not from the Soviet Union but from a counterideal shared by most Europeans and a significant number of American leaders: the belief in European unification. While there was nothing unworthy about this objective, he felt it was unrealistic. A United States of Europe modeled on the American experience was impossible of realization. To achieve any kind of success, European unification should be tied to an Atlantic community in which the United States would play a critical role.

The trouble with Achilles's goal was the goal itself, a federation in which the United States would subsume its own sovereignty under a larger rubric. He never explicitly outlined just how the Atlantic union would be governed, but it was the prospect of drastic change for the United States that precluded serious consideration of the Atlantic ideal. Like the partisans of a united Europe, Achilles had no objections to European nations sacrificing much of their sovereignty to a supranational body. It was indeed this prospect that made the unification of Europe such an attractive objective for American policymakers.

On one level it evoked the missionary impulse in America's outlook on the world. In the spirit of Carl Van Doren's advice, Americans could help Europeans achieve the blessings of a federal union, much as the thirteen states did in 1787. On another, more practical level, American Europeanists would help build a bulwark against Communist expansion before it reached the Atlantic. And on an even more practical level, members of Congress could find in the unification of Europe both a self-sufficiency that would relieve the United States of economic support and at the same time produce markets for American goods. This latter objective later impressed some Europeans as an American effort to use NATO to impose an imperial control over the continent.

If Clarence Streit was the pied piper of Atlanticists, the European visionary, Count Richard Coudenhove-Kalergi, provided the inspiration for an American cadre of support for the unification of Europe. Coudenhove-Kalergi, a scion of Austrian nobility with an ancestry that included Flemings, Greeks, and Japanese, had been a tireless propagandist for a unified Europe. Since 1923 he had produced books almost annually for his Pan-European Union, with few results to show for his efforts. The collapse of Europe and the danger of Communist control gave him access to American leaders that in an earlier period he would not have enjoyed. He claimed, with some exaggeration, to have induced the secretary of state to endorse his proposals for his European Parliamentary Union. Those caught up in his enthusiasm included Senator J. William Fulbright, who became president of the American Committee for a Free and United Europe. Other advocates shunted Coudenhove-Kalergi aside, but his American offshoot prospered. The American Europeanists became a force to be reckoned with among the various interest groups mobilized behind the Atlantic treaty.

Once it became apparent that an American alliance would become a reality, the true believers in a United States of Europe lost much of their audience. Fulbright and his associates sought nothing less than the full political integration of Europe. Although there were few in Congress or elsewhere in the United States who would oppose the concept of European federation in 1949, there were even fewer who considered the idea vital. It could be embraced by isolationists that wanted America to be freed from a dependent Europe, by realists that wanted maximal effectiveness from American aid, as well as by integrationists that saw in federation the beginnings of an Atlantic or even a world federation. In most cases an endemic suspicion of Europeans–their motives, their abilities, their innate character–accompanied professions of friendship for a federated Europe. Even such warm friends as Fulbright regularly rested their case for a federal Europe on the ground that its absence made economic aid wasteful, an argument that isolationists could share.

This fragile support for a federated Europe relieved the French and British leadership in 1949 of having to carry out any putative mandate for political integration. Neither Britain with its ambivalence toward Europe nor France with its campaign for refurbishing a national identity tarnished in World War II had a serious intention of creating a United States of Europe. The Western Union they created in 1948 was essentially a vehicle for assuring Europe the military aid that would ensure their national survival and not bury it inside a new Europe. If they were Europeanists, it meant that the alliance would be in the service of its individual members and not for the reordering of the European polity.

Yet the concept of a new Europe did not disintegrate into cynicism, even when the abortive European Defense Community (EDC) collapsed in 1954. The EDC was a French-inspired response to American pressure for a German military contribution to the alliance in the wake of the Korean War, rather than a serious effort to resolve Franco-German differences under a new supranational rubric. American concern for its realization was once again a means of extracting greater efficiency from a more coherent Europe. But at the same time, Europeanists from both sides of the

Atlantic recognized the virtues of Jean Monnet's functional approach to European unity. Monnet, a French economist with close connections to the American political establishment, saw the impracticality of a full-blown union without step-by-step preparation. The European Coal and Steel Community (ECSC) was just such an example; the European Defense Community went too far too fast. While Monnet was the source of both the Schuman Plan that spawned the former grouping and the Pleven Plan, from which the EDC grew, the latter emerged under the gun of American pressure for German contributions to the alliance. Monnet's solution was a gradual accretion of authority that would lead ultimately to a unified Europe.

Given Monnet's ties with the United States, there was none of the antagonism that Gaullist advocates of a new Europe displayed. His approach to European unity won a devoted following in the United States, led by George Ball, an influential figure in the State Department in the Kennedy and Johnson administrations. As the Coal and Steel Community blossomed into the broader European Economic Community, American supporters cheered its advances, even as they were put off both by President de Gaulle's efforts to hijack the movement and by Britain's continued ambivalence toward the continent. De Gaulle's exclusion of Britain from the EEC in 1963 and his identification of the United States as an alien entity in Europe combined with German doubts about American steadfastness as an ally to energize American Europeanists.

An important band of statesmen in the State Department and White House, consisting of such figures as Walt Rostow and Robert Bowie, along with Ball, became known as "theologians" for their devotion to the ideal of a United States of Europe in the 1960s. Their instrument was the Multilateral Force (MLF), an updated EDC as a consortium of NATO's European partners with its own medium-range nuclear missile. The hope was that the sharing of the nuclear weapon would serve a number of purposes by undercutting the French nuclear *force de frappe*, discouraging West Germany from considering a similar program, and integrating Britain's nuclear forces into the new entity. But the ultimate purpose from the perspective of the theocrats was not an improved military capacity for SHAPE or even the inhibition against nuclear proliferation. It was the extension of the concept of the European community.

The MLF, like the EDC, ended in failure, punctuated by the withdrawal of France from NATO's military organization in 1966. Key figures in Washington were uncomfortable with sharing nuclear technology, while European leaders saw elements of sham in a European-owned nuclear weapon with its warhead in America's exclusive possession. The European partners subsequently expanded their influence in NATO's second generation as the EEC widened its membership, enlarged its responsibilities, and in the 1980s and 1990s changed its name first to European Community (EC) and then to European Union (EU).

In the process, resentments against their American ally grew. Some of the resentment stemmed from the superpower's continuing control of the major offices in the alliance, even as the European members acquired the potential, if not the will, to function without the protection of their transatlantic ally. There had been inevitable tension been between donor and beneficiary in the early days of the alliance. This was magnified by the seeming success of European unification as new institutions were added to include also a military arm in the form of the formerly peripheral Western European Union (WEU). The end of the Cold War lessened the importance of military power and accelerated the movement toward a Europe united in every aspect. By the time the millennium arrives, there should be a single currency in place, if not a single government for the European Union. Conceivably, the Europeanists had succeeded so well that NATO itself had become dispensable.

The growing independence of Europe gratified those Americans who shared the vision of George Kennan in the 1940s and John F. Kennedy in the 1960s of two equal elements on each side of the Atlantic inside NATO. But their voices were considerably more subdued toward the end of the century. Those Americans who supported European integration to relieve the United States of an economic burden and to promote an economy that would buy American products were disconcerted by the ingratitude of the partners and by the hostility many of them displayed. Most unsettling was the opposition to American policies by the European Community itself as it competed with the United States in the world market. Americans had difficulty in accepting the notion that the European junior partners might regard NATO as an expression of American economic imperialism.

Too few Americans seemed to realize that they may have created a Frankenstein monster in their zeal to rebuild and remold Europe along American lines after World War II. Democracies may be inherently benign in military relations, but politically and economically their differences could breed bitter conflicts. The United States in the 1960s never appreciated that the Europeans did not regard the Vietnam War as an affirmation of America's loyalty to its commitments. In the 1970s, it deprecated Europe's receptivity to the Arab cause out of dependence on Middle Eastern oil. In the 1980s, it minimized European concerns about a Soviet-American entente at the expense of their collective interests. In the 1990s, the superpower expressed its support for greater European leadership in NATO but balked at an excessively independent Eurocorps or the idea of turning over its key military posts to a European authority. If the United States supported such European initiatives as the European Security and Defense Identity (ESDI) and the Combined Joint Task Force (CJTF), it was in the expectation that their activities would operate within a NATO framework.

Had the growth of a united Europe been at the expense of the transatlantic bond? This is a moot question in 1998, since it rests on the assumption that the United States of Europe is now in place or will be in the immediate future. European unity may be achieved by the beginning of the new millennium, but uncertainties abound. How centralized will the European Union become, given Britain's unwillingness to be bound by many of its rules or Norway's refusal even to join the union? What are the prospects of the European Union creating a viable military component in light of its hesitations over Bosnia before 1995 and over potential civil war in Kosovo? In brief, is Europe prepared to accept the obligations of a supranational sovereignty that would come with a United States of Europe?

A positive response is reasonable, though tentative, at this writing as long as NATO itself remains viable. The successful achievement of a federated Europe hangs on the continuation of the Atlantic Alliance. In this sense, the victory of the Europeanists over the Atlanticists is tempered by the perceived need for an American-led alliance. Security for Europe rests on tools for crisis management that NATO's military machine possesses. The issue is not fear of an immediate revival of Russian imperialism. It is a recognition that Europe by itself is unable to cope with the kinds of internal disorders that have characterized the Balkan tragedy. NATO, not the EU, the WEU, the Organization for Security and Cooperation in Europe (OSCE), or any of the collective security bodies that have grown up over the last generation, has the capability, if not the will, to manage other such crises on its periphery, whether in the Balkans or in the Mediterranean basin or in the Middle East. Without the Atlantic connection, the Western European Union, or any alternative military arm of the EU, lacks the technology that NATO controls. It may also lack the ability to choose its leaders. Would a supreme European commander be drawn from Germany, France, or Britain? National rivalries within the European Union could give rise to the self-defeating military command problems that plagued the Brussels Pact organization in 1948 when Britain's Lord Montgomery contended with France's Jean de Lattre de Tassigny for the role of supreme commander.

The current preoccupation with NATO enlargement obscures the fact that logically the former Warsaw bloc members would benefit more from entry into the European Union than into NATO. Admitting that the EU itself is not willing for a variety of reasons to admit new nations, it is obvious that Eastern Europe's anxiety to enter NATO is the Atlantic connection and the sense of security that connection brings. It is reasonable to assume that in a future unstable international environment, members of the European Union will continue to value the NATO ties as much as do the potential new NATO allies, despite the history of differences between the United States and Europe. It may be worth recalling that no member nation has asked to withdraw from the alliance, as would be permissible under Article 13 of the North Atlantic Treaty. It may also be worth recalling that President Jefferson in 1801 underlined the common values of both political parties by saying that "We are all republicans: we are all federalists." At the risk of making too pretentious a comparison, I should like to conclude that with NATO "We are all Europeanists; we are all Atlanticists."

ENDNOTES

1. Carl Van Doren, *The Great Rehearsal: The Story of the Making and Ratifying of the Constitution of the United States* (New York: Viking Press, 1948).

2. Escott Reid, *Time of Fear and Hope: The Making of the North Atlantic Treaty, 1947-1949* (Toronto: McClelland and Stewart, 1977), 132.

3. Walter Lipgens, *History of European Integration: The Formation of the European Unity Movement, 1945-1947* (Oxford: Clarendon Press, 1982), 107.

NATO'S EVOLVING STRATEGIC CONCEPT

Steven L. Rearden

NATO is still feeling its way as it adjusts to the post-Cold War world. The dissolution of the Warsaw Pact, the disintegration of East European communism, and the breakup of the Soviet Union have obviously created a new European political and military environment. No longer is the threat of an East-West confrontation, possibly involving nuclear weapons, the prime concern. But the post-Cold War world is by no means devoid of tensions or uncertainties that could lead to conflict. Rather than an East-West war, the danger today seems to lie in terrorism, ethnic rivalries, and a resurgence of nationalism. As the late NATO secretary general Manfred Wörner so aptly put it: "The paradox of the end of the Cold War is that there is less threat, but also less peace."[1] In these circumstances, as the NATO intervention in Bosnia attests, the alliance does not have far to look for things to do.

Where the alliance has run into problems is in finding an overall strategy for responding to this new situation. Though far from idle, NATO's leaders and planners have thus far met with mixed results in their search for a comprehensive and coherent post-Cold War strategic concept. While still committed to preserving collective defense, NATO also has had to grapple with other, more urgent problems associated with out-of-area peace-enforcement operations, crisis management, and the admission of new members. The general blueprint for undertaking these various tasks, adopted at Rome in November 1991, was at the time viewed as an interim response. Over the ensuing years, NATO has moved cautiously toward a more permanent solution, and while work is currently underway to draft a more up-to-date concept, it will probably not be until the April 1999 NATO summit that any results materialize.[2] Until then, NATO will have to make do with the ad hoc approach that has more or less governed its behavior since the Cold War ended.

THE ROME STRATEGIC CONCEPT

NATO's current strategic dilemma stems directly from the swift and extraordinary changes that swept across Eastern Europe and the Soviet Union in the late 1980s and early 1990s, changes that left the alliance in the unusual position of having no overt threat facing it. Though a perceptive observer might have seen the end of the Cold War coming, the extent of the transformation in the former Soviet empire took most people by surprise and required adjustments in thinking and behavior that proved hard for some in the West to accept. For NATO planners two tasks appeared uppermost: to redesign the alliance's force and command structure to meet the new needs of the post-Cold War environment; and to provide a rationale around which these decisions could be made in the most expeditious and practical fashion. Some, including the British and the French, believed it premature to move too far too fast from established policy and doctrine. But by and large there was a strong and growing consensus that the alliance had to act–and act positively–if it were to stay ahead of events.

The decision to embark upon a full-scale strategy review–the first review of its kind in more than twenty years–had its immediate origins in the NATO Defense Planning Committee (DPC) meeting of May 1990. At that time the defense ministers made known their intention of reexamining NATO's military strategy in the light of the "radically altered" security environment in Europe, and indicated that one of their goals would be to revise downward NATO's force-posture needs.[3] Subsequently, at American instigation, allied leaders added a political dimension to this review: the London Declaration of July 1990, which affirmed their intention of pursuing reconciliation between East and West and of recasting NATO's role as that of "agent for change" in the quest for "new partnerships." The declaration further confirmed that NATO would move away from forward defense, where feasible, and modify its traditional flexible response posture to reflect reduced reliance on nuclear weapons in keeping with recent arms control agreements.[4]

The job of preparing specific recommendations fell to a multinational committee known as the Strategy Review Group (SRG), chaired by Michael Legge, NATO's assistant secretary general for defense plans and policy. Working methodically, the SRG organized "brainstorming" exercises to help develop ideas and established contacts with the NATO Military Committee through the latter's Military Strategy Working Group. According to Legge, a consensus quickly emerged "that the new military strategy would not only have to reflect the present security environment, but also the Alliance's political response to the changed circumstances."[5] Or, as one senior British diplomat is said to have put it, NATO was looking ahead to 1994 and beyond "when the Russians are gone from Eastern Europe."[6]

Some of the SRG's findings were preordained. One, of course, was that NATO would largely abandon its practice, dating back some forty years, of relying on nuclear weapons for deterrence and defense. Ending reliance on nuclear weapons had been underway ever since NATO had announced in 1979 that it was unilaterally reducing its atomic arsenal by 1,000 warheads. However, most of the weapons withdrawn at that time later fell into a special deployment category—warheads without military utility belonging to retired or about-to-be-retired delivery systems. This process had accelerated steadily during the 1980s as the accuracy of conventional replacement systems increased and as more and more "smart bombs" and precision-guided munitions entered the inventory. Arms control contributed also, but the weapons covered in the 1987 Intermediate-range Nuclear Forces (INF) treaty were theater-range missiles, a small fraction of the stockpile. Through these various means, by the end of the decade, NATO had reduced its nuclear arsenal to around 4,000 warheads.[7] The strategy review took this process several steps further, and at its meeting in October 1991 at Taormina, Italy, the Nuclear Planning Group agreed to cut NATO's substrategic nuclear stockpile by roughly 80 percent. This included the total elimination of ground-launched, short-range nuclear missiles and artillery and a reduction by one-half in the number of air-dropped weapons. Henceforth, instead of for deterrence, NATO would keep a small arsenal of nuclear weapons, carried aboard dual-purpose aircraft and British nuclear-powered ballistic missile submarines (SSBNs), for possible retaliatory purposes "to preserve peace and stability."[8]

A second predictable outcome was a reduction in the size of NATO's conventional forces, partly to comply with the ceilings set by the 1990 Conventional Forces in Europe (CFE) agreement, and partly for reasons of economy. Of the two, it was the latter that provided the strongest impetus. The controversies surrounding the U.S.-led military buildup of the 1980s had taken a heavy political toll in Europe, and by the early 1990s public support for such policies had declined sharply. Cutting back costs thus became a top priority. Instead of defense, attention now focused more on meeting the rising needs of social programs and, in Germany, on the enormous added tasks associated with reunification. Meanwhile, in the United States, the bills were starting to come due for many of the high-ticket military end-items ordered during the Reagan years. With budget deficits soaring and with the Cold War winding down, the Bush administration knew it could ill afford to maintain a defense establishment at a size and level of readiness as that achieved during the Reagan years. A smaller force at a somewhat lower level of preparedness would have to suffice.

While it was apparent that NATO defense spending would no longer remain at the high levels it had reached in the 1980s, it was less clear how far it should drop. Not uncommon were predictions of reductions ranging as widely as 25 to 50 percent in NATO's overall force size. The example of the Persian Gulf War (1990-91) pointed up the value of strong, ready forces, and lent support to those who saw NATO's future in out-of-area expeditions, with a mobile force posture tailored accordingly. But the Gulf War, despite its brevity, proved a hugely expensive undertaking mounted not by NATO but by a separate U.S.-led coalition including some, though not all, alliance members. When the crisis erupted in August 1990 because of Iraq's invasion of Kuwait, NATO had equivocated and eventually declined to become officially involved. Yet the overall success of the Desert Storm campaign further reinforced the belief that NATO should prepare itself for similar contingencies in the future.

The lessons of the Gulf War apparently did not bulk large in the strategy review, but they did play a role, especially in reconfirming the need for restructuring NATO's forces. Indeed, the earliest concrete accomplishment of the strategy review was a refurbished force structure, announced at the end of a joint meeting in Brussels in May 1991, consisting of the Defense Planning Committee (DPC) and the Nuclear Planning Group (NPG), using the Desert Storm exercise as a partial model. The major change manifested itself in a shift away from forward-deployed forces to a more mobile three-tier structure consisting of main defense forces, immediate and rapid reaction forces (IRF and RRF), and augmentation forces.[9] Within the RRF, which was to be up and running by 1995, NATO envisioned initially a four-division corps under a United Kingdom commander, with its assets shared between the Major NATO Commands (MNCs). Half the corps would be entirely British–an armored division stationed in Germany, and an air-mobile division based in the UK. The other two divisions would be multinational, one in the north, composed of British, Dutch, Belgian, and German units; the other in the south, organized around Italian, Greek, and other forces.[10]

Although NATO already had a rapid reaction capability, known as the ACE (Allied Command Europe) Mobile Force, or AMF, it constituted little more than a headquarters organization, with assigned forces from eight NATO nations, equaling a light brigade.[11] Under the new arrangement, AMF would become NATO's "immediate" reaction force and would be backed up by a new and larger command with its own standing force, the British-led Allied Rapid Reaction Corps (ARRC). Though comprising no more than about 10 percent of the total NATO force, reaction units would serve as the alliance's shock troops in future contingencies–the first on the scene and therefore the ones most likely to make a difference.[12] The decision to place the ARRC under British command reflected the culmination of considerable debate and bureaucratic maneuvering at Supreme Headquarters Allied Powers Europe (SHAPE). According to published reports and interviews, SACEUR (supreme allied commander Europe) informally offered the rapid reaction force command to the UK as early as December 1990, mainly to assuage the British over the impending loss of the Channel command, which would go out of business as NATO streamlined its command structure; and because the Falklands campaign had given the UK more recent experience than anyone else in organizing and leading such operations. The Germans, who then provided the commander of the AMF, objected to the designation of the ARRC as a standing force and likewise opposed the idea of a permanent British officer in charge. They preferred a rotating command that would give all participants a chance at heading it and suggested that its field components be assembled as needed from other formations, depending on circumstances. But with prodding from London and the promise that the Germans would have command of ARRC's air component, Bonn gave in to SHAPE staff planners' insistence that the matter be settled as proposed in time for the DPC-NPG meeting in mid-May 1991. Thus the decision was made with little further deliberation.[13]

Left unresolved by the May 1991 reorganization was the role of U.S. forces in ARRC and other reaction force activities. Although it was difficult to imagine that the United States would not participate to one degree or another, CFE-mandated troop cuts and the threat of congressionally imposed ceilings combined to limit what the United States could do. President George Bush and his military advisers, the Joint Chiefs of Staff, wanted to keep about 250,000 troops in Europe, but there was strong feeling in Congress that the number should be closer to 100,000, roughly comparable to a medium-sized corps.[14] At the same time, U.S. authorities were said to be reluctant for "political reasons" to take too prominent a part in organizing the rapid reaction force.[15] Indeed, while the ARRC was to be part of NATO, available to both MNCs, it was generally assumed that the European forces assigned to it would be used under the aegis of the Western European Union (WEU).[16] Expected U.S. contributions fell into such technical support categories as strategic lift, satellite surveillance, and communications–areas where, as the Gulf War demonstrated, the United States possessed superior resources and capabilities to those of its allies. Yet in developing detailed plans for NATO's future military structure, U.S. military authorities seem to have intentionally stayed in the shadows.

The culmination of the strategy review was the adoption of the new concept at the Rome council meeting of November 1991, which as German defense minister Volker Rühe characterized it, marked the formal turning point "from confrontation to cooperation with the Alliance's former adversaries."[17]   At the heart of the new strategy was the assumption that the recent changes in Europe's political climate had significantly reduced the "threat of a simultaneous, full-scale attack on all of NATO's European fronts," and that it was therefore feasible to contemplate not only large-scale force reductions but also a redirection of the alliance's energies and resources into other areas. Although collective defense would remain first and foremost, NATO now envisioned new missions, part of "a broad approach to security," resting on the ability "to respond flexibly to a wide range of possible contingencies." Toward this end, NATO would continue to keep credible main defense forces and minimal sub-strategic nuclear capabilities but would give priority to developing multinational formations oriented toward crisis management and conflict-prevention functions. The new guidance did not specifically endorse out-of-area engagements as such but did confirm that NATO would, if called upon, contribute to "global stability and peace" by providing support for the United Nations.[18]

This was, on the face of it, a rather formidable agenda that seemed to commit the alliance to new and almost open-ended tasks at a time when diminishing resources called into question NATO's capacity to act effectively. Commenting publicly, SACEUR General John Galvin, USA, described NATO's new strategy as one of "crisis response," a less demanding mission than in the past but a no less urgent one. While Galvin talked as though the chances of another major war in Europe were now exceedingly remote, he declined to rule out the possibility, observing that under the CFE Treaty, Russia would still have about thirty divisions and 6,000 to 8,000 tanks. Still, his main concern was "the amount of instability" resulting from the "enormous transitions" then under way in Eastern Europe and the former Soviet Union, and the need for the alliance to be prepared to act should the turmoil spill over into NATO Europe. Whether he considered the forces available to him under the new strategy to be adequate for such purposes, he did not say.[19] Michael Legge, who chaired the drafting of the new concept, downplayed its potential military limitations. He thought its chief contribution was its "broad approach to security," which would require NATO to pay more attention to the political and diplomatic aspects of problems and comparatively less to their military side. What Legge seemed to be saying, reading between the lines, was that the days of NATO being primarily a military alliance, dominated by the SACEUR and other military authorities, were over.[20]

This, of course, remained to be seen. What became clear was that NATO was in a transition period, caught between the end of the Cold War, on the one hand, and an uncertain future, on the other. With the Soviet threat still a vivid memory, it proved hard for many NATO planners to get away from viewing the alliance as a front-line military organization committed to mutual defense and collective security. Yet with the threat from the East steadily receding, it was almost impossible for NATO to justify the claim on resources it had exercised in the past. In the circumstances, NATO had no choice but to make do with a slimmed-down force structure, reconfigured to the more urgent requirements of crisis management. The new strategic concept endeavored to cope as best it could with these diverse realities. The result was an all-too-obvious compromise that wound up straddling two stools in an effort to accommodate as many viewpoints as possible. As the first full post-Cold War reassessment of NATO's strategic needs, the Rome concept probably went as far as alliance leaders dared at the time in reordering their priorities and in making the institutional changes they knew to be necessary. But it was only the first step toward facing up to changes yet to come.

MEETING THE NEEDS OF CRISIS RESPONSE

Since the adoption of the Rome concept, NATO's strategic posture has undergone further evolution, with two sets of problems predominating. One is the alliance's current preoccupation with enlargement, growing out of the Partnership for Peace (PFP), NATO's military cooperation program with nonmember European states. The other is, strictly speaking, organizational rather than strategic: the development of a force posture and command structure to meet the needs of the Rome concept, especially in the increasingly critical and active areas of peacekeeping and crisis response. Taken together, these problems vividly illustrate NATO's unresolved strategic dilemma and how pressures at work within the alliance continue to push it in two directions at the same time.

Meeting NATO's organizational requirements under the crisis response strategy has not proved easy and certainly has taken longer than most observers anticipated. The reasons for this situation are complex, but basically they all revolve around one central fact: that European defense and security responsibilities are no longer a NATO monopoly. Instead, they are now the active concern, to one degree or another, of a growing list of organizations, including not only NATO but also the Western European Union defense organization, the European Union (EU), the United Nations (UN), and the Organization on Security and Cooperation in Europe (OSCE).

If NATO were to collapse tomorrow, its successor as the guarantor of European security would likely be the WEU. Founded in 1954, the WEU remained practically moribund until the 1980s, when interallied friction over the Reagan administration's handling of Soviet policy and the NATO nuclear buildup led the French, with German support, to revive the WEU as a means for providing an alternative, independent European voice in defense affairs (including arms production) and for improving overall cooperation. The emerging goal became the development of a distinctive European Security and Defense Identity (ESDI), linked to NATO but capable of operating wholly on its own.[21] As an indication of what to expect, France and Germany announced in October 1991 that they would soon form a Franco-German "Eurocorps," which in certain respects would rival the rapid reaction force planned by NATO.[22] The Eurocorps idea immediately caught NATO leaders' attention, and at their Rome summit the following month, they agreed to explore other ways of reinvigorating the WEU, starting with the reinstatement of regular, biannual meetings between NATO and the WEU Council.[23]

It was clear that, behind the Eurocorps and measures to strengthen the WEU, stood the French, whose criticisms of NATO and of American involvement in the alliance were well known. From the French standpoint, the end of the Cold War had rendered NATO largely superfluous and urgently in need of wholesale reform. This meant, above all, doing away with the integrated command structure, long the symbol of American domination in French eyes, and developing an alternative security system framed around ESDI principles.[24] Most Europeans agreed that, owing to the drawdown of U.S. forces, Europe would have no choice but to assume an ever larger share of responsibility for its security and defense–hence the growing emphasis, supported by the United States, on multinational formations like the ARRC. But whether the command and control of these multinational formations should rest with NATO or with some other mechanism became the source of considerable tension and almost endless bickering within the alliance.

Over the course of the ensuing debate, positions gradually mellowed, but not to the point that either side felt totally comfortable with the outcome. On the matter of the Eurocorps, the French in January 1993 gave way to an agreement with NATO providing that French forces within the corps would come under NATO's "operational command" in time of crisis.[25] Observers at the time cautiously hailed this agreement as the possible blossoming of a French rapprochement with NATO, and indeed, in the months that followed, such appeared to be the case.[26] Nonetheless, France remained as committed as ever to promoting the interests of the WEU, and in an effort to engineer a compromise that would bring NATO and the WEU into a closer working partnership, American defense planners suggested the adoption of the combined joint task force (CJTF) concept. Approved at a meeting of NATO's Defense Planning Committee at Travemünde, Germany, in October 1993, the CJTF proposal received formal endorsement by the NATO ministers at their Brussels summit in January 1994.[27]

Though well established in U.S. military doctrine, the joint task force concept was relatively new to European defense planners, whose previous experience with such operations was mostly confined to small-scale NATO naval and/or air exercises. The CJTFs planned for NATO would be larger and somewhat different from those of the past in that they would mainly encompass multinational land-component forces and be dedicated initially to out-of-area peace-enforcement and crisis-response missions.[28] What many Europeans liked about the CJTF concept was that it seemed to bridge the gap between NATO and the WEU. CJTF operations involving a U.S. contribution would fall under NATO command and control, while those confined to European forces would be under the WEU. As one Western European Union official described them, CJTFs were a means of meeting "Europe's requirements for operations in which North Americans may not wish to participate."[29]

Although the theory seemed sound, implementing efforts languished for the next two years while U.S. and French military planners haggled over the details. In June 1996 NATO leaders tried to breathe new life into the CJTF concept by promising more operational control to the WEU.[30] However, thus far the results have been minimal, highlighted only by a trial exercise in November 1997. In Bosnia and during the Congo crisis in the summer of 1997–two instances where the use of CJTFs would have proved extremely useful–the NATO countries involved had to resort to ad hoc arrangements for conducting multinational operations. Generally speaking, the has to offer. Like many serious observers in the West, Kissinger feels that what the East Europeans really want out of membership in NATO is protection against a renascence of Russian power. What he fears they may be getting is a "U.N.-style talk shop" that could someday leave them sorely disappointed.[41] Others feel that the Clinton administration is seriously misleading both Congress and the American public about the costs and commitments that NATO enlargement will entail.[42] But despite the apparent drawbacks, NATO enlargement as it extends to the current candidates enjoys widespread support in Western Europe and appears to be gaining a credible following in the United States as well. How long this support will last, should enlargement costs skyrocket beyond current projections or should NATO decide to admit other new members (e.g., the Baltic states), provoking a confrontation with the Russians, is another matter.

WHAT ROLE FOR THE UNITED STATES?

As Jonathan Eyal has pointed out, the current NATO enlargement debate, though politically significant in the short term, is unlikely by itself to have a decisive bearing on the alliance's future prospects.[43] More important for the long term and from a strategic standpoint is the behavior of the United States, whether it remains as politically involved and active in European affairs as in the past, or whether it opts to pursue its interests elsewhere. At the moment, U.S. policy strongly supports both NATO enlargement and collective defense, while the United States spearheads the international peacekeeping effort in Bosnia. Secretary of State Madeleine Albright, a Czech by birth, still remembers how Britain and France capitulated to Hitler at Munich in 1938, and she is resolved that a similar fate should not await NATO's new East European members.[44] Time alone will tell how durable this commitment will prove. While more and more Europeans seem to feel that the United States exercises an inordinately strong voice in NATO affairs,[45] the truth is that American influence in shaping the alliance's policies and strategy is far less than what it used to be, now that NATO is no longer dependent on U.S. nuclear protection as during the Cold War. U.S. influence has been diminishing for some time and will probably diminish even further over the next decade if current trends continue. During the height of the Cold War, according to some estimates, the United States devoted around half its defense budget, in one form or another, to European defense. With the collapse of communism, that has ceased to be the case. Quite simply, NATO is no longer the focal point of U.S. defense planning. Not only has the U.S. military presence in Europe fallen sharply in recent years, down to a baseline force of around 100,000 troops set by the Clinton administration, but also there has been a dramatic shift in the American strategic perspective. The current U.S. involvement in Bosnia notwithstanding, the focus of American foreign and defense policy is moving steadily away from Europe.

One sign is the shift in American economic and commercial contacts away from Europe and increasingly toward Asia and the Pacific rim. In 1975, Western Europe accounted for nearly a third of American exports; by 1995, less than 20 percent. Imports from Europe over these same years experienced a similar decline, falling from 21 to around 13 percent.[46] Meanwhile, American trade around the Pacific rim and with the Far East continues to grow, with imports from Japan, China, and Taiwan leading the way. At the same time, the pattern of American immigration policy has changed. Growing numbers of legal immigrants today come not from Europe, as in years past, but from Latin America and Asia. Illegal immigration boosts the number of non-Europeans even higher. The net effect is that the makeup of the American population is changing to reflect increasingly a demographic and cultural base with fewer and fewer European political, cultural, and social ties.

Along with the loosening of economic and social links to Europe, U.S. military and policy planners find themselves looking more and more to Asia and the Pacific as the regions of future American interest. In fact, they have been doing so for some time, starting with the oil crises of the 1970s. Since then, American defense planners have accorded ever-growing attention to waging wars of one degree or another in and around the Persian Gulf and Southwest Asia. The creation of the Rapid Deployment Joint Task Force in 1980 (later, the U.S. Central Command), the reflagging and protection of Kuwaiti tankers in 1987, and, ultimately, the Gulf War of 1991 all testify to the close attention that that part of the world has acquired in American defense plans.

Projecting ahead, Asia and the Pacific are about the only places where Pentagon analysts are likely to find the justifications they need for maintaining a large standing force structure. Having already undergone substantial post-Cold War cutbacks, the military services would like to avoid a further round of reductions. As they canvass the globe, it is in such places as the Persian Gulf, the Korean peninsula, and the Taiwan Straits, rather than the Balkans or Eastern Europe, where military planners see U.S. forces most likely to become engaged. Official projections into the next century envision a sizable defense establishment, organized around ten army divisions, a "blue water" navy with twelve carrier battle groups, an air force of just over twelve active tactical fighter wing equivalents, and three Marine Expeditionary Forces, all backed by a vigorous research and development program with heavy emphasis on ballistic missile defense.[47] However, such a force will be increasingly hard to justify in Congress and to the American public if NATO-led peacekeeping and peace-enforcement missions to places such as Bosnia are the U.S. military's major justification for existence.

The United States is also saddled for the time being with a large and increasingly obsolescent strategic arsenal that continues to consume enormous resources but that contributes less and less to U.S. or NATO security. Part of the barrier to the further reduction of strategic nuclear forces is diplomatic—the refusal thus far of the Russian Duma to ratify the START II Treaty—and the delay this has caused to the conclusion of a START III agreement. Until then, as mandated by Congress, the United States is obliged to keep its nuclear forces at START I levels: eighteen Trident SSBNs, fifty Peacekeeper and five hundred Minuteman III intercontinental ballistic missiles, seventy-one B-52H bombers, and twenty-one B-2 bombers.[48] This represents a heavy burden and diverts resources that American defense planners would prefer to employ either in support of NATO or elsewhere. But it is all the more likely in the years ahead that, instead of channeling arms control-generated savings into general purpose forces, the United States will pocket the money or use it to fund domestic programs.

While a total American withdrawal from NATO appears unlikely, the next decade or so is very apt to witness a leveling-off, if not a further decline, in U.S. participation in NATO-sponsored activities. This will doubtless play into the hands of those, like the French and Russians, who have long sought to curb American power and influence in Europe. And it will also exacerbate NATO's fundamental strategic dilemma of how to honor growing commitments with a diminishing capacity to do so. The enlargement of the alliance and the acceptance of increased crisis-response and peace-enforcement obligations are not mutually exclusive enterprises. But they will require skillful balancing and judicious policy management if they are not to place NATO in the position of being unable to honor either.

ENDNOTES

1. Quoted in Guy B. Roberts, "NATO's Ambitious Response to the Proliferation of Weapons of Mass Destruction," *Airpower Journal* 11 (Fall 1997): 78.

2. See the Final Communiqué of the defense ministers meeting in Brussels, 2 December 1997, NATO Press Release M-NAC-D-2(97) 149.

3. DPC Final Communiqué, Brussels Meeting, 22-23 May 1990.

4. NAC Communiqué, Ministerial Mtg, Turnberry, UK, 7-8 June 1990. For the American role in shaping the London Declaration, see James A. Baker, III, *The Politics of Diplomacy: Revolution, War and Peace, 1989-1992* (New York: Putnams, 1995), 258-59.

5. Michael Legge, "The Making of NATO's New Strategy," *NATO Review* 39 (December 1991): 11. Also see Mark Stenhouse, "SHAPE's Role in the Strategy Review," in *Jane's NATO Handbook, 1991-92*, ed. Bruce George (London, 1991), 43.

6. Cited in Michael Clarke, "The Effects of the Gulf War and Reform Within NATO," in *Jane's NATO Handbook, 1991-92*, 216.

7. *The Military Balance, 1990-1991* (London, 1990), 214.

8. NPG Final Communiqué, Taormina, Italy, Meeting 17-18 October 1991. Also see Gregory L. Schulte, "NATO's Nuclear Forces in a Changing World," *NATO Review* 41 (February 1993): 17-22.

9. Joint DPC-NPG Communiqué, Brussels Meeting, 28-29 May 1991. Robert S. Jordan, "NATO's Structural Changes for the 1990s," in *NATO in the Post-Cold War Era: Does It Have a Future?* ed. S. Victor Papacosma and Mary Ann Heiss (New York: St. Martin's Press, 1995), 41-69, is the best overall look at NATO's post-Cold War organizational evolution.

10. Stenhouse, "SHAPE's Role in the Strategy Review," 43.

11. "NATO's Allied Mobile Force," in *Jane's NATO Handbook, 1991-92*, 68.

12. Jordan, "NATO's Structural Changes," 49; and Richard Vincent, "NATO's Multinational Rapid Reaction Force," *International Defense Review: Defense '92*, 29-32.

13. Anthony Forster, "The Ratchet of European Defence: Britain and the Reactivation of Western European Union," in *Western European Union 1954-1997: Defence, Security, Integration*, ed. Anne Deighton (Oxford: European Interdependence Research Unit, 1997), 38-39; *International Defense Review* 6 (1991): 545-46.

14. See Lawrence S. Kaplan, *NATO and the United States: The Enduring Alliance* (New York: Twayne, 1994), 163.

15. *International Defense Review* 6 (1991): 546.

16. See Jamie Shea, "Moving On From the London Declaration: The Political Role of NATO in the New Europe," in *Jane's NATO Handbook, 1991-92*, 86.

17. Volker Rühe, "Shaping Euro-Atlantic Policies: A Grand Strategy for a New Era," *Survival* 35 (Summer 1993): 131.

18. NAC Communiqué, Rome Meeting, 7-8 November 1991.

19. Brigitte Sauerwein, "Interview: 'Our New Strategy Is One of Crisis Response': SACEUR General John Galvin," *International Defense Review* 4 (1992): 319-21.

20. Legge, "Making NATO's New Strategy," 12.

21. Charles L. Barry, "Creating a European Security and Defense Identity," *Joint Force Quarterly* (Spring 1997): 62-69.

22. Charles G. Cogan, *Oldest Allies, Guarded Friends: The United States and France Since 1940* (Westport: Praeger, 1994), 186-87.

23. Catherine McArdle Kelleher, *The Future of European Security: An Interim Assessment* (Washington, DC: Brookings Institution, 1995), 54.

24. Robert P. Grant, "France's New Relationship with NATO," *Survival* 38 (Spring 1996): 58-60.

25. Cogan, *Oldest Allies*, 189.

26. See Grant, "France's New Relationship with NATO," 61-62.

27. Charles Barry, "NATO's Combined Joint Task Forces in Theory and Practice," *Survival* 38 (Spring 1996): 83.

28. See Roger H. Palin, *Multinational Military Forces: Problems and Prospects*, Adelphi Paper 294 (London: IISS, 1995), 65; Barry, "NATO's Combined Task Forces," 82-83.

29. Jose Cutileiro, "WEU's Operational Development and Its Relationship to NATO," *NATO Review* 43 (September 1995): 11.

30. Paul Cornish, "European Security: The End of Architecture and the New NATO," *International Affairs* 72, no. 4 (1996): 760-62; Barry, "Creating ESDI," 67.

31. Grant, "France's New Relationship with NATO," 73.

32. Most East Europeans tend to be rather reticent on the anti-Russian aspects of NATO enlargement. See, for example, Emil Constantinescu, "Euro-Atlantic Integration as a Political and Strategic Objective of Romania," *NATO's Sixteen Nations–Special Issue* 42 (1997): 3-7; and Andrzej Karkoszka, "A View From Poland," in *NATO Enlargement: Opinions and Options*, ed. Jeffrey Simon (Washington, DC: National Defense University Press, 1995), 75-85. An exception is Czech president Vaclav Havel, who clearly sees the purpose of NATO enlargement as pushing the alliance's borders eastward to restrain and contain possible future Russian expansionism. See "Czech President Havel Says Dangers Justify Larger NATO," *Washington Post*, 4 October 1997, A9.

33. Boleslaw A. Boczek, "NATO and the Former Warsaw Pact States," in *NATO in the Post-Cold War Era*, 210-12. On the PFP's early goals, see Joseph Kruzel, "Peacekeeping and the Partnership for Peace," in *Peace Support Operations and the*

U.S. Military, ed. Dennis J. Quinn (Washington, DC: National Defense University Press, 1994).

34. Michael Dobbs, "Wider Alliance Would Increase U.S. Commitments," *Washington Post*, 5 July 1997, A1, A16.

35. Boczek, "NATO and the Former Warsaw Pact States," 214-15; Jonathan Eyal, "NATO's Enlargement: Anatomy of a Decision," *International Affairs* 73 (1997): 695-719; and James M. Goldgeier, "NATO Expansion: The Anatomy of a Decision," *Washington Quarterly* 21 (Winter 1998): 85-102.

36. "NATO Infrastructure Ill-Prepared for Partnership for Peace," *International Defense Review* 3 (1994): 9.

37. Millon paraphrased in Theresa Hitchens, "France Ties OK of Larger NATO to Reforms," *Defense News*, 9-15 October 1995, 6; see also Grant, "France's New Relationship with NATO," 67.

38. Robin Lodge and Michael Evans, "Yeltsin Compares Nato Expansion to Cuba Missile Crisis," *Times* (London), 9 May 1997.

39. "A New European Order," *Economist*, 17 May 1997, 55-56.

40. NATO Press Release M-1(97)81, 8 July 1997.

41. Henry Kissinger, "The Dilution of NATO," *Washington Post*, 8 June 1997, C9.

42. See for example Charles A. Kupchan, "Doing the NATO Shuffle," *Washington Post*, 31 August 1997, C1, C5.

43. Eyal, "NATO's Enlargement," 711.

44. "Madeleine s'en va-t-en guerre," *Economist*, 16 August 1997, 21-22.

45. See Stanley Sloan, "Transatlantic Relations: Stormy weather on the way to Enlargement?" *NATO Review* 45 (September-October 1997): 12-16.

46. Trade data from U.S. Bureau of the Census, *Statistical Abstract of the United States: 1976*, 97th ed. (Washington, DC, 1976), 842-45; and idem, *Statistical Abstract of the United States: 1996*, 116th ed. (Washington, DC, 1996), 799-804.

47. U.S. Department of Defense, *Report of the Quadrennial Defense Review* (May 1997), 29-30.

48. Ibid., 32.

EUROPEAN SECURITY COOPERATION:
THE EUROPEAN UNION'S EVALUATIONS
AND RESPONSES

Michael E. Smith

The attempt to enhance, if not replace, Atlantic multilateral security cooperation with a more regionally focused European initiative has proven to be one of the most contentious items on the post-Cold War political agenda. Divisions and disagreements over this issue have appeared among key actors on both sides of the Atlantic, allowing tragedies such as the carnage in Bosnia to take place. In 1914, it could plausibly be argued, the absence of an active European security institution in favor of bilateral alliances allowed a crisis in the Balkans to escalate into World War I. Earlier this decade, we faced the opposite problem: Differences over the division of labor between a number of security-related institutions–NATO, the European Union (EU), the Western European Union (WEU), the UN, and the Conference on Security and Cooperation in Europe–inhibited a coordinated response to the violence in this same region for years.[1] Even though the conflict was contained far more effectively than in 1914, this fact provides little comfort to those who expected the interlocking web of European security institutions to come to their aid quickly and effectively.

Superficially, these institutions seem to have learned from the events of recent years. Above all, NATO has shown remarkable adaptability in the way it defines and pursues its missions. The "out of area" problem has been addressed, while cooperation with Russia has taken place on the ground and the door has been opened to new members for the first time in years. Flexible provisions have been adopted and utilized to permit the participation of NATO nonmembers in its operations, overcoming the perceived problem of a lack of differentiated membership. The EU, as well, has advanced in its efforts to cooperate in security and defense policy from the days when such matters could not even be officially discussed by its members. In terms of a NATO-EU partnership, the 1996 NATO ministerial meeting in Berlin seemingly resolved the division of labor between the two institutions.

Yet there are still two major practical questions to be addressed with regards to this partnership. First, is it really conceivable that NATO in general–and the United States in particular–would agree to let the EU play a more independent role in critical matters of security cooperation, even to the point of using NATO resources? In other words, what kind of security problem would be serious enough to require some form of military intervention, but small enough not to invite the interest, if not involvement, of the United States and NATO? Second, if such a problem exists and agreement is reached for a more independent European response, would the EU be able to resolve effectively the situation on its own? Or would the absence of the United States and NATO undermine the credibility of whatever operation the Europeans were attempting to mount? And, more importantly, might the European attempt to go it alone make matters worse in the end?

This analysis addresses these questions from the EU's point of view, in terms of its most recent policy decisions, institutional reforms, and resources, all of which are inextricably bound in a constantly shifting and uncertain climate of political will. While the EU has demonstrated some capacity to adapt its mechanisms for external cooperation, though in carefully limited ways, there remain several major deficiencies on the part of the EU in all of these areas. Above all, the EU has distracted itself with a halfhearted attempt to bolster its military capabilities while ignoring its existing strengths in external relations. Contributions to NATO-EU security cooperation need not involve military instruments alone, a fact that policymakers on both sides of the Atlantic have overlooked. The EU's formidable economic capabilities and emerging social welfare structure could provide considerable support for European security cooperation, but this role appears to be far less ambitious than some Euro-enthusiasts hope for.[2] Indeed, in recent years overwhelming attention has been paid to the idea of merging the EU and the WEU, rather than to the more fundamental question of whether Europe requires any significant military capability of its own. These issues are examined in detail below. First, there is an evaluation of the EU's tangible efforts to cooperate in security and defense policy since the Maastricht Treaty entered into effect. Next, the latest efforts (the 1997 Amsterdam Treaty) to enhance such cooperation are reviewed. Finally, the prospects for future European security cooperation based on these reforms are analyzed.

THE EU'S SECURITY AND DEFENSE IDENTITY: A BALANCE SHEET

At a time when most EU states take for granted the idea of an enhanced European identity in security affairs in the face of problems such as Yugoslavia, it is easy to forget just how far the EU has changed in such matters since the end of the Cold War. The momentous events in world politics between 1989-91 jolted Europe out of its complacent, dependent role in Atlantic security affairs, leading to the 1991 Treaty on European Union (TEU) and its "second pillar," the Common Foreign and Security Policy (CFSP). Formally linked to the policies and institutions of the "first pillar," the CFSP included mechanisms for adopting common foreign policy positions and undertaking joint actions. Procedures for taking some CFSP decisions by qualified majority voting were a major innovation in the TEU. The role of the European Community's executive body, the Commission, in foreign affairs was slightly enhanced as well. It now shared with European Community member-states a legal right to initiate foreign and security policies under the rubric of the CFSP and could join in the implementation of them as necessary.

Maastricht also included a reference to "the eventual framing of a common defense policy, which might in time lead to a common defense" (Article J.4), despite the opposition of Britain, Denmark, the Netherlands, Portugal, and Ireland. The WEU was explicitly linked to the EU, and was requested to "elaborate and implement decisions and actions of the Union which have defense implications" (Article J.4[2]). A declaration attached to the TEU reiterated the WEU's commitment to strengthen itself in stages as the defense arm of the EU (which satisfied the French) *and* as the European pillar of the Atlantic Alliance (which satisfied the British and the Americans). Both decisions satisfied the Germans, long caught between the ambitions of France and the long-standing accomplishments of NATO. In a later decision at the

Lisbon European Council in June 1992, the EU managed to flesh out some of the operational details regarding specific areas for CFSP actions,[3] common interests of the new EU,[4] and domains falling under the security dimension of the CFSP,[5] which included defense issues.

The decisions within the EU itself, however, were secondary to the raging transatlantic debates over the relationship between the EU, the WEU, and NATO.[6] After years of negotiations in several fora between 1990 and 1997, measures to improve cooperation between the EU and the WEU, and between the WEU and NATO, were outlined, and the WEU itself moved from London to Brussels.[7] Although the language of the TEU satisfied two visions of an emerging European Security and Defense Identity (ESDI), which had been tentatively agreed to during the November 1991 NATO summit in Rome, the practicalities of these new relationships remained in doubt long after Maastricht entered into effect. To further enhance the ESDI, France and Germany proposed an upgrading of their joint army corps to the "Eurocorps," which now includes troop contributions from Spain, Belgium, and Luxembourg. After more wrangling over the role of these troops, NATO and the Eurocorps reached an agreement in December 1992, one which clearly favored NATO as the dominant European security institution. First, the Eurocorps would be assigned to NATO in the event of a European attack; second, the Eurocorps would also fall under NATO command during crises and NATO-run peacekeeping operations; and third, in peacetime the Eurocorps would not be under NATO command but NATO would have the right to review its operations so as to determine its compatiblity with NATO's planning, doctrine, and training.[8] At the Luxembourg European Council (EC) of 22 November 1993, the EU reiterated that the Eurocorps could be deployed in the framework of the WEU in the event NATO fails to act or if the Europeans decide to act alone, but the extent of such independence remained unclear.

How successful was the EU in implementing these changes?[9] Although the EU was able to undertake a number of joint actions in foreign policy,[10] these were mostly technical in nature. More specifically, it is clear that the CFSP has had very little to do with security or defense. By the start of the EU's Intergovernmental Conference (IGC) in March 1996, only four minor security-related issues had been directly addressed by the CFSP: a directive on assistance with UN mine-clearing efforts, preparation for the renewal of the nuclear Non-Proliferation Treaty, the control of exports of dual-use goods, and the goal to prohibit blinding laser weapons. The EU also negotiated a "Stability Pact" (or Balladur Plan) with Central/Eastern Europe, but this was an exercise in preventative diplomacy and has received little attention since its inception.

Concerning the EU/WEU link, results were even more modest.[11] Although the WEU sent minesweepers into the Persian Gulf in 1988, participated in a naval blockade during the 1990-91 Persian Gulf War, and helped enforce sanctions against Yugoslavia on the Danube River and in the Adriatic Sea, no WEU actions had been taken in conjunction with or at the request of the EU under Article J.4[2] by the start of the IGC.[12] In fact, only one EU decision under Article J.4[2] had been taken: the Council Decision of 27 June 1996 to have the WEU prepare contingency plans to support the emergency evacuation of EU citizens from a third country if necessary. This was not even published in the *Official Journal of the EU* due to Danish reservations about participating; it was as much a symbolic decision for the IGC process (to show critics of reform that nearly all CFSP instruments had been used at least once) as it was a practical CFSP action.[13] Moreover, the WEU has rarely if ever been present at General Affairs Council CFSP meetings, while institutional links between the Commission and the WEU are poorly developed. According to EU insiders, Commission relations with NATO have been much better than those with the WEU.[14]

In addition to a limited body of security actions and no significant joint EU/WEU actions, the EU has not been very successful in supporting its aspirations in terms of material resources. In the first place, protracted budgetary disagreements between EU states and institutions held up several joint actions, particularly the EU's administration of Mostar, after the CFSP entered into effect. Agreement on what constituted "administrative" and "operational" CFSP expenditures, and on whether such expenditures should be charged to EU member-states or to the EC budget, took a long time to reach.[15] Even then, the EU provided the CFSP with an operational budget of only 32 million ECU in 1995-96.

In the second place, the EU has not managed to coordinate a growing number of military units whose operational roles and command structures are ill-defined. The Eurocorps is still a small land force (50,000 troops), and it only became operational on 30 November 1995. It is independent of, but linked to, the WEU, and the two forces began joint exercises ("Crisex") on 15 December 1995. The "Eurofor" and "Euromarfor" (among others) complicate the question of command and control. Fortunately, later decisions by the WEU and NATO during ministerial meetings in mid-1996, following the French rapprochement with NATO, finally confirmed that the WEU, and/or "Combined Joint Task Forces" (CJTF) with NATO, could carry out military operations without U.S. involvement but with the logistical support of NATO.[16]

In the third place, the EU has been similarly confounded by the number of ad hoc arms production agreements involving small coalitions of its members. Article 223 of Maastricht, which permits state protection of domestic arms industries, effectively discourages mergers or acquisitions of defense manufacturers, but EU member-states seem unwilling to revoke it. Its most important purpose perhaps is as a bargaining chip to obtain a reciprocal pledge from the United States to give up its "Buy American" defense procurement policy, but neither the Americans nor the Europeans have been willing or able to confront this issue directly at present. The sensitivity of the issue and fears of Commission involvement in approving such acquisitions or mergers mean Article 223 will remain in force for some time. France and Britain are the most vocal opponents of revoking Article 223, while the other states are indifferent or only slightly in favor of it.[17]

Finally, it should be noted that although Maastricht provides for qualified majority voting (QMV) on CFSP matters (except for those concerning defense), no such voting has successfully taken place since the CFSP entered into effect. Article

J.3[2] of Maastricht requires unanimous decisions in Council on both specific actions and the definition of later CFSP decisions (implementation, duration, funding), which could be taken by QMV. No such decisions have been reached due to lingering fears of setting a precedent for QMV in the CFSP, although states have "refrained from insisting on a consensus" on several minor CFSP decisions.[18] Worse, when there is a clash between the voting rules of the EC (QMV) and those of the CFSP (unanimity), those of the CFSP tend to dominate. This inevitably complicates the CFSP decision-making process while diluting existing supranational EC procedures with intergovernmental ones. The controversies over security-related decision-making procedures have not been lost on the Commission, which has been on the defensive since Maastricht and has not yet asserted itself as forcefully in the CFSP as some had hoped.

With this limited record and the lingering practical problems involved in creating an ESDI, the stage was set in 1996 for another series of reforms. In their official contributions to the 1996-97 IGC, most EU states and institutions admitted serious disappointments with the CFSP in general and the security aspects in particular. The Commission[19] and the European Parliament[20] were the most critical of the difficulties encountered in implementing the CFSP, while even the official Council report on the functioning of the TEU also admitted the disappointment of some member-states with the performance of the CFSP.[21]

The criticisms outlined in these reports were taken into consideration by the Reflection Group charged with preparing the agenda for the IGC between June and December 1995.[22] However, the Reflection Group had been seriously divided over the question of merging the EU and the WEU, so the EU foreign ministers were unable to establish firm guidelines on this matter for their IGC negotiatiors.[23] Even by the end of the IGC negotiations in mid-1997, most of the reforms had not deviated too far from the ideas discussed in the Reflection Group a year earlier; the same could be said about the final Amsterdam Treaty approved by the Amsterdam European Council of 16-17 June 1997 and signed by EU member-states on 2 October 1997.

THE AMSTERDAM REFORMS

It is beyond the scope of this essay to discuss the positions, negotiations, and outcomes of the Amsterdam Treaty in great detail.[24] Instead, this examination limits itself to the major debates and reforms concerning the EU's external political relations and its links with the WEU. Overall, the Amsterdam Treaty enhances and clarifies existing provisions of the TEU, yet in some areas it represents only a modest step forward.[25] The general EU/CFSP provisions will be considered first and then the relationship between the EU and the WEU.

EU/CFSP Reforms

First, Amsterdam includes more details about the EU's interests to be served by the CFSP and/or WEU. Article J.1[1] states that the CFSP must:

> safeguard the common values, fundamental interests, independence, and integrity of the Union in conformity with the principles of the United Nations Charter; strengthen the security of the Union in all ways; preserve peace and strengthen international

security, in accordance with the principles of the United Nations Charter, as well as the principles of the Helsinki Final Act and the objectives of the Paris Charter, including those on external borders; promote international cooperation; develop and consolidate democracy and the rule of law, and respect for human rights and fundamental freedoms.

In addition, the so-called "Petersberg tasks" (humanitarian and rescue tasks, peacekeeping tasks, and tasks of combat forces in crisis management, including peacemaking), outlined by the WEU at a meeting on 19 June 1992, were formally incorporated in the new treaty under Article J.7[2].

Second, in terms of CFSP policy instruments, no major changes were made other than to expand slightly the concept of CFSP joint actions. According to Article J.4[1], "joint actions shall address specific situations where operational action by the Union is deemed to be required. They shall lay down their objectives, scope, the means to be made available to the Union, if necessary their duration, and the conditions for their implementation." As will be discussed below, the WEU was brought closer to the EU (compared to Maastricht), yet EU member-states still could not agree to a full merger of the two institutions or a timetable for such due to the continued opposition of Britain and the neutral EU member-states. Nor could the EU commit itself to establishing an independent defense capability. Instead, Article J.7[1] alludes to the "progressive framing of a common defense policy . . . which might in time lead to a common defense, should the European Council so decide," wording which closely matches that in the Maastricht Treaty.

Article J.7[1] does affirm that the WEU is an "integral part of the development of the Union," providing the EU with an operational capability for the Petersberg tasks noted above. The WEU also "supports the Union in framing the defense aspects" of the CFSP. However, as with the TEU, member-states could not agree to instruct the WEU to serve the EU; instead, the Amsterdam Treaty says the EU "will *avail itself* of the WEU to elaborate and implement decisions and actions of the Union which have defence implications." Institutional links are supposed to be enhanced "with a view to the *possibility* of the integration of the WEU into the Union, should the European Council so decide" (emphasis added). Once more, this tortured wording reflects lingering differences over the specific institutional links between the EU and the WEU, and the long-term goal of a common defense policy.[26] A protocol attached to the new treaty concerning the defense provisions of Article J.7 states that the EU "shall draw up, together with the Western European Union, arrangements for enhanced cooperation between them, within a year from the entry into force of this Protocol" (see below). In addition, the delicate question of security clearances for Council Secretariat-General personnel has been breached, with specific arrangements to be decided later.[27] Finally, as with the Maastricht Treaty, any such arrangements or merger must respect the obligations certain member-states have regarding NATO.

Equally important provisions were outlined regarding decision-making and compliance, but these do not go as far as extending real QMV procedures to security or defense cooperation, as some suggested.[28] Instead, the Amsterdam Treaty follows the new doctrine of "flexibility" in such matters, effectively opening the door to two classes of membership in the EU's CFSP/ESDI pillar. First, all member-states are entitled to full participation when the EU "avails itself" of the WEU in the service of Petersberg tasks; those states who do participate (even if not members of the WEU) may also be involved in planning and decision making. Second, the EU still relies on unanimous Council decisions when taking CFSP decisions (Article J.13[1]), but Amsterdam permits abstentions by member-states so as not to prevent the adoption of such decisions by the majority. Such "positive abstention" would theoretically allow for "coalitions of the willing" to proceed with a particular action. Third, when abstaining in a vote, any member of the Council may qualify its abstention by making a formal declaration to do so. In that case, the member is not obliged to apply the decision but must "accept that the decision commits the Union." To enhance compliance, abstaining states must "refrain from any action likely to conflict with or impede Union action based on that decision and the other Member States shall respect its position." However, if such abstaining members represent more than one-third of the votes weighted in Council, the decision will not be adopted.

The new procedures do improve the provisions for QMV in the CFSP, but only slightly. If enough members decide to go ahead with a CFSP decision, the Council can act *automatically* by qualified majority under two circumstances: when adopting joint actions, common positions or taking any other decision on the basis of a common strategy; or when adopting any decision implementing a joint action or a common position. This removes the cumbersome procedure under the previous Article J.3[2] of Maastricht, which required an initial decision to act, then another unanimous decision of all EU member-states to define later decisions that could be taken under QMV. However, as noted, if a set of abstaining states amounts to more than one-third of the votes in Council, a coalition easy enough to engineer, the EU cannot act. Moreover, as always, there is a powerful escape clause that may paralyze the EU: If a member of the Council declares that, "for important and stated reasons of national policy, it intends to oppose the adoption of a decision to be taken by qualified majority, a vote shall not be taken." The Council may, acting by a qualified majority, request that the matter be referred to the European Council for decision by unanimity, but this use of QMV requires at least sixty-two votes in favor, cast by at least ten members. This means that three large states, two large states and two small states, or six small states (plus other combinations) can block CFSP decisions. As usual, none of these provisions applies to decisions having military or defense implications, which must be taken by consensus.

Amsterdam also modifies the issues of policy implementation and external representation. As under Maastricht, the new treaty (Article J.8) provides for the Presidency to represent the EU in CFSP affairs, including international organizations and conferences. As before, the Commission is "associated" with the Presidency in these tasks. IGC negotiators had also hoped to reform the "Troika" arrangement for external representation (consisting of the previous, current, and next member-states to hold the Presidency). They succeeded in part: now the Presidency can be assisted by its successor alone if necessary, which should have reduced slightly the number of officials representing the EU abroad. However, Amsterdam confused the issue in Article J.8[3] by providing that the Presidency should "be assisted by the

Secretary-General of the Council who shall exercise the function of High Representative for the common foreign and security policy." This provision provoked much debate in the context of the Reflection Group and the IGC,[29] but at least Amsterdam did not reflect the French proposal to establish a new grand political official to speak for the CFSP. Instead, this high representative can also assist the Council by contributing to the formulation, preparation, and implementation of CFSP policy decisions, and, when appropriate and acting on behalf of the Council at the request of the Presidency, through conducting political dialogue with third parties. Moreover, the Council may, whenever it deems it necessary, appoint yet another special representative with a (temporary) mandate to handle particular policy issues.

Given the CFSP's budgetary problems over the past several years, the Amsterdam Treaty outlines specific provisions in the area of CFSP financing (Article J.18). Under this article, both CFSP administrative expenditure and operational expenditure are to be charged to the budget of the EC, under its normal procedures, which inevitably involve the Commission and the European Parliament. There are, as usual, key exceptions to this procedure for expenditures arising from operations having military or defense implications and cases where the Council, acting unanimously, decides otherwise. In keeping with the doctrine of "flexibility," EU member-states that formally abstain from military or defense actions according to the above provisions are not required to finance such actions. As before, in cases where expenditure is not charged to the EC budget it will be charged to the member-states in accordance with a GNP scale, unless the Council, acting unanimously, decides otherwise. This is not likely to happen, considering the past difficulties with funding the Mostar operation.

After years of debate, the Amsterdam Treaty also includes an inter-institutional agreement between the European Parliament, the Council, and the Commission concerning CFSP financing.[30] The new CFSP budgetary procedure is described in detail in this agreement, and it includes sections regarding the funding of:
  (a) the observation and organization of elections or participation in democratic transition processes;
  (b) EU envoys;
  (c) prevention of conflicts/peace and security processes;
  (d) financial assistance to disarmament processes;
  (e) contributions to international conferences; and
  (f) urgent actions.

Considering the haphazard nature of CFSP funding over the past four years and disagreements among EU member-states regarding this issue, this agreement could be a great step forward and go a long way to improving the budgetary process. It will be only a modest improvement, however, if EU states do not agree to a substantial increase of the CFSP budget.

The new treaty also creates a CFSP Policy Planning and Early Warning Unit, to be established in the General Secretariat of the Council under the responsibility of its secretary general, the new high representative for the CFSP.[31] The decision to establish this unit was the easiest one for the IGC negotiators to reach, as most felt the EU's difficulties in situations such as Yugoslavia were due in part to the lack of a common definition of the problem.[32] This unit, in conjunction with the existing Political Committee, which prepares all CFSP issues for the Council, is intended to help remedy this perceived deficiency. Under the new treaty, cooperation with this unit will be established with the Commission, EU member-states, and the WEU in order to ensure the coherence of the EU's external economic and development policies. It will be staffed by personnel from the General Secretariat, EU member-states, the Commission, and the WEU, and the institutions these officials represent are expected to share relevant, even confidential, information. The tasks of the unit will include the following:

(a) monitoring and analyzing developments in areas relevant to the CFSP;

(b) providing assessments of the Union's foreign and security policy interests and identifying areas where the CFSP could focus in the future;

(c) providing timely assessments and early warning of events or situations that may have significant repercussions for the Union's foreign and security policy, including potential political crises; and

(d) producing, at the request of either the Council or the Presidency or on its own initiative, argued policy options papers to be presented under the responsibility of the Presidency as a contribution to policy formulation in the Council, and which may contain analyses, recommendations, and strategies for the CFSP.

Finally, Amsterdam also states (under Article J.7) that member-states will support armaments cooperation in the hopes of framing a common defense policy, but there is no formal commitment to a common arms procurement policy or organization yet. Predictably, this controversial topic did not see much consensus in the Reflection Group nor during the early IGC talks, but there was recognition that if Europe wants to increase its share of the shrinking global arms market it must change its research and procurement practices, given the very large economies of scale required by these industries. Opposition to direct Commission involvement or to the revocation of Article 223 does not preclude other cooperative measures of course; Britain was approved to join the proposed Franco-German arms agency (set up in 1995) on 4 June 1996, while France and Germany (at their Dijon summit, 6 June 1996) formally agreed to give a new push to defense cooperation and to "review" their twenty-seven bilateral arms programs, which would extend to joint procurement.

Similarly, the Commission is already poised to take steps toward improving the competitiveness of the EU's approximately 50 billion ECU defense industry, having outlined a number of proposals in a January 1996 communication. According to it, between 1984 and 1992 domestic demand in EU defense industries fell by 30 percent, exports were cut in half, and the industry shed 37 percent of its workforce. As Martin Bangemann, EU industry commissioner, bluntly put it, "If the EU wants a CFSP, then it has to choose between a domestic arms industry or buying military hardware from America."[33] The Commission wants to apply single market rules to the defense industry and foster joint armaments research and production, but since France and Britain still fear potential Commission influence in military affairs through the "back door" channel of industrial policy, major change in the near future is unlikely. There was wide agreement that some sort of coordination–and potentially a formal European armaments agency or West European armaments organization–should be established among these groups and industries, but this objective did not find its way into the Amsterdam Treaty in any substantial way.

WEU Reforms Concerning the EU

It is worth taking a look at the EU's post-Amsterdam relationship to the WEU in some detail. After its "reawakening" in 1984, the WEU has steadily attempted to define and enhance its role in European security affairs. It provided a forum for allied European Community states to discuss security and defense matters among themselves outside of the NATO framework, particularly when they did not see eye-to-eye with the United States (such as over Euro-missiles).[34] Yet the WEU still saw itself as part of the broader Atlantic Alliance (for example, see the 1987 WEU *Platform on European Security Interests*). The WEU participated in military operations during these years, such as in "Operation Cleansweep" in 1988 at the time of the Iran-Iraq war, and its membership grew. However, WEU member-states were not yet prepared to define its role in clearer terms. In addition, the WEU clearly lacked the resources to play a larger role in European security; it was particularly deficient in reconnaissance, intelligence, and transport.

Since Maastricht the WEU has attempted to define possible missions for itself, such as the Petersberg tasks of 1992 and a common European defense policy on 9 May 1994, while attempting to clarify its relationship to NATO and the EU. The WEU also established several new permanent organizations to support itself: a Planning Cell, a Situation Center, a Satellite Center, and the Institute for Security Studies.[35] The Italians and the British, who held the EU Presidency and the WEU Presidency, respectively, during the first half of 1996, managed to adopt a joint declaration on taking steps to increase EU/WEU institutional links, adapt the WEU's "Humanitarian Task Force" for use by the EU, and conduct WEU military exercises.[36] Similarly, the 7 May 1996 "Birmingham Declaration" of the WEU made it clear that the organization was ready to serve as the defense arm of the EU and to perform Petersberg tasks with NATO's logistical support. These plans were attached to the Amsterdam Treaty.[37]

In particular, Amsterdam reiterates the goal of building up the WEU in stages as the defense component of the EU. When the EU "avails itself of the WEU," the WEU acts according to the guidelines of the European Council (set by unanimity, of course); as noted above, all EU member-states are entitled to participate, while the role of WEU Observers is to be defined later. New arrangements for "enhanced cooperation" between the EU and the WEU include:

(a) consultation/decision making, particularly in crisis situations;

(b) joint meetings of EU/WEU organizations;

(c) harmonization of presidencies, rules, and practices of EU/WEU organizations;

(d) coordination of staff of WEU Secretariat-General and EU Council Secretariat-General, including exchange and secondment of personnel;

(e) arrangements to allow relevant bodies of the EU, including its new Policy

Planning and Early Warning Unit, to draw on the resources of the WEU's Planning Cell, Situation Center, and Satellite Center;

(f) cooperation in the field of armaments, potentially involving a European Armaments Agency;

(g) practical arrangements for ensuring cooperation with the European Commission; and

(h) improved security arrangements with the EU.

Regarding NATO, Amsterdam's "Declaration Relating to the WEU" reaffirms that NATO is the "essential forum" for Atlantic defense. The WEU is "an essential element" of the development of the ESDI "within the Atlantic Alliance," and it will "continue its efforts to strengthen institutional and practical cooperation with NATO." Cooperation with NATO is to be developed in the following areas:

(a) mechanisms for consultation between the WEU and NATO in the context of a crisis;

(b) the WEU's active involvement in the NATO defense planning process;

(c) operational links between the WEU and NATO for the planning, preparation, and conduct of operations using NATO assets and capabilities under the political control and strategic direction of the WEU, including:

(1) military planning;

(2) a framework agreement on the transfer, monitoring, and return of NATO assets and capabilities;

(3) liaison between the WEU and NATO in the context of European command arrangements.

The WEU has also worked out "preliminary conclusions" on the formulation of a common European defense policy. Along these lines, several EU member-states agreed to a three-stage plan to create a common defense union with a military capacity. As the Amsterdam Treaty was being finalized, France, Germany, Italy, Spain, and Belgium, with some support from the Netherlands and Luxembourg, announced on 21 March 1997 their proposal for "a common European defense," including the full integration of the WEU into the EU. In the first stage, the EU would be able to "request" the WEU to carry out security missions on its behalf. In the second stage, the EU could give "instructions" to the WEU regarding military operations. In the final stage, the WEU would be integrated into the EU along with a "common armaments policy" and a mutual security clause. The first stage of this plan is supposed to begin as soon as the Amsterdam Treaty is ratified by all EU member-states; dates for later stages were not specified.[38]

Yet this coalition is still solidly blocked by another one opposed to a rapid merger of the EU and the WEU: Britain, Portugal, and the WEU Observers (Austria, Denmark, Finland, Ireland, and Sweden). Presumably, EU members who are not full members of NATO (Austria, Finland, Ireland, and Sweden) could also "opt in" to this defense structure at a later date. At least these countries agreed to include the Petersberg tasks in the Amsterdam Treaty, and they have contributed to security operations in the Balkans and elsewhere.

PROSPECTS: PARTNERSHIP OR RIVALRY?

The Amsterdam Treaty continues a long tradition in the institutional development of European political cooperation, resulting in incremental reforms based largely on a lowest-common-denominator consensus among EU states. There are real improvements, such as the new CFSP budgetary process and the elimination of Article J.3[2]. There are cosmetic changes, such as the new Policy Planning and Early Warning Unit. There are complications, such as the new High Representative for the CFSP. And there are omissions, such as a legal personality for the EU so that it can conclude international agreements (at present such agreements must be signed by all member-states or by the EC on behalf of the EU), and more democratic accountability for the EU's ESDI. One could quibble over the details still left to be worked out, such as the idea of "separable but not separate" forces for WEU/NATO, or "double-hatting" of officials in these domains. However, assuming the details can be worked out, is it really conceivable that the EU could play a leading, if not independent, role in European security? Given the EU's record in this area over the past half decade, there are serious reasons to be skeptical about such a role.

First, there is the question of resources. To put it bluntly, the EU cannot afford its own independent defense capability. Military budgets in the EU are under heavy strain, while economies in general have struggled to meet the criteria of Economic and Monetary Union. According to some estimates, a European intervention force of 50,000 troops would cost from $18 to $49 billion over the next twenty-five years, and a satellite intelligence system would cost between $9 and $25 billion over the same period. Another estimate puts the costs of European military independence at $107 billion per year.[39] The EU cannot pay this price, even if it wanted to (and public opinion would have something to say about it as well). It also goes without saying that the WEU has very limited operational resources compared to NATO. There is also no supreme commander of WEU, no peacetime headquarters, and no unified and joint commands.

In addition to limited financial resources, there is not enough cooperation among defense companies in Europe to support military independence. European states are still supporting national champions (with limited domestic consolidation and restructuring) while inhibiting cross-national mergers and acquisitions under the protection of Article 223. For example, Western Europe has ten prime contractors for warplanes and helicopters, while the United States has five; Western Europe has eleven missile companies and the United States has four. Most French armaments firms are still state-owned, making partnerships with Britain and Germany problematic. In fact, British and German cooperation is now on the rise compared to long-standing Franco-German cooperation. Also, the French are much less inclined to make partnerships with American firms, which further distances them from British and German cooperative efforts. These partnerships also help to alleviate pressures for a common European arms industry. Thus, external cooperation and lingering domestic barriers to reform prohibit a robust Europeanwide arms industry. For now only the Eurofighter is going forward, and probably the "Horizon" air-defense Eurofrigate and the Eurocopter.[40] The EU also lags way behind the United States in the development and integration of new warfare technologies, such as digital communications, a global positioning system (guidance and navigation), computers, precision-guided munitions, and stealth technology to evade radar.[41]

Second, without its own resources the EU must increasingly rely on NATO to support its ambitions, an option that presents another set of difficulties. NATO and the United States (that is, Congress) are unlikely to give the EU a blank check to use NATO resources. The many layers of decision making required for the CJTF concept to become operational, combined with Europe's limited military assets, mean that most security-related missions (Petersberg tasks or otherwise) that require military force will also require U.S. involvement, whether by legislative approval or active participation in the operation. Even if France "won" the exclusion of a clause in the Berlin agreement saying that NATO could "supervise" or "oversee" European operations, there are three important limitations here concerning CJTFs: (1) the North Atlantic Council must unanimously approve the use of NATO assets; (2) NATO will be able to monitor and review the use of NATO assets; and (3) NATO has the right to recall forces in the event of a "grave security crisis."[42] Moreover, it should be recalled that NATO has few assets of its own; most of its assets are national assets, and most of those are American. Thus Europe will probably have to borrow military equipment from the United States if the CJTF concept is to have any relevance. In short, there will be no "Europeanization" of NATO yet, in terms of all-European commands and independent European commanders (linked to the EU or not).[43]

Third, even if the EU developed its own significant capabilities, and/or NATO agreed to lend the required assets, there has been a distinct lack of collective political will whenever an opportunity to act independently presents itself to the Europeans. For example, the EU stood by during the military confrontation between Greece and Turkey over the Aegean islet of Imia/Karadak in early 1996. This would have been a perfect opportunity for Europe to get involved in a security/defense matter, but the United States had to step in. Similarly, when Commissioner Hans van den Broek suggested in early May 1996 that the EU take over the peacekeeping mission in Bosnia after the Americans left, he was soundly criticized from all sides (even Britain and France) for the idea and for speaking out like this without consultation from governments.[44] The Europeans would not conceive of staying in Bosnia without the Americans.

The flip side of this problem with political will is when an EU state decides to go it alone, without the involvement of NATO or the EU. France has most often demonstrated this tendency, with its unilateral actions in the Middle East and Africa, its decision to halt conscription and withdraw troops from Germany without consulting the Germans, and its highly controversial nuclear tests in the Pacific in defiance of its EU/UN partners, yet all EU states are susceptible to this temptation. Most recently, the EU could not agree to use the CFSP to help alleviate the growing crisis in Albania, one which seemed to be tailor-made for the EU's new ambitions. After an exodus of 14,000 refugees to Italy by March 1997, several EU states (Denmark, Italy, France, and Greece) wanted to send thousands of troops once

Albania appealed to the European members of NATO. But Britain, Germany, Sweden, and neutrals were able to block the idea. Instead, 7,000 multinational troops, led by Italy and France, were deployed on 14 April (Operation Alba, or "Sunrise"). Yet these troops stayed only long enough to assist with elections and to distribute food and medicine; there was no support for a peacekeeping or peacemaking mission.[45]

Fourth, even if enough EU states mustered the will to act as a unit independent of NATO, Amsterdam's decision-making procedures still allow one state to block collective action for "important and stated reasons of national policy." Although this provision might reduce the use of the veto to make trivial ideological points about CFSP procedures (as has taken place under Maastricht), it is still too tempting an option when EU states do not agree on a policy's fundamentals. Moreover, the EU still requires unanimity in questions of defense; while the EU's non-NATO members (Austria, Finland, Ireland, and Sweden) have been willing to contribute to external security operations, one cannot expect that this willingness will automatically carry over in situations where another member of the EU is directly threatened.

Fifth, even if the required number of EU governments decided to mount a military-related security operation, domestic politics can interfere with collective action. At the very least, elections, domestic problems, and changes of government periodically prevent the rotating EU Presidency from exerting the leadership required for Europe to act. This could be seen during Italy's Presidency the first half of 1996, where its weak government did nothing about the Greco-Turkish Aegean crisis. At the most, domestic public opinion or constitutional provisions get in the way of European collective action in defense matters, as Denmark, Germany, and Ireland have demonstrated. Germany managed to change its constitutional interpretation regarding defense matters, but only after a protracted debate that complicated if not delayed NATO/WEU decision making on peacekeeping in Bosnia.[46] Austria has done this as well to some extent. However, as noted above, it takes only one EU member-state to prevent the EU from acting if, "for important and stated reasons of national policy," it intends to oppose the adoption of QMV decisions. This has happened before, and there is little reason to believe it cannot happen again.

Sixth, even if the previous problems were resolved, the EU is about to confront other challenges that may work against an effective ESDI capacity. Enlargement and Economic and Monetary Union will seriously complicate matters and water down the EU's independent efforts in security and defense.[47] Six new members in the short term (Cyprus, the Czech Republic, Estonia, Hungary, Poland, and Slovenia), which will add over sixty million to the EU's population, and a new currency will impose major costs on the EU, diverting monies that could be used for military personnel and equipment. An intertwined set of "hard cores" in Europe (the single currency, free movement of persons, social provisions, and so on) with varying memberships could make it very difficult to mount a collective security operation with so many other pressing concerns. The EU will also "import" the security problems and external interests of its new members, while at the same time giving them an effective veto over decision making regarding the CFSP/ESDI. How these new members will be represented in the Commission's external relations departments (not to mention the EU's other institutions), which involve up to seven Commissioners and four Directorates-General, presents another extremely difficult issue. Thus, given the current mix of limited resources, weak decision-making procedures, competing interests, and the pending difficulties related to enlargement,[48] the idea of a truly operational ESDI seems to be an increasingly insurmountable obstacle.

CONCLUSION

The preceding comments should not imply that the EU can play no important role in security affairs. The Union plays a far more important role in economic security through its common market, trade, aid, and development programs. And despite the complexities of the next enlargement, the EU has proven highly successful in encouraging new and potential member-states to reform their political and economic systems, as we have seen with Greece, Portugal, and Spain. There is nothing wrong with enhancing the EU's characteristics as a civilian, economic power; in fact, there are strong reasons for doing so at the expense of military power. Despite the provision incorporating the Petersberg tasks in the CFSP, the EU can be a more powerful force for long-term security, not crisis management, using socioeconomic tools, not military ones. Other noncombat-related support tasks, such as policing, customs patrols, information-sharing, support operations, training, and humanitarian aid, are also possible.

Above all, the EU must be careful to recognize its limitations. At present, the WEU is in serious danger of becoming superfluous as a separate "European arm" of NATO *and* as the "defense arm" of the EU. Its functions should be brought into the EU as part of the CFSP; otherwise its existence simply produces unnecessary institutional confusion in Europe. Given recent changes in the EU and NATO, the added value provided by the WEU for its members is rapidly diminishing. It is a forum for defense ministers, but they are not prevented from meeting in the EU. A combined Council of Foreign and Defense Ministers could be permitted, as the Italian Presidency and Commission have suggested, perhaps with the neutral member-states admitted as observers or nonvoting members. The WEU is also important for confidence-building and information-sharing, but these functions can be handled within the framework of the CFSP.

But the WEU is really an insurance policy. Like most insurance policies, its value is the peace of mind it provides, even if no "claims" are made against the policy. NATO can handle defense matters and less-serious security-related tasks, and the United States will still support its allies in these matters. The WEU does have symbolic value in that it gives neutral EU states an outlet for participation in security affairs without the burden of security guarantees, and without provoking a negative reaction in Russia. It could also be useful as a means to bring associated states in Central and Eastern Europe into a collective security arrangement (but not an alliance) at about the same time they join the EU. In this sense it could act as a teaching tool to educate new EU/WEU members of their responsibilities in joining the European integration experiment.[49]

However, assuming EU enlargement to the East proceeds in the next decade, the same proposed changes in EU decision-making rules that would allow the neutral states to participate selectively in security-related CFSP tasks could be used as a transitory mechanism for the new member-states. Meanwhile NATO, through the Partnership for Peace and Russian participation in the Implementation Force in Bosnia, seems to be managing its practical relationship with Russia quite effectively, although conservative Russian politicians will probably still be able to gain by NATO-bashing in the foreseeable future.[50] And NATO expansion to include, for example, Ukraine and the Baltics is highly unlikely in the short to medium term. All these factors are working against the maintenance of the WEU as an autonomous unit, inside or outside the EU.[51]

Thus the EU should not delude itself; without major changes in the relationship of the WEU to the EU/CFSP, NATO's unmatched resources and ability to perform new tasks, combined with the CJTF concept, threaten to make any independent defense or security component of the CFSP irrelevant in practice, although it may remain an ambition for years to come. In short, what really matters is the sequence of institutional decision making when a potential military crisis or security problem presents itself. In such cases, it would not be unreasonable to argue that NATO should have a "right of first refusal" for any operations that might involve combat. Bosnia has shown it is possible to have an excess of institutional arrangements, so that responsibility is passed around and no one takes the lead. The United States has not helped matters, of course, by vacillating over participation in Bosnia and threatening to reconsider its commitment to NATO. But these acts were meant for a domestic political audience. Broadly speaking, the United States has learned from the mistakes of Bosnia and it knows there are strong reasons for staying involved in Europe.

The EU as well can take modest steps to satisfy a lingering desire to have an independent capability if necessary, and there is also nothing wrong with this goal as an insurance policy in the long term. But Europe must face realities: It is not ready, able, or willing to assume a more prominent role in military operations. A "capability-expectations gap" need not be a liability either, for such a gap can encourage the EU to continually develop and refine its capabilities.[52] But if Europe's unrealized ambitions prevent others from acting, or needlessly complicate multilateral cooperation in security affairs, it would be necessary for expectations to be scaled down.[53] As Bosnia tragically demonstrated, Europe must realize the consequences of making inflated claims about its willingness or ability to take on more responsibility in world politics.

ENDNOTES

1. On Europe and Yugoslavia, see Simon Nuttall, "The EC and Yugoslavia: *Deus ex Machina or Machina sine Deo?" Journal of Common Market Studies* 32 (August 1994): 11-25; and Geoffrey Edwards, "European Responses to the Yugoslav Crisis: An Interim Assessment," in *Toward Political Union: Planning a Common Foreign and Security Policy in the European Community*, ed. Reinhardt Rummel (Boulder, CO: Westview Press, 1992); and Pia Christina Wood, "European Political Cooperation: Lessons from the Gulf War and Yugoslavia," in *The State of the European Community*, vol. 2: *The Maastricht Debates and Beyond*, ed. Alan W. Cafruny and Glenda Rosenthal (Boulder, CO: Lynne Rienner, 1993).

2. For ambitious views, see Jacques Delors, "European Integration and Security," *Survival* 33 (March-April 1991): 99-109; Hans van den Broek, "The Common Foreign and Security Policy in the Context of the 1996 Intergovernmental Conference," speech given at the Royal Institute for International Relations, Brussels, July 1995; and Hans van den Broek, "Why Europe Needs a Common Foreign and Security Policy," *European Foreign Affairs Review* 1 (July 1996): 1-5.

3. These include: strengthening democratic principles and institutions; promoting regional stability and regional cooperation; assisting international efforts to deal with emergency situations; strengthening existing cooperation against arms proliferation, terrorism, illicit drugs, and supporting good government. See the *Report to the European Council in Lisbon on the Likely Development of the Common Foreign and Security Policy* (hereafter Lisbon Report), 27 June 1992.

4. Factors that determine common interests include: geographical proximity of a given country or region; an interest in the political and economic stability of a region or country; and the existence of threats to the security interests of the Union (Lisbon Report).

5. These are: disarmament and arms control in Europe (including confidence-building measures); nuclear nonproliferation; and economic aspects of security (especially technology transfer) (Lisbon Report).

6. For more on this debate, see Charles Krupnick, "Explaining European Defense Cooperation: Analysis of the 1991 NATO and EC Negotiations on Security and Defense," paper prepared for delivery at the Fourth Biennial International Conference of the European Community Studies Association, Charleston, SC, 11-14 May 1995 (hereafter Fourth Biennial Conference); Robert J. Art, "Why Western Europe Needs the United States and NATO," *Political Science Quarterly* 111 (Spring 1996): 1-39; and Simon Duke, "The Second Death (or Second Coming?) of the WEU," *Journal of Common Market Studies* 34 (June 1996): 167-90.

7. "Declaration on Western European Union," attached to the Treaty on European Union.

8. Art, "Why Western Europe Needs the United States and NATO," 29. This agreement between the Eurocorps and NATO is mentioned in the "Communique Issued

by the Ministerial Meeting of the North Atlantic Council," Brussels, 17 December 1992, reprinted in the *NATO Review* 40 (December 1992): 29-30.

9. For detailed assessments of the performance of the CFSP, see Roy H. Ginsberg, "The European Union's Common Foreign and Security Policy: An Outsider's Retrospective on the First Year," *ECSA Newsletter* 7 (Fall 1994): 13-16; Roy H. Ginsberg, "Principles and Practices of the European Union's Common Foreign and Security Policy: Retrospective on the First Eighteen Months," paper prepared for delivery at the Fourth Biennial Conference; Elfriede Regelsberger and Wolfgang Wessels, "The CFSP Institutions and Procedures: A Third Way for the Second Pillar," *European Foreign Affairs Review* 1 (July 1996): 29-54; Philip H. Gordon, "Europe's Uncommon Foreign Policy," *International Security* 22 (Winter 1997-98): 74-100; and Stephanie B. Anderson, "Problems and Possibilities: The Development of the CFSP from Maastricht to the 1996-IGC," and Michael E. Smith, "What's Wrong with the CFSP? The Politics of Institutional Reform," both in *The State of the European Union*, vol. 4, ed. Pierre-Henri Laurent and Marc Maresceau (Boulder, CO: Lynne Rienner, 1998).

10. Between 1 November 1993 and 1 July 1996 the CFSP produced twenty-six common positions, thirty joint actions, and nearly 200 declarations. However, nearly half of the positions and actions were related to ex-Yugoslavia and Mostar (eleven positions, thirteen actions).

11. For more detailed discussions, see Trevor Taylor, "West European Security and Defense Cooperation: Maastricht and Beyond," *International Affairs* 70 (January 1994): 1-16; and Mathias Jopp, "The Defense Dimension of the European Union: The Role and Performance of the WEU," in *Foreign Policy of the European Union: From EPC to CFSP and Beyond*, ed. Elfriede Regelsberger, Philippe de Schoutheete de Tervarent, and Wolfgang Wessels (Boulder, CO: Lynne Rienner, 1997).

12. WEU support of the EU's administration of Mostar was not an official request by the EU made under Article J.4[2].

13. Denmark "opted out" of this decision, but the Danes also said they would not impede the development of closer cooperation among member-states in this area. *Agence Europe*, 29 June 1996; *European Report*, no. 2045, 3 July 1996; interview with COREPER official, Brussels, 1996.

14. Interview with a Commission official, Brussels, 1996.

15. Interviews with Commission and COREPER officials, Brussels, 1995-96. Also see Thomas Hagleitner, "Financing the Common Foreign and Security Policy (CFSP): A Step Towards Communitarisation or Institutional Deadlock?" *CFSP Forum* 2 (1995): 6-7; and Jörg Monar, "The Finances of the Union's Intergovernmental Pillars: Tortuous Experiments with the Community Budget," *Journal of Common Market Studies* 35 (March 1997): 57-77.

16. *European Report*, no. 2083, 11 November 1995; ibid., no. 2085, 18 November 1995; ibid., no. 2131, 11 May 1996; ibid., no. 2137, 5 June 1996. Also see the "Birmingham

Declaration" of the WEU ministerial meeting (7 May 1996); and the final communiqué of the North Atlantic Council ministerial meeting in Berlin (NATO doc. M-NAC 1-96-63), 3 June 1996.

17. For more on this issue, see Pierre de Vestel, *Defence markets and industries in Europe: Time for political decisions?* (Paris: Institute for Security Studies of the WEU, 1995); and Saferworld, *The Future of the European Defence Industry* (Brussels: Club de Bruxelles, 1994).

18. According to interviews with Commission and COREPER officials (Brussels, 1995-96), member-states did not insist on unanimity on the antipersonnel mine-clearing directive, financial sanctions against Bosnia-Herzegovina, some disbursement decisions for Mostar, and a decision on the prohibition against making payments under contracts caught by the embargo against Haiti.

19. See Commission of the European Communities, *Commission Report on the Functioning of the Treaty on European Union* (Luxembourg: Office for Official Publications of the EC, 1995); Commission of the European Communities ("High Level Group of Experts on the CFSP"), *The Foreign and Security Policy of Europe for the Year 2000: Ways and Means to Establish Real Credibility* (Durieux Report) (Brussels: Commission's Spokeman's Service, 28 November 1995); and Commission of the European Communities, *Commission Report on Reinforcing Political Union and Preparing for Enlargement* (COM[96]90) (Luxembourg: Office for Official Publications of the EC, 1996).

20. European Parliament, *Report on Progress Made in Implementing the Common Foreign and Security Policy (November 1993-December 1994) of the Committee on Foreign Affairs and Security* (Matutes Report). *EP Documents* 211/241 (24 April 1995).

21. Council of Ministers, *Report of the Council on the Functioning of the Treaty on European Union* (Luxembourg: Office for Official Publications of the EC, 1995).

22. Reflection Group, *Reflection Group's Report for the 1996 IGC* (Brussels: European Community, 5 December 1995).

23. Interviews with Reflection Group members and IGC negotiators, Brussels, 1995-96. Also see Michael Hennes, "The Reflection Group of the European Union," *Aussenpolitik* 47, English edition (Winter 1996): 33-42.

24. Subsequent references in the text to the Amsterdam Treaty are from the Intergovernmental Conference of the Amsterdam European Council (16-17 June 1997), *An Effective and Coherent External Policy*, downloaded from the European Union website.

25. For a more detailed discussion of the CFSP reform debate, see Smith, "What's Wrong with the CFSP?"

26. For example, the Irish draft treaty revisions, which preceded the Amsterdam Treaty, had suggested that the wording of Article J.4 should be changed to "the *pro-*

gressive framing of a common defence policy *in the perspective of* a common defence. . . . The Union *will avail itself of* the WEU to elaborate and implement decisions and actions of the Union which have defence implications" (emphasis added to reflect textual changes).

27. This subject is addressed in the "Declaration on enhanced cooperation between the European Union and the Western European Union," attached to the Amsterdam Treaty.

28. During the Amsterdam negotiations, Commissioner Hans Van Den Broek suggested a "big bargain" to enhance decision making: the idea of eliminating the veto in the CFSP in exchange for giving bigger countries more voting weight in it. The idea was soundly rejected by the smaller states. *Economist*, 22 March 1997.

29. Interviews with Reflection Group members and IGC negotiators, Brussels, 1995-96.

30. See the "Interinstitutional Agreement between the European Parliament, the Council, and the European Commission on provisions regarding financing of the Common Foreign and Security Policy," attached to the Amsterdam Treaty.

31. See the "Declaration to the Final Act on the establishment of a policy planning and early warning unit," attached to the Amsterdam Treaty.

32. Interviews with members of the Reflection Group and with IGC negotiators, Brussels, 1995-96.

33. The Commission's plans for enhancing the competitiveness of EU defense industries are outlined in the *Commission communication on the challenges facing the European defense industry*, released by the Commission's Spokesman's Service, Brussels, 25 January 1996. The quote is from *European Report*, no. 2094, 20 December 1995. Interviews with members of the Reflection Group and with IGC negotiators, Brussels, 1995-96. Also see *European Report*, no. 2102, 27 January 1996, and *Agence Europe*, 26 January 1996.

34. Duke, "The Second Death (or Second Coming?) of the WEU."

35. For more on these reforms, see Joseph I. Coffey, "WEU After the Second Maastricht," in *The State of the European Union*, vol. 4.

36. *Agence Europe*, no. 6622, 8 December 1995.

37. *European Report*, no. 2131, 11 May 1996. Also see the Amsterdam Treaty, "Declaration relating to Western European Union," which notes and incorporates the "Declaration of the Western European Union on the role of Western European Union and its relations with the European Union and with the Atlantic alliance," adopted by the Council of Ministers of the WEU on 22 July 1997.

38. John Palmer, "Paris and Bonn Launch European Defence Plan," *The Guardian*, 22 March 1997.

39. These estimates are from M. B. Berman and G. M. Carter, *The Independent European Force: Costs of Independence* (Santa Monica: RAND Corporation, 1993); and the Royal United Services Institute cited in the "The Defence of Europe: It Can't Be Done Alone," *Economist*, 25 February 1995.

40. Charles Grant, "A Survey of the Global Defence Industry," *Economist*, 14 June 1997.

41. For more on this point, see "The Future of Warfare," ibid., 8 March 1997.

42. On the NATO/CJTF debate, see *European Report*, no. 2083, 11 November 1995; ibid., no. 2085, 18 November 1995; ibid., no. 2131, 11 May 1996; ibid., no. 2137, 5 June 1996; and the final communiqué of the North Atlantic Council ministerial meeting in Berlin (Doc. M-NAC-1 96-63), 3 June 1996.

43. For far more pessimistic assessments of Europe's willingness and ability to become more independent of NATO and the United States, see John Mearsheimer, "Back to the Future: Instability in Europe After the Cold War," *International Security* 15 (June 1990): 5-56; and Art, "Why Western Europe Needs the United States and NATO."

44. *Agence Europe*, 7 May 1996.

45. The troops that left after the Albanian elections in July were replaced by 600 policemen, mostly Italians (with some help by the WEU).

46. On Germany's domestic debate, see Clay Clemens, "Opportunity or Obligation? Redefining Germany's Military Role Outside of NATO," *Armed Forces and Society* 19 (Winter 1993): 231-51; Hans W. Maull, "Germany and the Yugoslav Crisis," *Survival* 37 (Winter 1995-96): 99-130; and Michael E. Smith, "Sending the Bundeswehr to the Balkans: The Domestic Politics of Reflexive Multilateralism," *German Politics and Society* 14 (Winter 1996): 49-67.

47. For more on enlargement problems, see David Allen, "Wider but Weaker or the More the Merrier? Enlargement and Foreign Policy Cooperation in the EC/EU," paper prepared for delivery at the Fourth Biennial Conference; and Christopher Preston, "Obstacles to EU Enlargement: The Classical Community Method and the Prospects for a Wider Europe," *Journal of Common Market Studies* 33 (September 1995): 451-63.

48. For its part, the Commission has called for an "integrated approach" to external relations so that its political capabilities can match its economic resources. Qualified majority voting in the CFSP is a necessary part of that approach, as is a strengthening of the WEU's operational resources. See the Commission's report, *Agenda 2000: Volume 1, For a Stronger and Wider Union* (DOC/97/6, Strasbourg, 15 July 1997), part 4, "The Union in the World." Yet not all EU member-states are fully committed to these ideas.

49. For more arguments along these lines, see Philip H. Gordon, "Does the WEU Have a Role?" paper prepared for delivery at the conference, "European Security, Defense, and Integration: Western European Union, 1954-1996," St. Antony's College, Oxford, 21 June 1996.

50. On this point see Bruce Clark, "Bonn says Russia easing NATO stance," *Financial Times*, 5 June 1996.

51. For more on the WEU issue, see Lawrence Martin and John Roper, eds., *Towards a Common Defence Policy* (Paris: Institute for Security Studies of the WEU, 1995).

52. The phrase is from Christopher Hill, "The Capability-Expectations Gap, or Conceptualizing Europe's International Role," *Journal of Common Market Studies* 31 (September 1993): 305-28. Also see his "Closing the Capability-Expectations Gap?" paper prepared for delivery at the Fifth Biennial International Conference of the European Community Studies Association, Seattle, WA, 29 May-1 June 1997.

53. For a similar argument, see David Allen and Michael Smith, "The European Union's Presence in the European Security Order: Barrier, Facilitator, or Manager?" paper prepared for delivery at the Tenth International Conference of Europeanists, Chicago, IL, 14-16 March 1996.

NATO IN THE NEXUS
OF TRANSATLANTIC SECURITY RELATIONS
Stanley R. Sloan[1]

In spite of the end of the Cold War, for better or worse, NATO remains the most important single ideological and institutional link between the United States and Europe. Many other institutions, including the European Union (EU), the Western European Union (WEU), and the Organization for Security and Cooperation in Europe (OSCE), play unique and important roles in the emerging European security system. But it is NATO that keeps the allies working together on a day-to-day basis and gives them the option of acting together in a principled defense of their common interests.

Promoting the values articulated in the Treaty of Washington remains a shared U.S.-European interest. The NATO nations have so far successfully used the enlargement process to help spread and solidify those values among a much wider group of nations. Continued defense cooperation in the alliance gives policymakers options that they would not otherwise have, facing a diverse array of potential future disturbances to international stability. Defense cooperation also serves as a policy tool to help create new patterns of relationships in Europe and holds out the prospect of moving Russia's relationship with the NATO countries beyond the Cold War foundations of arms control policies and onto qualitatively new ground.

As the NATO allies address the challenges of enlarging alliance membership and seeking successful outcomes in Bosnia, NATO will probably hold together. But underlying structural imbalances–reflected in U.S. complaints about burdensharing and European protests about U.S. hegemonic behavior–could threaten the long-term health of the transatlantic relationship.

NATO, the Cold War bastion of Western values and deterrence strategy, remains the core institution of European security today. The reasons for NATO's persistence are many and can be expressed in a variety of ways, depending on one's inclination toward optimism or pessimism, idealism or cynicism. Some would say that NATO's resilience has to do with the fact that it has become much more than a traditional military alliance. A Dutch defense expert, for example, argues that the process of growth can be traced to the report of the "three wise men" in the mid-1950s, which advised that "NATO must become more than a military alliance" and warned that if it did not, "[NATO] would disappear with the immediate crisis which produced it."[2] The assertion that NATO was more than a traditional alliance was, in fact, made repeatedly by administration witnesses during U.S. Senate consideration of the original treaty in 1949.

Others might say that NATO persists because the Europeans want the United States to stay engaged in Europe, or, less generously, because they don't want to pay the political and economic costs of defense autonomy. Some critics say that NATO persists because the United States hopes to preserve hegemony over Europe. It could also be argued that simple inertia is more important than all these arguments put together.

Today, a vast array of perspectives on NATO enlargement, European defense, transatlantic defense cooperation, NATO-Russia relations, and related issues routinely grace the pages of leading newspapers and journals. Behind each one lies a set of assumptions about what NATO is. This essay begins by examining that question, in part to expose more clearly the author's prejudices. It then moves on to a discussion of some of the challenges immediately ahead and concludes with some observations about longer term trends.

WHAT IS NATO?

As we move beyond the immediate "post-Cold War era," there are many diverse views about what NATO is and what it should become. The debate over NATO's essence recalls the Indian fable about the king who asked a group of blind men to feel various parts of an elephant and to describe the elephant based on the part they had touched. Naturally, each blind man produced a different description of the elephant. NATO is a bit like that elephant, and we all are in some respects like the blind men–each hoping to produce a noble overview. This discussion starts from the premise that an objective assessment of NATO's purpose and mission should draw on several sources, including the provisions of the 1949 North Atlantic Treaty, the fact that an organization is in many respects defined by its activities and the declared goals and intentions of its members.

NATO as a Community of Values

The North Atlantic Treaty, otherwise known as the Washington Treaty (4 April 1949) from the fact that it was signed in Washington on 4 April 1949, was clearly designed to counter Soviet expansion and military power. But the treaty itself identified no enemy, protected the sovereign decision-making rights of all members, and was written in sufficiently flexible language to facilitate adjustments to accommodate changing international circumstances. Secretary of State Dean Acheson argued that "The central idea of the treaty is not a static one" and that "the North Atlantic Treaty is far more than a defensive arrangement. It is an affirmation of the moral and spiritual values which we hold in common." During 1949 Senate hearings on the treaty, Acheson and other administration witnesses argued that what they were proposing was very different from previous military alliance systems.[3]

The North Atlantic Treaty would not have been signed in the absence of a Soviet threat. But what made NATO different from previous military alliances was that it was based on the treaty's clearly articulated support for "democracy, individual liberty and the rule of law." A value basis for the alliance was necessary to help overcome forces in the United States that might have successfully resisted U.S. participation in a purely military alliance. It is true that, during the Cold War, the values of democracy, rule of law, and individual freedom occasionally took second place when authoritarian regimes in NATO were tolerated in the interest of maintaining a militarily strong alliance. But NATO's survival beyond the end of the Cold War suggests that its value foundation remains an important part of the glue that holds the alliance together and attracts new members.

NATO as a Flexible Framework

The treaty, drafted in relatively simple language, does not spell out in great detail how its objectives should be implemented. There is no specified military strategy, no requirement for any particular set of bureaucratic arrangements or military organization beyond the creation of a North Atlantic Council and a defense committee, both called for in Article 9. This suggests substantial latitude for reform or elimination of bureaucratic and military structures, or creation of new cooperative arrangements, as seen fit by the members. The only limits on such changes are imposed by national interests, inertia, and other human and institutional factors, not by the treaty.

NATO's flexibility has been demonstrated, for example, by the military buildup and elaboration of an integrated command structure in the early 1950s (which had not been anticipated when the treaty was signed and was judged necessary only after North Korea invaded the South), the adjustment to the failure of the European Defense Community (EDC) in 1954, and by the substantial reorientation of NATO's missions and structures in the 1990s. In the mid-1960s, NATO was forced to adjust to France's departure from the Integrated Command Structure. At the same time, the allies revamped NATO's strategy with the doctrine of "flexible response" to a possible Warsaw Pact attack. In 1967, the allies approved the Harmel Report, which gave the alliance the mission of promoting détente as well as sustaining deterrence and defense.

NATO as a Collective Defense System

At its founding, the most prominent aspect of the treaty was its requirement for individual and collective actions for defense against armed attack. Article 3 of the treaty provides that the allies "separately and jointly, by means of continuous and effective self-help and mutual aid, will maintain and develop their individual and collective capacity to resist armed attack." In Article 5, the treaty's collective defense provision, the parties agreed that "an armed attack against one or more of them in Europe or North America shall be considered an attack against them all . . . ." They agreed that each party to the treaty would "assist the Party or Parties so attacked by taking forthwith, individually and in concert with other Parties, such action as it deems necessary, including the use of armed force, to restore and maintain the security of the North Atlantic area."

The Article 5 provision is frequently described as requiring an automatic response by the United States to hostilities in Europe. The term "automatic" is inconsistent with a strict interpretation of Article 5, which leaves the precise actions taken by each party subject to their sovereign decision, and this was the interpretation of those who supported treaty ratification in 1949. In the case of the United States, a decision to go to war to help defend a NATO country against attack would still require decisions taken within the constitutional framework involving congressional as well as presidential decisions.

During the Cold War, NATO's strategy and the way in which the United States deployed its forces in Europe gave Article 5 more substance in practice than suggested by the words in the treaty. Beginning in the early 1950s, the United States deployed its military forces and nuclear weapons forward in Europe, mainly in Germany, in a fashion that ensured a Soviet attack on the West would in its early stages engage U.S. forces, therefore constituting an attack on the United States as well as on the host nation. In the mid-1950s, the United States threatened "massive [nuclear] retaliation" against the Soviet Union should it attack a NATO country. After the credibility of massive retaliation was undermined by Soviet acquisition of long-range nuclear weapons, NATO adopted a strategy of "flexible response," which suggested that battlefield nuclear weapons might be used early in any European conflict. Such weapons were deployed well forward in West Germany to ensure that they were seen as part of NATO's first line of defense.

Today, with no imminent Soviet-style threat, NATO strategy and force deployments have fundamentally altered the circumstances under which the United States would be making decisions on the use of its conventional and, especially, its nuclear forces in Europe. During the Cold War, the nuclear umbrella was designed to appear likely to be forced open in the case of a Warsaw Pact attack; prudent Soviet leaders had to assume that nuclear weapons might well be used early in a European conflict. Today, the nuclear umbrella is much less automatic.[4] NATO strategy now calls nuclear weapons "weapons of last resort." The allies have promised Russia that neither substantial NATO forces nor nuclear weapons would be deployed forward in new member-states. The United States has withdrawn all but a token deployment of some two hundred free-fall bombs from Europe.

All this suggests that, although the words of Article 5 have not changed, the threat that might invoke the article and the alliance strategy and deployments in support of Article 5 have changed quite radically. Now, the activities of the alliance have turned toward purposes of defense cooperation that lie beyond collective defense.

NATO as a Cooperative Defense Organization

NATO has been and always will be a political as well as a military alliance. In recent years, it has been popular to say that NATO would have to adapt to new circumstances by becoming "more political." But NATO's activities today continue to illustrate its unique utility as an instrument to promote and implement political/military cooperation among member- and partner-states. The goals of such cooperation today, however, are substantially different than those during the Cold War.

Policy Options for Crisis Management

In the early 1950s, the NATO countries developed a civilian organization and an integrated military command structure to help manage the alliance and to establish that there would be a united front in response to any Warsaw Pact attack. At the end of the Cold War, the allies asked themselves if they still needed such a system at a time when the Soviet threat had all but vanished. Their answer, recorded in the 1991 "New Strategic Concept," was that defense cooperation, so essential in the Cold War, could be turned to other purposes. Since that time, most of NATO's military activities have been focused on "non-Article 5" requirements, most significantly in Bosnia.[5] NATO cooperation is widely accepted as having facilitated an effective U.S.-led coalition response to Iraq's invasion of Kuwait.

NATO remains an organization of sovereign nation-states, and no member can be compelled to participate in a military operation that it does not support. Defense cooperation therefore cannot guarantee that the allies will respond to any given political or military challenge. But NATO can be used to build political consensus and create military options to back up or implement political goals. U.S. and allied policymakers would have fewer credible coalition military options if their military leaders and forces were not working together on a day-to-day basis, developing interoperability of those forces, planning for contingency operations, and exercising their military capabilities. This day-to-day work develops habits of cooperation at the political and military level that underpin the ability to work together when required to do so under pressure or, more importantly, under fire.

Defense Cooperation as an Instrument of Political Change

Beyond this explanation of NATO as a mechanism for building multinational military coalitions, defense cooperation is now being used for political goals as well. The Partnership for Peace (PFP), premised initially on the development of individual defense cooperation arrangements with partner countries in Europe, has begun to weave the military systems of new democracies into the web of NATO cooperation. Through the PFP, countries have been learning how to develop systems of democratically controlled security establishments as well as habits of cooperation with NATO states and neighboring partners. The partnership approach has helped the first wave of candidates meet the requirements for NATO membership.

In the face of Russian opposition to NATO enlargement, the allies are attempting to use political/military cooperation with Russia as a means to change Russian perceptions of the alliance and, it is hoped, to change the political relationship between Russia and NATO. The process of developing NATO-Russian cooperation began with military cooperation in Bosnia and now is developing further in the framework of the Russia-NATO Founding Act. In a sense, the allies are updating the goal of using NATO to promote improved relations among states in Europe that was added to NATO's mission by the 1967 Harmel Report. If NATO's current policy succeeds, the defense cooperation relationship with Russia could leapfrog over the Cold War-based arms control accords that were designed to regulate relationships between parties otherwise in conflict with one another. Moving from a Russia-NATO relationship governed by arms control to one characterized by the transparent, predictable, and confidence-building nature of defense cooperation would mark a sea change in the European security system.

Other Agendas

It is clear that NATO serves a variety of purposes for individual member states beyond these broadly stated goals. Many such "secondary" agendas help explain why current members of NATO want the alliance to continue, and why so many countries want to join. For example, former members of the Warsaw Pact do not fear attack from today's Russia, but they see NATO as a guarantee against falling once again into the Russian sphere of influence as well as an insurance policy against any future resurgence of a Russian threat. Most European governments hope that the process of European unification will lead to more intensive security and defense cooperation. But they recognize that integration of European defense and foreign policies faces many obstacles. This is an evolutionary process that might require several more decades before Europe could become a unitary actor on the world stage. In the foreseeable future, most European allies see the transatlantic link as essential to security in and around Europe, even though they support the development of a stronger European role in NATO.

Further, many Europeans believe that the U.S. role in Europe, particularly as translated through NATO, provides an important ingredient of stability that facilitates cooperation among European states. For example, Germany is not seen as a threat by its neighbors, but both Germany and other European states feel more comfortable with a Germany that is thoroughly integrated within the framework of both the European Union and the transatlantic alliance. From the U.S. point of view, NATO can be regarded as a way to help ensure that the burdens of maintaining international stability are fairly shared. Ironically, it can be, and frequently is, seen as a source of burdens to the United States. The burdensharing debates of yesterday, today, and tomorrow bear witness to this. NATO can also be seen as a way for the United States to retain influence over events in a region of the world that remains vitally important to U.S. political, economic, and security interests.

Is NATO a Collective Security Organization?

The term "collective security" is widely and loosely used in the discussion of NATO's future role. According to its classic definition, collective security is a system of relations among states designed to maintain a balance of power and interests among the members that will hopefully ensure peaceful relationships within the system. The League of Nations, established after World War I without U.S. participation, is usually regarded as such a system.

NATO has always been designed as a system of cooperation among member-states to deal with challenges and problems originating *outside* that system, not within it. Granted, NATO has to some extent tried to promote peaceful settlement of problems within the system in support of its mission of defending against external threats. It is credited with having helped heal World War II wounds inflicted by Nazi Germany on its neighbors. NATO has also attempted to mitigate conflicts between Greece and Turkey. But when the allies began preparing for enlargement, they made clear to potential applicants that they should resolve differences with their neighbors *before* they could be seriously considered for NATO membership.

From a legal perspective, NATO does not have principal responsibility for collective security in Europe–the North Atlantic Treaty does not suggest such a role. The Organization for Security and Cooperation in Europe (OSCE) was designed to promote peaceful relations among states "from the Atlantic to the Urals." The 1975 Helsinki Final Act established a series of agreed principles ("rules of the road") to govern relations among states in Europe. The OSCE member-states (all European states plus the United States and Canada) have adopted further agreements and principles, given the organization some diplomatic tools for conflict prevention, and convene regular meetings under OSCE auspices to try to nip problems in the bud before they develop more serious proportions. As a Euro-Atlantic cooperative security system develops, the OSCE can serve as the "constitution" and collective security framework for that system.

It should, however, be acknowledged that several aspects of NATO's activities contribute to the goal of collective security. The Russia-NATO Founding Act, the Partnership for Peace, and the Euro-Atlantic Partnership Council, for example, make important contributions to the goal of maintaining peaceful and cooperative relations among all states in Europe.

Today's NATO

In sum, the collective defense commitment in the North Atlantic Treaty is an obligation taken on by all members, even though Article 5 leaves much room for nations to decide collectively and individually what to do in any given crisis scenario. Continuing defense cooperation in NATO keeps alive the potential to mount collective responses to aggression against alliance members. Defense cooperation creates nonobligatory policy options for responses to crises beyond NATO's borders. Defense cooperation also serves as a tool for changing political relationships between NATO countries and other nations, particularly Russia. NATO is not a collective security organization; it is not designed to keep peace among its members but rather to protect and advance their interests in dealing with the world around them. Some of NATO's activities nonetheless contribute to the goal of collective security. To many, the North Atlantic Treaty represents the values and goals currently being articulated by the United States and its allies. Viewing the entire NATO "elephant" today, the alliance appears to be: a transatlantic community of values; a collective defense system; a system for defense cooperation; and a key part of an emerging cooperative Euro-Atlantic security system.

However, at this time of rapid change, issues of direction and mission are sources of contention among experts and policymakers on both sides of the Atlantic. The allies now are undertaking the momentous step of opening NATO's membership to countries that once belonged to the Soviet-led Warsaw Pact. This process has already placed strains on the relationship with Russia, and Russian opposition to enlargement has led many in the West to urge caution about moving too fast. But the process of enlargement also puts a strain on relationships among current members of the alliance because it raises fundamental questions about the purposes of NATO and whether the burdens of maintaining and enlarging the alliance are going to be shared equally.

TRANSATLANTIC RELATIONS IN THE ENLARGEMENT DEBATE

The debate in the U.S. Congress on NATO enlargement has been about much more than who should join NATO. The Senate's consideration of the protocol to the North Atlantic Treaty to admit the Czech Republic, Hungary, and Poland became a debate about the respective roles of the United States and its European allies in the post-Cold War world. Arguments in the committees and on the floor of the Senate scrutinized the purpose of NATO and the appropriate balance of burdens and responsibilities in the alliance. Senatorial attitudes toward NATO enlargement have, in some respects, been influenced more by senators' perceptions of the state of transatlantic cooperation than by the qualifications of the candidate states.

At the same time, a parallel challenge has been brewing across the Atlantic. There appears to be growing sentiment in Europe that the alliance is increasingly out of balance. From this view, the important structural and procedural changes celebrated at the Madrid summit as creating a "new NATO" do not diminish the dominant power and influence of the United States in NATO councils. The accusation that the United States behaves like a hegemonic power in relations with its allies, once heard mainly from French quarters, now echos elsewhere in Europe. When the United States declared its insistence on including just three candidates in the initial round of enlargement, even those allies who supported the outcome said quietly that they "liked the package but not the way it was wrapped."

Ironically, the answer to the American burdensharing demand and the European hegemony complaint is the same: a more coherent and responsible Europe. But that Europe is not likely to emerge from the current economic and political trends over the next decade. This suggests that, as the alliance moves through the enlargement process, allied unity could be severely tested by an increasingly acrimonious debate that could be made even worse by the challenge of achieving "success" in Bosnia–the tough testing ground for post-Cold War NATO.

The Burdensharing Demand

The most difficult issue in consideration of NATO enlargement is an old, familiar one: burdensharing. It was at the center of the debate over the membership applications of the Czech Republic, Hungary, and Poland, and it is likely to be a recurring theme as the enlargement process moves on to include other countries.

As Senator William V. Roth, Jr., chairman of the Senate NATO Observer Group, noted: "How the costs of NATO expansion will be shared will be critically important in the ratification debates, particularly in the U.S. Senate." He cautions that the issue could emerge "as the Achilles' heel–not only of NATO enlargement but of the alliance itself."[6] Senator Joseph Biden, co-chairman of the Senate NATO Observer Group and a supporter of both NATO and enlargement, has warned that "for NATO to remain a vibrant organization . . . the non-U.S. members must assume their fair share of direct enlargement costs and for developing power projection capabilities. To do otherwise would cast the United States in the role of 'the good gendarme of Europe'–a role that neither the American people, nor the Senate of the United States, would accept."[7]

The burdensharing issue has focused on several aspects: direct costs of NATO enlargement; force improvements required for adaptation to new missions; and arrangements for continued implementation of the Dayton Peace Accords in

Bosnia. In addition, many members of Congress believe that the main responsibility for bringing the new democracies into the Western fold belongs to the European Union. They may understand that the difficult and expensive task of "deepening" the EU through creation of the European Monetary Union is a high priority with European governments. But they nonetheless expect to see an EU enlargement process that will bring qualified East and Central European states into the EU fold as soon as possible.

Costs of NATO Enlargement

With regard to the direct costs of NATO enlargement, the Clinton administration, in its February 1996 report to the Congress, projected the total cost of an initial "small" group (similar to the one approved at Madrid) at $27-35 billion between 1997 and 2009.[8] Of this total, a projected total of $9-12 billion was called "direct enlargement" costs: those improvements in command, control, and communications facilities required to link the new allies to the current members. Such costs would be allocated according to traditional NATO cost-sharing formulas, which, according to their estimate, would cost the United States some $150-200 million per year. At the end of 1997, NATO, with U.S. agreement, produced its own estimates of this category of costs, and the results projected much lower totals. According to the NATO estimate, the costs falling under NATO's common budgets would amount to just $1.5 billion over ten years. The difference between this figure and the early-1997 U.S. estimates was explained as due to better than expected existing infrastructure in the candidate states, different methodologies for calculating costs, and the fact that the United States had based its estimates on four, not three, candidates. Whatever the figure, members of Congress expect NATO allies to carry without complaint their "fair share" of such relatively modest expenses.

The U.S. study projected another $10-13 billion in costs to the new members to restructure their own forces to make them more interoperable with NATO forces for both collective defense and peace operations. NATO did not produce an estimate of costs in this area because they are the national responsibility of the new members, not shared expenses of the alliance. Many analysts and the applicants themselves see this portion of the costs as expenses that they would incur in any case to modernize their military capabilities over the next decade.

Cost of Force Projection Improvements

The most controversial and difficult issue posed by the Clinton administration's cost estimates, and one on which members of Congress will continue to focus, is the cost of improvements to the military capabilities of current allies. These costs, estimated in the U.S. study at some $8-10 billion, are not a new product of the enlargement decision. Rather, these costs result from NATO's 1991 New Strategic Concept's requirement for all allies to restructure their militaries to make them more capable of projecting force beyond national borders. The United States has judged the improvements essential not only to support NATO's new missions but also to fulfill collective defense commitments to the new allies. Some allies, France in particular, already are reforming their defense establishments to move in this direction. None of the European allies is likely to have "new" money available for developing force projection capabilities. They will have to meet the Strategic Concept's goals by developing greater efficiencies and reprioritizing current expenditures. But NATO's future political viability and military effectiveness will depend on whether all the allies make serious contributions to the new missions now identified for the alliance.

Bosnia

Perhaps the most difficult continuing issue could be the question of how to allocate the costs of maintaining for an indefinite period a NATO presence in Bosnia. Many members of Congress would have preferred that the United States leave Bosnia when the mandate of the Stabilization Force (SFOR) ran out in June 1998. But the decision to stay was based on the judgment, supported by most expert opinion and NATO military leaders, that the withdrawal of SFOR as planned would have destabilized Bosnia, possibly bringing a return to civil war or, at a minimum, de facto partition of Bosnia and a failure of the Dayton Accords.

Many members of Congress, who agree that some external military presence will be required in Bosnia for years to come, think that the European allies should demonstrate that they are willing and able to assume more responsibility for security in Europe by taking over Bosnian military operations. Most European governments, however, believe that the presence in Bosnia should remain a NATO operation and are reluctant to remain in Bosnia without a clear and present U.S. commitment. Given the uncertain future for Bosnia under even the best of circumstances, the Europeans fear they might be left holding the bag of failure to implement Dayton and perhaps even face U.S. criticism from the sidelines for the outcome.

Under these circumstances, a transatlantic debate about who will carry future burdens of peace implementation in Bosnia could continue in parallel with discussion of future enlargements of NATO. There will be a persistent danger that transatlantic discussions of burdensharing could become quite fractious. Members of Congress may complain about the reluctance of the Europeans to take responsibility for a continuing military presence in Bosnia. The European allies would likely respond that they indeed had tried to help the United States implement the Dayton Accord, and it is not their fault alone that the goals of the accord were not accomplished. Such a debate could put great strain on transatlantic relations.

American Leadership or Hegemony

Meanwhile, at the same time that American members of Congress are pressing the allies for more effective burdensharing, European allies may be quite sensitive about diktats from the U.S. administration and Congress. It has always been difficult for the United States to achieve the "perfect" level of alliance leadership that builds consensus without seeming to dictate American preferences. It is even more so today, when there is no imminent threat to help build consensus behind U.S. preferences.

The United States now has such overwhelming strength in the international system that, like a bull in a china shop, it must walk very carefully not to break alliance dishes. Self-confident U.S. behavior–ranging from touting the strength of the U.S. economy at the G-8 summit to limiting the first round of NATO enlargement to three states–has rubbed many Europeans the wrong way. When the Clinton administration revealed its choice of the Czech Republic, Hungary, and Poland to participate in the first wave of NATO enlargement, many allies privately applauded. Even France, which was a strong proponent of including Romania and Slovenia, was not surprised that the United States and several other allies would only support a smaller group.

But the fact that the United States appeared to have abandoned the process of NATO consultations to make its choice clear, and then said its decision was nonnegotiable, troubled even the closest allies of the United States. It strengthened the hand of those in Europe who claim that the United States is acting like a hegemonic power, using its impressive position of strength to have its way with weaker European allies.

U.S. officials say that they wanted to keep the issue within alliance consultations but that their position was being leaked to the press by other allies, particularly France. They decided to put an end to "lobbying" for other outcomes. Their choice to go strong and to go public may have been understandable and even defensible. However, the acknowledged leader of a coalition of democratic states probably needs to set the very best example in the consultative process if it wants other sovereign states to follow its lead willingly. Perhaps it is just hard being number 1, and U.S. officials have observed that the United States is "damned if it does, and damned if it does not" provide strong leadership. Perhaps the style of the decision reveals too clearly what appears to be a Washington culture in which the bright and brash more often than not move ahead in the circles of power. But the style does not work well in an alliance of democracies.[9]

Whatever the explanation, U.S.-European relations would have been better served by a U.S. approach that allowed the outcome to emerge more naturally from the consultative, behind-the-scenes, consensus-forming process. In NATO councils, votes are weighed, not counted, and the U.S. vote still carries more weight than any other. The final result would have been the same, and the appearance of a U.S. diktat to the allies would have been avoided.

LOOKING AHEAD
The Twenty-first-Century World and NATO
NATO will enter the twenty-first century in transition, changing from an alliance once focused primarily on deterring the Cold War Soviet threat to its new role at the center of the emerging cooperative Euro-Atlantic security system. The allies have pointed the way toward a system that will be inclusive, rather than exclusive, and therefore toward a NATO that has begun and will continue to enlarge its membership to include qualified candidates. Moreover, the allies have confirmed the construction, still in process, of a "new NATO" that is compatible with, and even critical to, the new political, economic, and security realities in Europe. But neither the process of enlarging NATO nor of building a new NATO are completed. The choices scheduled to be made at the planned April 1999 NATO summit meeting concerning further enlarge-

ment, particularly about NATO's future means and missions as embodied in a new strategic concept, will define further the NATO that enters the next century.

What kind of world faces the NATO allies as they approach the twenty-first century? So far, there is no consensus concerning how best to characterize the international system that is emerging after the end of the Cold War. The NATO allies are working to shape the emerging international system in ways that will support their interests and reflect their values. But the end result is far from clear. This is a transitional period, one which calls on governments to ensure that the system that emerges in the next century is as favorable as possible.

On balance, the world is a much more congenial place than it was during the Cold War. The military confrontation in Europe is gone. It is progressively being replaced by a system of cooperative security, underwritten by growing defense cooperation, political consultation, and economic integration. From this perspective, there is a strategic breathing space. But, if taken for granted, that space clearly could dissipate, inviting new potentials for tensions and conflict. It is the task of elected officials and policymakers to anticipate new problems and to mitigate their potential impact on the interests of their nations.

Relations between NATO countries and both Russia and China are poised precariously between elements of cooperation and conflict. Either relationship could go sour in the future, and either eventuality could destabilize the international system. Russia's reform process is threatened by strong nationalist and former Communist elements, and the direction of its political evolution is largely beyond NATO's influence or control. China is becoming a major player in the international economic system. However, its large and growing market stands in stark contrast to its relatively closed political system that denies citizens the human rights taken for granted in Western democracies. China, therefore, remains a potentially disruptive factor in international politics. In addition, North Korea presents a continuing threat to peace on the Korean peninsula.

The Middle East is a bubbling cauldron. The Middle East peace process holds hope for increased stability in the region, but fundamental differences and tensions between Israel and its neighbors appear likely to persist well into the next century. Radical regimes in Libya, Iraq, and Iran could endanger regional stability as well as international access to vital sources of energy. All three have been, and presumably continue to be, sources of support for international terrorists who, with access to modern weapon technologies, have a widening range of means for attacking civilian targets.

Threats of terrorism and motivations to acquire nuclear, chemical, and biological weapons grow out of dissatisfaction with the status quo. A variety of nonproliferation regimes, including the 1968 Treaty on the Non-Proliferation of Nuclear Weapons, exist, and the dangers of the spread of these weapons are well understood in the international community. But weapons of mass destruction can be powerful tools for those who hope to gain advantage over their adversaries. The poor condition of Russian military forces and potential political instability in Russia raise concerns that Russian nuclear weapons might fall into the hands of radical regimes or terrorists. Chinese political objectives and desires to profit from the international arms market may conflict with NATO nonproliferation goals. Instability in Russia or China, as well as threats to peace in the Middle East, therefore raise profound challenges for the future.

In addition, conditions of poverty, famine, and internecine conflict in many regions of the world remain time bombs on an otherwise stable globe. Until underlying economic, social, and political problems are resolved or ameliorated, these conditions in Africa, Asia, and elsewhere will continue to challenge Western values and interests. Natural resource availability will remain a source of tension and potential conflict.

The twenty-first-century world will undoubtedly be host to an even more rapid pace of technological change than that experienced in the last century. Technological advance can be for either ill or good of societies and their security, but it is in any case inevitable. The NATO allies in the next century will be challenged to decide which technologies present threats to their interests and which can be deployed to the advantage of their security and well being.

Although technology may be giving rise to new challenges, it is likely that political and economic relationships will carry forward familiar challenges from the twentieth century. In spite of an immense area of common interests built on a foundation of shared values, the NATO nations are all unique products of their historical experiences and cultural backgrounds. This diversity, which brings to the alliance many strengths, also poses difficulties. Those difficulties will, in the twenty-first century, likely continue to include varying outlooks, for example, on dealing with questions of when and how to use force on behalf of alliance goals, how to deal with unfriendly regimes, and how best to relate to one another in the alliance.

One particular political problem likely to carry over into the next century is the fact that no one nation is likely to match the political, economic, and military strength of the United States. This unique position of the United States in an alliance among equals will continue to raise concerns in Europe about excessive American influence and issues in the United States about inequitable burdensharing.

In the coming decades, it is possible that the process of European integration will produce a sufficiently cohesive Europe to yield a more equitable sharing of both responsibilities and burdens in the alliance. The imminent steps toward the European Monetary Union will likely exert a strong force toward greater political union. But at the same time, the parallel process of enlarging the membership of the European Union will make political union more elusive. Europe is therefore likely to remain a collective of individual states that find themselves increasingly dependent on one another and on their common institutions, but that are not ready to take the final political steps into full political union.

Another issue that will carry over from the twentieth to the twenty-first century is how to maintain an international economic system that meets the individual and common needs of the states in that system. Some have speculated that the end of the Cold War would inevitably lead to greater frictions among participants in the international trading system. They argued that the Western nations resolved economic differences among themselves because they faced a common military and ideological threat from the Soviet Union. But this analysis overlooks the fact that the international economic system is essentially one that invites competition, and therefore a degree of conflict, but which works successfully only when the competition is tempered by compromise and then cooperation. The system is in many respects self-regulating. Nevertheless, in the next century it seems likely that trade and economic frictions will from time to time threaten relations among NATO nations, and that policymakers will continually be challenged to maintain a balance of costs and benefits that ensures continued political commitment to the system.

The Challenge

Whether or not the burdensharing demands and the hegemony complaint turn transatlantic relations sour in the coming years will depend on how much value the United States and its allies place on the alliance relationship. No longer does a Soviet threat force the transatlantic partners to cooperate. But the values that underlie the partnership still appear to be alive and well on both sides of the Atlantic. The twenty-first-century world projected above suggests the need for Euro-Atlantic cooperation to deal with the challenges facing the interests of the allies. From the European perspective, there is no credible answer to Europe's security needs in the foreseeable future than thoroughgoing cooperation with the United States. From the U.S. perspective, there currently is no more effective way to share international security burdens than defense cooperation through the NATO structure. The United States and Europe have little practical choice other than to continue their cooperation. But the potentially contentious debate about how to share costs and responsibilities equitably will play a major role in determining what kind of NATO emerges in the early years of the coming century.

THE NECESSITY FOR CONTINUED ADAPTATION

In the longer run, simply managing transatlantic relations might not be an adequate response to the challenges facing the allies. Bitter emotions about burdensharing and hegemony could deteriorate into perceptions of diverging interests and deprive the alliance of its political content, the will to act together on behalf of shared principled interests. In 1985, in what seems like a lifetime ago, I called for "a new transatlantic bargain" designed to rebalance the transatlantic relationship. Rereading what I wrote then is both reassuring and depressing: reassuring that I was on the right track; depressing to see how slowly we have been able to move toward the goals I identified. Nonetheless, with the exception of one reference to the Soviet Union, the words of the book's last two paragraphs ring true today:

> The new bargain must bring greater European responsibility and leadership to the deal; it must ensure continued American involvement in European defense while at the same time constructing a new European "pillar" inside, not outside, the broad framework of the Western alliance. The new bargain requires evolutionary, not revolutionary change–NATO must remain able to serve the fundamental purposes for which it was designed. And, the bargain must bring together Europe's full potential, attracting the active participation of France, West Germany, and Great Britain, while benefitting from the substantial combined assets of the other West European allies.

Will the European allies find the vision and courage to take on added responsibilities? Will the United States be wise enough to accept a more independent European partner? Will we have the patience to allow the evolutionary change to occur? Perhaps not. However, if the allies do not move in this direction, the imbalance in the transatlantic relationship will likely lead the alliance from one crisis of confidence to another. The alliance may withstand such a permanent crisis, *mainly because the Soviet Union will probably make it necessary*. But the only way to maximize the benefits of alliance will be to encourage a process of gradual evolutionary change in US-European relations toward a new transatlantic bargain.[10]

There is no Soviet Union to provide the rationale for overcoming future crises of confidence in the alliance, and we certainly hope that today's Russia will never raise the sorts of challenges posed by the Soviet Union when I first wrote the lines reproduced above. And we should note that progress has been made. France is a few steps closer to full participation in the alliance. The reform of NATO's structure to embrace the Western European Union has begun. The possibility of European-led Combined Joint Task Forces now exists. The revolutionary concept[11] of dual-hatting the deputy supreme allied commander to create the potential for European military leadership of operations from within the NATO structure has been accepted and implemented.

But the questions I raised in 1985 remain alive and well today. It is not clear that the process of European integration has the political energy to push ahead on defense cooperation. There simply is insufficient motivation. The Soviet threat is gone, and all other threats seem far less by comparison. As a result, resources made available for defense are in free-fall in Europe. The idea of collaborating to counter U.S. influence, a motivation that from time to time seems to energize the French, is a treacherous ground on which to build European defense cooperation because it puts the transatlantic relationship at risk. It is also not clear that the United States is prepared to give up real influence and responsibility to its allies until they demonstrate the will and ability to take on burdens that have been carried largely because the United States has been willing to do the heavy lifting (one has only to refer to the on-going dispute between France and the United States about whether the commander of Allied Forces South should continue to be an American officer).

The ironic conclusion that I reach as we approach the twenty-first century is that my recommendation for an evolutionary process of change remains the best advice for today and tomorrow. If things go reasonably well in the international system, and the level of threats remains in the current neighborhood, it is very unlikely that European defense cooperation will take any dramatic leaps forward in the foreseeable future. And so, in an age where instant gratification has become a standard by which progress is measured, the worry remains: Will we be sufficiently patient to accept an evolutionary process that moves ever-so-slowly toward that new transatlantic bargain; and will we be sufficiently persistent to continue to push in that direction even if not absolutely required by contemporary circumstances to do so?

ENDNOTES

1. Stanley R. Sloan is the Senior Specialist in International Security Policy for the Congressional Research Service and Consultant to the Senate NATO Observer Group. These views are his own.

2. Rob de Wijk, *NATO on the Brink of the New Millennium, the Battle for Consensus* (London: Brassey's, 1997), 1.

3. North Atlantic Treaty, Hearings Before the Committee on Foreign Relations, U.S. Senate, 27, 28, 29 April, 2 and 3 May 1949.

4. Credit to Larry Chalmer, Director of the National Defense University's NATO Staff Officer Orientation Course for the nuclear umbrella imagery.

5. For background on the process of NATO adaptation see Stanley R. Sloan, *NATO's Future: Beyond Collective Defense*, McNair Paper 46, National Defense University, December 1995 (originally published under the same title as Congressional Research Service Report to Congress 95-979, 15 September 1995).

6. Senator William V. Roth, Jr., "Roth's Rx for NATO," *Christian Science Monitor*, 18 June 1997, 20.

7. Senator Joseph R. Biden, Jr., "The Prospects for NATO Enlargement," address to the Atlantic Council of the United States, 18 June 1997.

8. Other studies have produced broader ranges of potential costs based on much wider ranges of threat scenarios. The often-quoted cost of $125 billion for enlargement comes from the high-end of the U.S. Congressional Budget Office's (CBO) calculation of what it would cost to integrate the new allies in a much more challenging threat environment such as that posed by the Soviet Union during the Cold War. Given the current state of Russian military forces and presuming the continued development of NATO-Russia defense cooperation, such circumstances appear out of the question over the next decade, a consideration unfortunately not addressed in the CBO study.

9. These arguments were originally developed in the author's article entitled "Steering NATO–Not a One-Country Job, *Christian Science Monitor*, 25 July 1997, 19. See also Stephen S. Rosenfeld, "American Power Plays," *Washington Post*, 26 December 1997. This op ed piece summarizes Sloan's report for Congress entitled *The U.S. Role in the World: Indispensable Leader of Hegemon?* CRS Report 97-1046, 10 December 1997.

10. Stanley R. Sloan, *NATO's Future: Toward a New Transatlantic Bargain* (Washington, DC: National Defense University Press, 1985), 191 (emphasis added).

11. To those of us searching for ways to bring about the new bargain, the idea now may seem logical rather than revolutionary. But when, in 1995, I first broached the idea, I found that it ran directly counter to the way senior military officers traditionally think about a deputy: someone to be seen but not heard, unless it is an echo.

THE RISKS AND DIFFICULTIES OF NATO ENLARGEMENT:
THE VIEWS OF CONSERVATIVE DISSENTERS

Richard L. Kugler

When the organizers of this conference approached me about participating, they asked for a paper that would identify and evaluate the major dissenting arguments being marshalled against NATO enlargement. I have written such a paper, but it is not intended to play the role of cheerleader for these arguments. As almost everybody familiar with this debate knows, I have been a vocal proponent of NATO enlargement for some time. Indeed, I was a member of the RAND team that played a major role in designing the policy and strategy for enlargement that the United States and NATO are pursuing today. Because my strategic views remain the same, I do not agree with those critics who claim that their dissent adds up to a convincing case for scuttling enlargement. Nor do I agree that NATO enlargement is fundamentally off course or headed toward a calamity.

Nonetheless, I see value in the active presence of dissenters who responsibly criticize official policies for NATO enlargement. When their arguments are well-formed, the dissenters serve as more than naysayers and irritants. They perform the vitally important function of subjecting official policy to outside scrutiny. In doing so, dissenters identify the risks and difficulties that threaten to prevent NATO enlargement from unfolding successfully. As such, their arguments help point out how to design better enlargement policies, so that the troubles ahead can be overcome and the strategic goals of enlargement can be fully achieved.

It is from this constructive perspective that my assessment unfolds. I am not trying to make a case against enlargement. Instead, I am searching for ways to make it better by taking a clear-eyed look at the pitfalls ahead–as seen by dissenters who have made an art form of foreseeing all the many ways that NATO enlargement can go wrong. Sometimes it is a good idea to listen to one's critics, for they may have a degree of truth on their side.

THE CHANGING SHAPE OF DISSENT

My central thesis is that a major change has occurred in the dissent community in recent months. Prior to the Madrid summit (July 1997), the most vocal and influential opposition to NATO enlargement was based on "liberal" dissent. That is, it stemmed from arguments that NATO enlargement is not necessary and will greatly damage relations with Russia. Principal exponents of this dissent included, for example, George Kennan, Michael Mandelbaum, and John Matlock. Since Madrid, this dissent has lost steam because worry about Russia's reaction has declined. It is now being replaced by a different dissent: a "conservative" dissent.

This new dissent does not quarrel with the idea that NATO enlargement may be a sensible strategic step, and it is not worried about ruffling Russia's feathers. But it is worried that enlargement will be carried out in a weak and unwise fashion that damages both NATO and Europe in the process. This new dissent often may be expressed in crude terms that fail to capture the nuances of daily policy, but even so, the United States and NATO should listen to it, not dismiss it as wrongheaded and evil-minded. Over the previous two years or so, NATO's leaders were wise to react to a cacophony of simplistic liberal dissent by creating better outreach policies to Russia. They now need to treat the emerging conservative dissent in the same responsive way–with policies that lessen the potential risks and difficulties being identified. The consequence can be not only less dissent, but also better policy.

Who are these conservative dissenters? At the moment, they are mostly Americans, and only a few Europeans. Henry Kissinger and Sam Nunn have been prominent members of this school for some time. Recently, U.S. senators Jesse Helms, John Warner, Kay Bailey Hutchison, and Ted Stevens have joined the fold. Some journalists (e.g., Jim Hoagland of the *Washington Post*), former government officials (e.g., Fred Charles Ikle), and a few academics (e.g., Jeffrey Record) fall into this category. France's François Heisbourg is an example of a European who worries that NATO risks unraveling itself by enlarging. Whether American or European, these dissenters are not from the extreme right or left: they mostly fall on the center-right of the political spectrum. They tend to be hardheaded internationalists who favor ambitious security and defense departures only when these departures are well-considered, fully supported, and capable of succeeding. They thus are not questioning the strategic goals that animate NATO enlargement. Instead, they are questioning whether the United States, the Europeans, and NATO have the willpower and skill to implement it effectively.

For the most part, these dissenters are not trying to block NATO enlargement. In contrast to the liberal dissenters, most of whom are opposed to enlargement in principle, the conservative dissenters often are more interested in shaping NATO enlargement to suit their tastes, rather than preventing it from unfolding. Thus they tend to be conditional supporters of NATO enlargement, but their conditions can be stiff in ways that have important policy implications. My intent here is not to identify the full membership of this growing group or to examine specific positions taken by individuals. Instead, it is to finger the substantive issues that this group as a whole is now voicing in increasingly strong and influential ways. These dissenters have different concerns and viewpoints. Not all of them would agree with the full list of positions developed below; others might add additional arguments. When the central thrust of their combined voices is assessed, however, they as a group are advancing a dozen separate but interrelated arguments, as follows:

1. Current policy for NATO enlargement is too idealistic and insufficiently realistic.
2. Collective security is replacing collective defense as NATO's raison d'être.
3. Russia will be given too much influence over NATO policy.
4. Owing to the open-door policy, NATO will be enlarging too far eastward.
5. NATO will be diluted, and its solidarity damaged.
6. A hollow commitment to new members is being made.

7. The European Union (EU) is not enlarging fast enough to keep pace with NATO.

8. Key defense reforms will not take place.

9. The budget costs will be too high.

10. The West Europeans will not share the burdens fairly, and the new members will be free riders.

11. NATO will be left unable to attend to urgent security challenges elsewhere in different regions (e.g., the Persian Gulf).

12. Enlargement will interfere with the modernization of U.S. and allied forces.

These arguments differ in their particulars, but they reflect a common theme: They are contending that NATO enlargement is a very serious step that should be taken only if it is carried out with great resolve and steady forcefulness. Additionally, they are asserting that NATO should adopt policies that reflect its own interests, and that it should attend to new defense requirements as it enlarges. Simply stated, the conservative dissenters doubt NATO's capacity (including that of both the United States and Europe) to carry out this agenda in effective ways. As a result, many are worried that enlargement is headed toward failure or at least deep trouble. Indeed, some feel so doubtful that they are willing to leave the region of the Central and East Europe countries (CEEC) region as an unstable security vacuum rather than risk enlarging NATO into it.

Right or wrong, this growing conservative dissent now poses a greater threat to parliamentary approval of enlargement than does the old, now-fading liberal dissent. Most likely it will not be sufficiently powerful to prevent the U.S. Senate and European parliaments from ratifying the admission of new members into NATO. But it could prove sufficiently influential to result in many conditions and riders being attached to parliamentary approval, in ways that will influence how NATO enlargement is carried out. It also could produce parliaments and publics that are skeptics of NATO enlargement rather than fully in support of it. If so, the consequence could be to damage the manner in which enlargement is implemented.

Dissent, however, need not always produce damaged policies and weak consensus. It can be a vehicle for producing better policies and a stronger consensus. The attractive feature of the emerging conservative dissent is that it provides a number of powerful ideas for strengthening U.S. and NATO policies so that enlargement will unfold as a success, not as a mess or a dud (i.e., a "mess" of never-ending controversies and a "dud" of frustrated expectations).

With this viewpoint in mind, this paper begins by briefly discussing the liberal dissent against NATO enlargement. It then appraises the conservative dissent and its various manifestations. Finally, it analyzes how NATO's approach to enlargement might be affected, and of how the United States and NATO can use the dissenters' arguments to develop better, more effective policies.

THE FADING LIBERAL DISSENT

The original liberal dissent flourished from 1993, when the idea of enlargement was born, until recently. It was anchored in two premises. The first held that NATO enlargement is not necessary. It argued that the new European security order requires not a larger NATO but instead the creation of a strong collective security system, one in which an unenlarged NATO will play only a subordinate role. The second premise held that NATO enlargement will offend Russia to the point of destroying democracy in that country and provoking a new cold war. It argued in favor of leaving the CEEC region as a neutral zone shored up by collective security assurances, thereby mollifying Moscow that this zone will not fall under the control of a traditional enemy of Russia.

The first of these premises subsided as a barrier to NATO enlargement fairly early. Most participants in the European debate came to accept that a better security architecture is needed in the CEEC region, one stronger than can be created by the Organization for Security and Cooperation in Europe (OSCE). Rather than arguing against NATO enlargement per se, many believers in this premise began talking in terms of transforming NATO itself into a collective security body as it enlarges. As discussed below, debate is still raging over the role to be played by this idea in shaping NATO's future, but at the moment, the collective security vision is not acting as a major liberal dissent against enlargement. The second premise took a lot longer to subside. Indeed, it did not pass from the scene until early summer 1997. At this juncture, negotiations finally produced agreement that although Moscow does not favor NATO enlargement, it will not provoke a confrontation in reaction to Poland, Hungary, and the Czech Republic joining NATO. This agreement produced the Founding Act and the NATO-Russia Permanent Joint Council, thereby setting the stage for the Madrid summit at which NATO announced enlargement by 1999.

The effect has been to neutralize liberal dissent—at least for the moment. This does not imply that all controversy over Russia and collective security concepts has been permanently resolved. What it means is that these issues likely will not paralyze NATO enlargement in the coming months. A key point is that this liberal dissent did not pass from the scene on its own. It lessened because NATO adopted policies that responded to the dissenters' legitimate concerns. During 1994-97, the United States and NATO took steps to upgrade the OSCE and to equip NATO with several outreach policies and institutions. These include Partnership for Peace (PFP), the new Euro-Atlantic Partnership Council, and the NATO-Ukrainian Council. Equally important, the United States and NATO took strong steps to make clear that they truly are seeking a genuine partnership and cooperation with Russia. These measures helped bring about the goals being advocated by the liberal critics of NATO enlargement. In the process, they made liberal dissent a less potent foe of NATO enlargement.

THE GROWING CONSERVATIVE DISSENT–IDEALISM VS. REALISM

The new conservative dissent began gaining prominence in late 1996. It has many different offshoots, but at its core, it perceives U.S. policy for NATO enlarge-

ment as being too captured by a naive ideology of Wilsonian idealism, and as insufficiently motivated by realism. Henry Kissinger has especially articulated this theme,
but he is not alone. The conservative dissenters view Russia in more guarded terms
than does the Clinton administration. As a result, they want an enlarged NATO that
has the strength to counterbalance a menacing Russia, if necessary. They view the
Clinton administration as being too soft on Russia and too willing to sacrifice a strong
NATO so that Russia will accept enlargement. But Russia is far from the only issue
at stake. Kissinger and other dissenters are also motivated by deeper-seated, philosophical disagreements that go to the heart of how Europe and modern-era global politics are perceived.

Many conservative dissenters are realists in the sense that they view Europe
as influenced by its troubled history, and as vulnerable to still-existing fault lines and
dangerous new geopolitical trends. Their desire to prevent such geopolitics (e.g., competition between Russia and Germany) from gathering momentum is a principal reason why many favor enlarging NATO into the CEEC region. Moreover, they fear that
today's tranquil atmosphere could give way to a tense situation tomorrow. They want
NATO to be prepared for the worst, or at the least to be capable of reacting effectively to downward trends. Consequently, they want to carry out a NATO enlargement that is strong-minded and firmly backed by adequate military strength to get the
job done. They thus strongly disapprove of a purely political enlargement, one in
which NATO welcomes new members in diplomatic terms but leaves its military
power at home.

What many dissenters perceive in the Clinton administration is the opposite:
not a mature awareness of Europe's troubled essence, but instead a sophomoric belief
that Europe has now surmounted its history to the point where old-style geopolitical
thinking is no longer needed. In the eyes of the dissenters, the Clinton administration naively views NATO enlargement as a triumphalist exercise in spreading democracy and Western economic values to the exclusion of a responsible old-style assertion
of power and security involvements. As a result, the Clinton administration allegedly
does not grasp the trouble that could be encountered or the need to ensure that as
NATO enlarges, it is prepared for tough security challenges. Distrust of the Clinton
administration's maturity and motives leaves many conservative dissenters suspicious
about the administration's specific policies, even when the policies look sound on the
surface. These dissenters do not speak with a single voice, but, as a group, they primarily argue in favor of measures aimed at making enlargement stronger and more
assertive–in ways that reflect how NATO traditionally has gone about the business of
protecting its members and making Europe stable.

COLLECTIVE DEFENSE VS. COLLECTIVE SECURITY

Owing to their realism, the conservative dissenters strongly feel that if
NATO is to enlarge, it should be the old NATO that does the enlarging. They do not
perceive NATO as militarily threatened today, or as facing a new confrontation any-
time soon. Even so, they want an enlarged NATO that reaffirms Article 5 of the
Washington Treaty–the collective defense clause that mandates a powerful alliance-

wide response in the event that any member is threatened. To these dissenters, collective alliance defense is the glue that bonds NATO together, and that makes it an effective alliance. If collective defense is abandoned, they feel, NATO will fall apart sooner or later. Equally important, they judge that collective defense is the primary mechanism by which an enlarged NATO will be able to achieve its peacetime strategic goals in the CEEC region. To them, enlargement's key strategic goals are to promote regional stability, to prevent competition and conflict, and to deter aggression. They argue that these goals will be achieved only if Article 5 remains NATO's heart and soul. Moreover, they feel that a strong collective defense capacity is needed if NATO is to become more effective at performing security interventions outside its borders.

The conservative dissenters are deeply concerned about NATO's future essence. They fear that the great strengths built up during the Cold War will be lost if NATO moves eastward in flawed ways. They have a special distaste for collective security pacts that provide allegedly vacuous political reassurances without the military capability to carry them out. To them, NATO is the model of a properly functioning alliance. By contrast, the League of Nations is seen as a classical case study in how to mishandle strategic affairs through collective security mechanisms that fail to work when the chips are down. The alleged problem with collective security is that it fails to create binding commitments by participants, and it also gives rogues the power to veto collective action because they are a member of the institution. The result is that when a crisis occurs, rogues are free to commit aggression, and responsible countries lack the unity and military power to make a stand.

To the dissenters, the idea that NATO might be drifting from collective defense toward collective security is abhorrent. Yet in their eyes, the Clinton administration seemingly is headed in this direction. To them, the Clinton administration is doing more than merely moving NATO's borders eastward. Directly or indirectly, it allegedly is using enlargement as a vehicle to weaken or even dismantle NATO's collective defense mechanisms and to erect a loose collective security pact in its wake. In this worried view, NATO's current members may retain a semblance of collective defense, but new members will receive mostly political commitments, and NATO's main focus will be on peacebuilding activities outside its borders. This new NATO allegedly will have widespread institutional ties to virtually every country in Europe, but its old-style integrated command and alliancewide defense planning will be allowed to atrophy. This atrophying presumably will begin in the CEEC region, where the failure to erect collective defense mechanisms will initiate NATO's steady transformation into a very different body.

The conservative dissenters' nightmare is a new NATO that functions merely as a political debating society and a forum for building democracy and launching peacekeeping operations rather than as a true alliance that assures its members of their security through credible military guarantees. Owing to their fear that the Clinton administration is trying to bring this nightmare to life, they are sounding a vocal warning that there are good ways and bad ways to enlarge. They aspire to the kind of enlargement that retains NATO as a collective defense alliance that can deal with new threats, should they emerge, while also being capable of protecting power outside alliance borders on behalf of strategic purposes. What they do not want is NATO becoming a modern-day League of Nations: an institution so devoted to cooperating with all countries that it cannot protect or stand up to any of them.

RUSSIA'S INFLUENCE

Another argument being put forth by the conservative dissenters (e.g., Kissinger and Senator Helms) is that Russia is being granted too much influence over NATO's plans for enlargement, perhaps to the point of rendering NATO unable to carry out its security commitments to new members. To the dissenters, one of enlargement's key strategic purposes is to reassure CEEC about their security against Russia. As a result, they place highest priority on NATO's defense preparedness, and they relegate measures to reassure Russia to second position. Indeed, they mostly regard Russia as a country with an uncertain future and as capable of again becoming authoritarian and imperialistic. They therefore want to keep Russia at arm's length until its credentials as a cooperative democracy are firmly established.

This stance leaves many of them deeply suspicious of the NATO-Russia Permanent Joint Council. What they fear is that this council will acquire the authority to issue strategic guidance to the North Atlantic Council and other NATO policy bodies. For example, they fear that Russia will be given undue influence over NATO's decisions to develop military infrastructure in the CEEC region, and to move combat troops there in an emergency. Beyond this, they worry that Russia will become empowered to block almost any NATO defense departure that it opposes. The practical effect allegedly will be to prevent NATO from carrying out new security commitments, not only in the CEEC region but also in any region where Russia judges that its self-interest is not served by a NATO presence.

Their recommendation is not to scuttle NATO enlargement, but instead to scuttle the Joint Council, or at least to keep its deliberations far removed from NATO's daily defense affairs. The dissenters seemingly doubt NATO's ability to keep the Joint Council removed in the proper ways. One reason is their belief that Russia will be intrusive and meddlesome about the defense dimensions of NATO enlargement. Another is their belief that the Clinton administration and NATO headquarters are enamored of befriending Russia to the point of being willing to grant Russia whatever influence it seeks. Evidently the dissenters hope that by complaining from the sidelines, they can pressure NATO into making sure that the Joint Council does not grow out of proportion.

ENLARGING TOO FAR

The conservative dissenters have grave doubts about the wisdom of NATO's "open door" policy, which proclaims that the door to alliance membership will be kept open to any European country that meets NATO's standards for democracy and cooperative conduct. Because the dissenters think in geopolitical terms, they believe that NATO should enlarge its security perimeter only when this step makes sense for NATO's own interests, defined in pragmatic ways. They also believe that NATO should admit new members only if the alliance can truly defend them from attack. As a result, the dissenters argue that NATO should set firm limits on how far to expand

and how fast. Most support the Madrid summit's decision to admit only three new members, but they worry that, once the initial tranche is admitted, the enlargement process will continue, thereby greatly increasing NATO's roster of new states.

The dissenters are not opposed to any new members beyond the Madrid three. Their stance depends upon the specific country being considered. Most seemingly have mixed feelings about Romania and Slovenia. They mostly regard the former as a valuable strategic asset and the latter as too small to be consequential. They mostly are reluctant to admit the Baltic states for the simple but powerful reason that NATO cannot defend these three countries. As for the idea of admitting such Balkan countries as Bulgaria and Albania, the dissenters are strongly opposed. They also are opposed to the idea of moving NATO into the former Soviet Union by admitting either Ukraine or Russia. Thus the dissenters might support a limited second tranche of enlargement, but nothing further in the foreseeable future.

The dissenters are suspicious of private assurances that the open-door policy is merely a rhetorical principle that will not be applied in actual practice. One reason is their fear that the open-door policy will be used as an instrument to pursue NATO's transformation into a collective security pact that houses virtually every country in Europe. Another reason is their concern that aspiring countries will use this principle as a device to build pressure on NATO to enlarge beyond prudent limits. The dissenters note that already twelve countries have applied for membership. When the three invitees join the alliance in 1999, the other nine will be loudly clamoring at the door. Moreover, some of these countries will have sponsors within NATO's fold. In this setting, the dissenters doubt NATO's ability to say no. As a consequence, the dissenters would have NATO set limits on enlargement as a matter of policy so that decisions to refuse admission do not have to be made on an individual basis.

DILUTING AND WEAKENING NATO

The conservative dissenters want to preserve NATO's internal solidarity and its political capacity to act strongly in a crisis. They value NATO precisely because of its strength in these areas. They judge that these positive features were created as a result of patient effort over many years and that they could be lost if NATO pursues unwise policies. What they do not want is a diluted NATO that lacks solidarity: the kind of diffuse alliance that not only has lost its collective defense focus but also lacks the capacity to work effectively together on other departures owing to internal disagreements about strategic priorities.

Enlargement leaves them nervous on this score. They fear that the admission of at least three more members may make it harder for NATO to reach a unanimous decision to act in crisis. Most likely, the new members will support NATO interventions in their own CEEC region. But what about NATO actions in the Balkans, the Mediterranean, or even the Persian Gulf? The dissenters fear that larger membership–especially if more than three countries are admitted–is a ticket to institutional paralysis. They fear creation of a bloated alliance that is anchored largely in Central Europe, that looks inward at itself and not outward at the larger menaces that could threaten Western interests.

The dissenters also are nervous about whether NATO's current members are sufficiently unified to carry out new enlargement missions in the CEEC region. They fear that although some countries will be willing to support enlargement in a committed fashion, others will have no desire to defend the CEEC region or even become actively involved there. For example, the United States, Germany, and Britain might become active in the CEEC region, but France and the Lowland Countries might do little. The dissenters thus judge that enlargement may open a deep rift within NATO that creates two distinct strategic camps, one willing to accept new security involvements and the other unwilling. To them, this outcome is a one-way ticket to a diluted NATO, and perhaps to a destroyed NATO.

HOLLOW COMMITMENTS

Apprehension about "hollow" military commitments to new members is another theme of the conservative dissenters. To them, a hollow commitment is a security pledge that exists only on paper, without the military power to back it up. In particular, they regard the Article 5 commitment as meaningful only if NATO possesses the military power fully to carry out this commitment in peace, crisis, and war. As a result, the dissenters place major emphasis on NATO's military preparedness, even though Europe is no longer threatened in a major way. They want a NATO that can respond militarily in the event that relations with outside powers suddenly go sour, or that a slow downhill spiral in relations takes place. They also reason that robust coalition military planning is needed if NATO's members are to make sound individual decisions about their force postures in ways that promote the collective good.

Concern about a hollow commitment starts from the premise that NATO has quite large forces to defend its current borders. For example, NATO is capable of defending Germany's borders with a posture of about twenty-five divisions and eighteen hundred aircraft, all of which are well-trained and well-equipped. NATO has parallel plans for defending its northern region and southern region. The dissenters are urging that similar high standards of preparedness be applied to the defense of Poland, Hungary, and the Czech Republic when they join NATO in 1999. To an important degree, the new members will be able to defend themselves, but they will need quality improvements in interoperability, readiness, modernization, and infrastructure. NATO's current members also will need to develop the capacity to send reinforcements eastward in order to strengthen the CEEC region's defenses in ways that meet the alliance's strategic preparedness standard. The dissenters favor appropriate plans and programs in both arenas.

The dissenters tend to look at this issue from a political perspective, not through military details. For the most part, they seemingly have not yet become absorbed in the technical studies prepared by the Pentagon, RAND, and Congressional Budget Office (CBO) on specific force commitments needed fully to meet requirements. As a consequence, the dissenters question whether the United States and NATO are prepared to carry out the new commitments at all. One reason is their perception that current policy favors a purely political enlargement without accompanying military actions. Another reason is their fear that the Clinton administration will sacrifice defense preparedness in the CEEC region as a step to reassure Russia of NATO's peaceful intent. These concerns leave the dissenters worried. Their deepest fear is that of a truly "hollow" (i.e., worthless) commitment. A less menacing but more realistic fear is that NATO will create two tiers of security. That is, old members will be defended at a quite high level of preparedness, but new members will be defended at a lower level. The dissenters question whether NATO could survive in the face of such arrangements for long. The effect would be to uproot NATO's bedrock strategic principle that security is indivisible within the alliance. If some members can be given lesser security guarantees, why not others? In the minds of dissenters, the answer to this question illustrates why NATO's ability to meet new military requirements in the CEEC region has important implications for the alliance's future health as a whole.

THE EUROPEAN UNION'S ROLE

Thus far the NATO enlargement debate has not been defined in ways that draw attention to the EU's role in moving Western institutions eastward. As a result, some conservative dissenters have complained about the EU's failure to enlarge faster, but their complaints have mostly been low grumbles rather than loud bellows. Even so, these dissenters are accusing the West Europeans of wanting NATO to enlarge first in order to postpone the greater expense of enlarging the EU. The only issue is whether their complaints about the EU's slow progress will get louder as NATO enlargement draws near.

EU enlargement into the CEEC region will have a big impact on determining whether the West's strategic goals are achieved. Whereas NATO provides military security, the EU provides a foundation for economic recovery. The two institutions thus are best seen as working together, in tandem. For example, Western businesses may be reluctant to invest in Eastern Europe unless NATO is present to protect those investments. Likewise, NATO's new members will be hard-pressed to afford the defense expenses of enlargement unless their economies recover. This recovery is more likely if they gain admission into the EU soon.

The risk is that NATO will enlarge in 1999, but the EU will delay enlargement until several years later. During the intervening years, NATO enlargement may be weakened because it lacks a properly supportive economic climate. In the CEEC region, the consequence could be loss of respect for NATO and for Western institutions as a whole. This is a fate that the conservative dissenters want to avoid by urging the EU to move faster. At issue is whether their appeals will have any effect on an EU that seems more influenced by self-involved technicalities and legalities than by compelling strategic requirements. Once the EU has resolved its debates over European Monetary Union (EMU) and other internal matters, the dissenters argue, it needs to surmount its procedures and accelerate its own enlargement.

BUDGET COSTS

Concern about budget costs has been a growing preoccupation of many conservative dissenters–especially U.S. senators that must pay the bill when new members are admitted into NATO. Yet cost seems mostly a metaphor for larger strategic issues in their minds. As prodefense conservatives, few are penny pinchers. Most are willing to spend modest amounts to support NATO enlargement, but they do not want to see the bank vaults emptied. They are aware that many other defense innovations started out with projections of affordable expense but then fell victim to soaring costs as a result of new requirements, gold-plating, and other dynamics. The dissenters do not want the same for NATO enlargement. Because there is no threat, they want a NATO enlargement that not only makes sense militarily but also can be done on the cheap. The bottom line is that they have two opposing fears: that NATO will not attend to its new defense requirements at all, or, conversely, that NATO will go over-board by spending far more than is needed. The consistency in these positions seem-ingly lies in the fact that the dissenters want a cost-effective defense posture for enlargement: enough to get the job done but at no wasted expense.

The Clinton administration has issued a study forecasting that the costs of NATO enlargement will be $27-35 billion through 2009. The new members are to pay about $13-17 billion, the West Europeans about $12-16 billion, and the United States, the remainder. The dissenters draw comfort from this moderate forecast, but they also take it with a grain of salt. One reason is that RAND has forecasted costs up to $50 billion, and the CBO issued a study predicting that the costs might be much high-er—up to $125 billion. Another reason is that initial estimates have a way of being low because many investments are not foreseen. What matters is how defense require-ments are defined once the political heat to control costs is turned off.

In contrast to liberal dissenters, conservative dissenters want NATO enlarge-ment to be supported by a high level of military preparedness. But few are willing to pay big dollars. The prospect of having to pay more than currently expected is a fur-ther chill on their enthusiasm for enlargement. In theory, this stance should leave them curious about the military details of NATO enlargement and prone to fine-tun-ing it in ways aimed at blocking measures that are too costly while endorsing measures critical to NATO's new requirements. In practice, however, there has been no con-crete impact thus far, for few conservative dissenters have said much about the details of either military programs or costs. Perhaps they will start saying more when they come to conclude that the details have policy importance.

DEFENSE REFORMS

The conservative dissenters are heavily preoccupied with ensuring that the defense requirements flowing from NATO enlargement are met. If these require-ments are to be met, both old and new members will have to reform their military pos-tures. For both, the dissenters are fretting that the necessary reforms will either not be made or be pursued too slowly and incrementally. Hence, the dissenters foresee lack of progress on this important issue as a potential cause of NATO enlargement possibly turning into a dud.

The military reforms that must be made by new members are especially imposing. The force postures of the CEEC region all suffer from their Warsaw Pact legacy. As a result, they are not interoperable and compatible with NATO's forces.

They also suffer from nearly a decade of low defense budgets, in which chronically inadequate funds were used in a failing effort to support forces that were too large by almost any measure. What the new members need is to reduce their bloated postures while elevating their quality to NATO's levels. The dissenters are skeptical that these reforms will be accomplished. This owes to lack of civilian control over the military and to indifference about defense issues in Hungary and the Czech Republic.

The dissenters also doubt that the West Europeans will embrace the reforms needed to make their forces capable of projecting power eastward in adequate amounts and in a timely fashion. Because West European forces were originally designed to defend nearby Cold War borders, they lack the logistic support and mobility assets to perform projection missions. The dissenters suspect that the West Europeans are inward looking and are not truly committed to defending Eastern Europe. In any event, the allies' lack of money and political support allegedly will prevent major changes. The dissenters consequently expect stagnant defense policies from both Western Europe and Eastern Europe, the opposite of what is needed to make enlargement succeed.

BURDENSHARING

Many conservative dissenters–especially U.S. senators–fear a coming transatlantic struggle over burdensharing, and even a disaster that could damage NATO. They are concerned that the United States will be left unfairly shouldering the expense of enlargement and carrying out its responsibilities. Their immediate impetus has been French president Jacques Chirac's caustic comment, which suggested that, because the United States created the idea of enlarging NATO, it should pay the bill. But Chirac is far from the only European who has led them to reach this conclusion. Indeed, many other European governments seem less than eager about providing money and forces to support NATO enlargement.

To the United States, the act of getting the Europeans to shoulder their fair share of the military burden was a tough struggle during the Cold War, when the threat was clear. Now that the threat is gone, the task has become far harder. The dissenters perceive the Europeans as apathetic about increasing their defense budgets in order to fund enlargement or even diverting funds from elsewhere in their defense programs. They fear that equally apathetic but clever new members will take advantage of NATO's security blanket to disarm in unhealthy ways, and thereby become free riders. The alleged result will be a NATO alliance in which nearly everybody runs from burdens and responsibilities, and the United States is left holding the bag.

For these reasons, the dissenters are skeptical of the Clinton administration's assurances that NATO enlargement will cost the U.S. taxpayer only $150-200 million per year, and that only small U.S. forces–one division and one fighter wing–need be committed to defense of the CEEC region. They fear that when the real bills come due, the U.S. expense will be well higher because other countries will have contributed far less than originally expected. They also fear that if a war must eventually be fought over the CEEC region, it will be mostly U.S. forces that do the fighting. Burdensharing worries significantly dampen their ardor for NATO enlargement and enhance their determination to forge satisfactory transatlantic agreements before admission of new members is formally approved by parliaments.

DEALING WITH OTHER REGIONS

The argument that preoccupation with enlargement may render NATO incapable of dealing with other regions is another theme of some conservative dissenters. This argument holds that the principal dangers facing NATO and Europe do not lie in the CEEC region. Instead, they allegedly lie elsewhere: the Balkans, the Mediterranean/North Africa, and the Persian Gulf. Proponents of this argument favor NATO enlargement if it offers the promise of stabilizing the CEEC region, thereby allowing NATO to pivot on its Central European axis and begin looking southward. But an entirely different evaluation applies if the effect of enlargement is to entangle NATO in CEEC imbroglios to the extent that it cannot deal with other regions.

Conservative dissenters fear that draining entanglements may be the case. For example, Germany, France, and Britain might become so consumed by East European missions that they lack the forces, money, and political energy to address other regions. The same could be true of NATO's remaining powers. The result could be that the United States is left alone defending the Persian Gulf to an even greater degree than already is the case today. Today at least some European allies have forces that could be sent to the Persian Gulf in an emergency. But what will be the situation if they acquire new missions in the CEEC region? The dissenters worry that the answer will work against U.S. interests.

The dissenters are not necessarily arguing for NATO to choose between an eastward focus and a southward focus. Indeed, the term "double enlargement" has been coined to suggest a reformed NATO that moves in both directions. But the dissenters want NATO enlargement into the CEEC region to be a facilitator of a southern reorientation, not a barrier to it. To the extent that the opposite is the case, they regard eastward enlargement as a potential drain on NATO's flexibility and ability to set priorities.

IMPACT ON MODERNIZATION

This issue has been raised by Senator Stevens, but not yet by many other conservative dissenters. The core argument is that defense funds spent on enlargement will come at the expense of modernization by procuring new weapons in the coming decade. Stevens is primarily focused on U.S. forces, for whom enlargement missions will add to the already significant expense for maintaining a strong European presence of 100,000 troops. But the effect could be even greater on the European allies.

According to the Pentagon, the U.S. expense for enlargement will be $150-200 million annually, only about one-third of 1 percent of the money slated to be spent on procurement. The main effect of enlargement thus will not be to slow U.S. procurement appreciably but instead to underscore the need to keep 100,000 troops in Europe, rather than deploying some of them elsewhere. For the European allies, the annual expense of $1 billion will be about 2.5 percent of the $40 billion that they spend on procurement. Thus, allied procurement could be slowed in more significant ways, thereby accelerating the growing gap between U.S. forces that are undergoing the "Revolution in Military Affairs" (RMA) and allied forces that are not experiencing this change.

What is to be done? As of yet, the conservative dissenters are unclear about how to answer this question. Some are likely to conclude that the impact on procurement is too small to worry about. Others may urge that NATO should give top priority to enlargement, but that NATO also should limit the costs so that procurement accounts are not unnecessarily drained. Still others may recommend modest cuts in allied force structures, rather than less spending on either enlargement or procurement. Balanced perspectives of this sort are likely to be the case, provided the costs of enlargement remain moderate. But a different reaction could emerge if the costs soar and the negative impact on procurement becomes truly major. In this event, the conservative dissenters might decide to start reversing their strategic priorities by cutting back on enlargement measures in order to fund more modernization.

POLICY IMPLICATIONS

The emergence of this conservative dissent means that the political climate for judging NATO enlargement is likely to begin changing. This change will take place during the period in which the U.S. Senate and European parliaments will be evaluating whether to ratify the admission of Poland, the Czech Republic, and Hungary into NATO in 1999. The future is uncertain, but the likely outcome is that if this dissent gathers energy, it will move U.S. and NATO policy in the directions that it seeks. These dissenters are not arguing merely to get themselves heard or to annoy those in power. Most want to influence policy. If they continue to speak out, they are likely to do so in some measure.

The larger questions are substantive: To what degree are these conservative dissenters on the mark? Do they exaggerate the troubles facing NATO enlargement, or have they fingered major fault lines in U.S. and alliance policy? Should their recommendations be adopted? In this complex arena, truth lies in the eyes of the beholder. My own reaction is that the conservative dissenters are putting forth fears that, at the moment, seem exaggerated. The dissenters are right in saying that idealism must be balanced by realism. However, their specific complaints are directed not at current enlargement policy but instead at how this policy might evolve if it mutates in disastrous directions. Such a mutation has not yet begun, and if the United States and NATO keep their strategic bearings, it may not begin at all. Nonetheless, the conservative dissenters are performing a valuable service. They are pointing out the many ways in which NATO enlargement could fall victim to bad implementation decisions in the critical arena of defense planning and core security relationships. They are also putting forth useful ideas on how U.S. and NATO policy can be strengthened. For these reasons, their arguments and recommendations should be taken seriously.

Some dissenters seem to feel that NATO's collective defense posture is already gravely weakened, but the facts demonstrate otherwise. True, NATO has reduced its forces and defense budgets by about one-third since the Cold War ended.

But its Cold War defenses were so large that a one-third cut leaves quite large assets in its wake. Today, NATO's members (excluding the United States) are spending fully $165 billion on defense. NATO still deploys about 55 mobilizable divisions, 3,600 combat aircraft, and 300 naval combatants. This is a huge posture whose dominance is magnified further when compared against today's threats, which are much smaller than during the Cold War. NATO is capable of defending all three of its regions with great strength and high confidence. Some critics allege that NATO's forces are far larger than can be justified by any realistic analysis of threats or missions. The situation can be debated, but in the relative sense of having adequate capabilities for meeting requirements, NATO's collective defenses are probably in better shape today than at any time during the past.

Nor is NATO headed toward weak collective defenses in the CEEC region as it enlarges there. The NATO enlargement study of 1995 rejected the idea of permanently stationing large NATO forces on the soil of new members because such deployments are not needed. But this study endorsed a host of important military improvements in such areas as interoperability, command systems, air defense, common infrastructure, reinforcement, and readiness. The Clinton administration's study of early 1997 outlined a similarly robust defense plan in greater programmatic detail. Divided into three equal parts. it included measures aimed at upgrading new-member forces, improving European regional projection capabilities, and assembling a better common infrastructure. In their subsequent negotiations with the Russians over the Founding Act and the Permanent Joint Council, the United States and NATO offered reassurances that enlargement poses no threat to Russia. But they were equally firm in denying the Russians any improper influence over NATO's preparations in the CEEC region. As matters now stand, NATO is free to build a fully capable defensive military posture in the region as it enlarges there.

The proper conclusion is that when the details are examined, NATO enlargement policy currently is on a sound track. NATO is not now on the way to becoming a loose collective security pact. Russia is not being given improper influence over NATO's strategic directions. NATO's open-door policy is not yet a prescription for admitting everybody. Now that specific invitees have been selected at the Madrid summit, NATO is developing appropriate defense plans for ensuring that new military requirements are met, and that new roles and missions are carried out. The necessary defense reforms have begun in many places. The costs of enlargement appear to be affordable, and there is no inherent reason barring NATO from being capable of both defending the CEEC region and projecting power elsewhere.

This positive evaluation of the current situation, nonetheless, is no guarantee that the future will unfold smoothly or successfully. There undeniably are risks and difficulties ahead as well as many pitfalls. NATO policy may be on a sound course today, but it plausibly could be diverted on a wrong course tomorrow. One risk is that NATO will eventually lose its focus on collective defense and thereby evolve into a weak collective security structure, with too many new members and outreach activities and not enough real defense capability. Another risk is that the EU will continue to keep its head in the sand and not enlarge fast enough to enable NATO enlargement to succeed. Yet another risk is that Russia will succeed in watering down the defense dimensions of NATO enlargement. Even short of Russian meddling, NATO's own reluctance to pursue necessary military improvement measures and reforms could result in an insufficiently strong defense commitment to new members. NATO could be damaged by burdensharing debates among old and new members that do not want to accept the military consequences of new political commitments. Conversely, NATO might fall victim to the opposite risk: that of allowing the costs of enlargement to soar while not attending to other regions and requirements. Either way, the United States could find itself surrounded by burden-shirkers and free riders, and thereby left holding the bag in ways feared by the dissenters.

These risks add up to a wide spectrum of potential, unfortunate outcomes that vary in the degree to which the West's goals are frustrated. The most damaging outcome is one in which NATO is badly overextended, its solidarity and effectiveness are seriously damaged, new members are rendered no more secure and democratic than today, and the CEEC region is left facing a troubled future, including a menacing Russia. The least damaging outcome is one in which a limited NATO enlargement is carried out effectively but is accompanied by a host of lingering debates over defense plans, burdensharing, and costs. Even this outcome is nothing to savor, for nobody wants the success of a visionary enlargement to be dimmed by endless, dispiriting quarreling over details. The prospect of NATO enlargement becoming best known for its squabbles over NATO's infrastructure budget is enough to sober even the most committed zealot.

Nothing makes these disasters inevitable or even probable. If one of them transpires, the reason will be that NATO bungled the job of developing sound policies. NATO can avoid this fate by acting in the sensible ways that it has pursued in the past. The solution is one of using coalition planning and consensus-building to define key strategic objectives, to create a program for achieving these objectives at affordable cost, and to implement this program in a steady manner over a period of years. If NATO acts in this reassuring fashion, the fears being expressed by the conservative dissenters will diminish, and their legitimate arguments will find their way into NATO policy.

How can NATO best react to this dissent by improving its policies in the near term? There are some things that NATO cannot realistically hope to do. Regardless of positions staked out in official NATO communiques, debate over basic philosophical issues (e.g., the combination of collective defense and collective security that makes the best sense for Europe) is likely to rage unresolved for many years. Likewise, NATO will be able to calm fears of undue Russian influence only by demonstrating its firmness from one year to the next. What NATO can do, however, is to launch the Pentagon's ten-year plan for achieving a mature NATO defense capability in the CEEC region. If this step is taken, and if NATO's military authorities begin forging multinational accords on future roles and missions for enlargement, NATO undeniably will be on the right track for the issue of greatest importance to its character and effectiveness. Concern over NATO's future defense arrangements and burdensharing practices will diminish. The dissenters may not be completely mollified about all the potential troubles facing NATO enlargement, but at least they will not have legitimate cause for arguing that NATO is losing its essence as an alliance that, first and foremost, provides collective defense.

NATO might also be well-advised to accept the dissenters' argument that the open-door policy should be rethought. The reasons for undermining this reappraisal include, but go beyond, the issue of whether specific candidates are important to NATO's interests and whether NATO can defend them. If NATO is compelled to admit an ever-expanding number of new members, its effectiveness as an alliance capable of serious military operations almost inevitably will diminish. As the number of new members grows, the difficulty of making political decisions to use force will increase. Beyond the current invitees and perhaps Romania, most applicants will add little to NATO's military posture, which does not need additional strength. As a result, NATO will lose more than it gains if it allows the enlargement process to go too far.

A case can be made that if pressures arise for NATO to develop stronger security ties to more countries, NATO should turn to solutions short of membership. For example, it could sign bilateral security treaties with specific countries, a step that would grant these countries political guarantees by NATO without giving them undue influence over NATO's own defense plans. The United States employs such treaties in Asia, and they suffice for the setting there. This step provides one option for NATO to pursue instead of either carrying out the open-door policy or endorsing it in principle but not in practice. Being clear about where and when the door closes may allow NATO and rejected suitors to work together to find acceptable alternative arrangements.

Finally, the United States and NATO can respond to the dissenters by making sure that official policy is sober and realistic about Russia. Clearly, strong efforts must be made to develop a cooperative partnership with Russia. Just as clearly, Russia will remain separate from Europe–in political, economic, and cultural terms–for some time. If the misty vision of bonding Russia to Europe is allowed to influence policy, the inevitable result will be frustration for both NATO and Russia. Both sides will be better off by openly acknowledging their separateness and by working to build neighborly relations between an enlarging NATO and a Russia that primarily will be a regional European power.

Quite possibly the dissenters will prove wrong about their fear that Russia will perpetually try to interfere in NATO's business. The real challenge may be one of keeping Russia adequately engaged in European issues, in ways that counterbalance its tendency to sulk, withdraw into itself, and focus totally on Eurasia. A Russia that is withdrawn, living in a deteriorating Eurasian geopolitical ghetto but capable of lashing out angrily may be a greater menace than a Russia that is engaged in European affairs in sometimes irritating ways. We may be heading toward an era in which Russia is becoming too weak for the West's own good. As history shows, great danger can come from countries that once were powerful but find themselves sliding downhill. Countries of this mentality tend to strike out in frustration, often at moments that catch others by surprise. This is exactly how Austria and Russia bungled into war in

1914. The specific crisis at Sarajevo did not merit a big confrontation but both countries were resentful of earlier humiliations and wanted to make a point by slamming down their fists. The result was a calamity that never should have happened–something to be remembered today as Europe's future is being charted.

Along with pursuing a sensible diplomacy, NATO also needs to be realistic about the role of Russian military power in its defense planning for enlargement. At the moment, the too-simplistic judgment that Russia's military has fallen into the dregs is serving as a convenient excuse for not coming to grips with hard future realities. Russia remains a large country with 150 million people, a trillion-dollar economy, and lots of military assets. Even during the next few years of continuing readiness troubles, it could generate forces for limited offensive operations if it put its mind to the task and spent a few months preparing. By 2010, when NATO's defense plan will mature, Russia's efforts to acquire a modern army–one that is smaller but mobile and well-armed–may also have matured. As a result, NATO's new members will continue to fear Russia, and under Article 5, they will have a right to NATO military protection from Russia. NATO will not be able to fulfill its new defense requirements unless it openly acknowledges this reality. Otherwise, it will find itself issuing confused rhetoric about its true military intentions and perpetually left vulnerable to forging weak military plans. It can handle the situation by pointing out that although NATO does not regard Russia as a threat, it must have an adequate military capacity to safeguard all of its borders in the unlikely event that political relations with outside powers sour suddenly and unexpectedly. In other words, a small dose of candor and honesty may be just what the doctor ordered.

CONCLUSION

In summary, NATO enlargement makes strategic sense and is off to a good start, but its ultimate success is far from assured. If the enterprise is not managed carefully, it could wind up deteriorating into a mess and a dud. NATO could end up damaged, and Europe could be left less secure and stable than now. In this sense, the conservative dissenters are right to be concerned. A principal problem with these dissenters is that, at the moment, they are mostly offering worried hand-wringing about bad decisions that have not yet been made. They have not yet developed a set of specific, constructive policies for easing their worries and improving NATO's performance. When they do so, they may have a good deal more to offer than merely strong warnings of trouble ahead.

Regardless of how the conservative dissent evolves, the coming strategic agenda promises to be anything but easy. The United States and NATO face several years of hard but worthy strategic labor and many tough choices, as the alliance enlarges eastward. Their task is one of shaping NATO's future, and Europe's, too. Hopefully, they will get things right: a conclusion that the conservative dissenters doubtless can agree with.

EUROPEAN UNION ENLARGEMENT
Giancarlo Chevellard

EUROPEAN UNION ENLARGEMENT: THE STRATEGIC PERSPECTIVE

The current enlargement of the European Union (EU) is essentially dictated by security motives. In this respect, the EU is healthily rediscovering its original raison d'être. If we turn to the late 1940s, when the adventure of European integration started, we must admire the far-reaching vision of our transatlantic leadership of the time. Just a few years after the end of World War II, forgetting the atrocities of the recent past, this leadership gave birth to the first European Community. The then European Coal and Steel Community was explicitly created to make more difficult, hopefully impossible, any new intra-European conflict. Integration and mutual dependence of the former enemy countries was considered the best preventive therapy against new European civil wars. The first community, an immediate economic success, developed rapidly on the political ground with its supranational institutions proving their credibility and effectiveness. Only a few years later in 1957, the same countries created the European Economic Community, which embodied the ambitious design of creating a single European market accompanied by a range of common policies and common institutions endowed with real powers and able to function through weighted majority voting decision making. The original political objective was restated in the founding treaty: "to lay the foundations of an even closer union among the peoples of Europe."

The European Community has been a huge success, proved by its internal achievements and by its successive enlargements. The six founding countries have been joined over the years by nine new members. The area of stability in Europe, under a single rule of law and under common institutions, has thus progressively expanded. The initial objective of the Community has been fully realized. Today nobody can imagine Western Europe as a source of bloody conflicts. In fact, the European Union is more and more perceived by the outside world as a powerful, essentially civil, player. The United States and the other major international actors have invited it to play a more active role in preventing and managing conflicts on a global scale.

The present EU enlargement is determined by basically the same pressing motives. After the collapse of the communist system in Central and Eastern Europe, the Union has been requested to expand the area of stability in Europe eastward and has responded positively to the request. There is a further point of similarity with the conditions prevailing at the moment of the creation of the Community. At that time, one condition for membership was the internal stability of the countries concerned. Such stability was to express itself through democratic institutions and free market economy. The same is true today. The criterion upon which accession will be decided is again political and economic stability of the applicant countries.

With this enlargement, the Union is committing itself to the internal stability of the former communist countries. It functions not only as a magnet for political and economic reforms but also as a provider of assistance for it. Notwithstanding the complicated and costly implications of enlargement, the Union has said "yes" to the request of accession of ten Central and Eastern European countries (CEEC) and Cyprus. There is no uncertainty today about who will join the Union. All the countries willing and able to join are to become members, but it is clear that the Union is not acting out of pure solidarity motivations. It has fundamental interests, including the idea that increased stability on the European Continent will bring to it considerable political and economic benefits. If EU security will be increased through integration and cooperation, then its well-being will be facilitated by the opening of markets with more than 100 million consumers.

There are nonetheless major differences between this enlargement and the four previous ones. There is a quantitative difference, for never in the past has the Union been asked to open itself to so many applicants at the same time. This enlargement, unlike past ones, is more of an open and undetermined process. It will stretch over the next decade, gradually redesigning the map of Europe, and will dominate the internal agenda of future new members. Enlargement will have an impact on neighboring countries such as Russia, Ukraine, and those in the Balkans. It may extend itself to new applicants, and it will most certainly require fundamental internal reforms in the Union. But how and when all this will occur will be determined during the process itself. The notion of enlargement as a long-term, largely undetermined process is fundamental. The point of arrival will result, sometime in the next decade, in a European Union of twenty-six (or more) members. The steps to it are part of a long sequence, implying the internal transformation of the Union and the adaptation of the surrounding European environment.

More than in the past, this enlargement is and will be a twofold process whereby EU extension will go hand in hand with its reinforcement. Widening will require deepening. The applicant countries want to join a dynamic and politically mature European Union. Although differences exist among the current fifteen member-states about the final objectives of European integration, none of them want to endanger what has been achieved. Introducing as many as eleven new members into the Union without simultaneously strengthening its policies and institutions may mean that it will quickly be transformed into an unmanageable, diluted single market. These are the reasons why enlargement and reinforcement are today two inseparable components of the European integration process.

Economic and monetary union and enlargement are undoubtedly the major items on the Union agenda as the century ends. The creation of the single currency on 1 January 1999 represents an enormous step forward in the achievements of the Union. The progressive introduction of the euro, until the complete elimination of the currencies of the participating member-states in 2002, will take place in the very same time frame in which the Union plans to realize its first new CEEC accession. Doubtless, this is an ambitious and demanding program since it combines the strengthening of the internal cohesion of the Union through the single currency with its enlargement.

The single currency, however, is not enough. In its process of strengthening, the Union must also review its system of government. The Amsterdam Treaty, signed on 2 October 1997 and currently subject to national ratification, has bared some of the difficulties. The treaty provides for significant progress in EU common policies but does not address the fundamental question raised by enlargement. It is difficult to challenge the notion that the massive expansion of the EU will be a success if its current institutions are sufficiently adapted to the new dimension. The reason is simple: unlike the United States, the EU constitutional system is rigidly regulated by the founding treaties. This means that the enlarged EU will need the revision of the treaties in order to tailor its institutions and decision-making procedures to its new membership of twenty-six countries.

The Amsterdam Treaty negotiators did not succeed in agreeing to provisions adapting the Union institutions. The tension between reinforcing and enlarging the Union has emerged as a potentially disruptive force, and inasmuch as reinforcement implies transferring powers and responsibilities from member-states to Brussels, politically sensitive nerves of each nation are obviously touched. The agreement on institutional reform was not achieved because of fundamental differences among member-states on key issues such as the weight of national representation in the different institutions and the modalities of decision making.

All member-countries have recognized that the institutional reform is a precondition for enlarging the Union to twenty-six. While approving the Amsterdam Treaty, the Union heads of government have decided to set aside many issues for a later stage. They have given the green light to go ahead with the enlargement process on the condition that at least one year before the EU's membership exceeds twenty, a comprehensive review of the provisions of the treaties on the composition and functioning of the institutions will be carried out. The thinking in Amsterdam was that, in due time, the pressure of the candidates to become full members will be such as to force the EU institutional reforms. Reconciling the drive to enlargement with the need of reinforcing the Union, therefore, is going to be one of the fundamental challenge of the coming years.

One last comment concerning the strategic perspective of the Union enlargement: As part of the overall transformations in the international environment, EU expansion interacts with NATO enlargement. Strategically they are both part of the same process, namely the integration of CEEC into the Western structures. The Amsterdam Treaty commits the EU to frame progressively a common defense policy, and it indicates the areas (essentially, "out of area" crisis management) and the instrument, Western European Union (WEU), through which such a policy will be developed. The enlarging European Union will thus have increasing responsibilities for defense matters. The obvious challenge is to combine harmoniously these responsibilities with those of NATO.

EU ENLARGEMENT: THE WAY AHEAD

Following the Amsterdam decisions, the EU Commission presented in July 1997 its communication "Agenda 2000" together with opinions on each of the CEEC's application for membership. These papers have been the basis for the important decisions taken by the heads of government of the European Union at the

European Council held in Luxembourg 12-13 December 1997. These decisions enable the EU and the candidate countries to enter into a new phase of the enlargement process. The European Council in Luxembourg has followed the Commission approach and declared that in the next phase actions should be carried out in three complementary areas: (1) establishing an overall framework for the enlargement process; (2) preparing the future member-states for accession; and (3) opening the negotiations for accession.

The Overall Framework for Accession

As "Agenda 2000" points out, EU enlargement will be successful if it is part of a larger package of internal reforms. These reforms include actions to increase economic stability and employment in the Union, to develop a fully operational foreign policy, to revise the common agricultural policy, and to establish a new financial framework. The Luxembourg European Council emphasized in particular the need to prepare the Union for enlargement by means of "strengthening and improving the operations of the institutions."

Externally, enlargement is a process that in different degrees concerns the whole of Europe. The European Council has consequently decided to set up a European conference that will bring together the Union and other European countries that are prospective members and wish to share its values and objectives. Cyprus, all applicant CEEC, and Turkey have been, for the time being, invited to take part in the conference, which, meeting once a year at the level of heads of government, will be a multilateral forum for political consultation on a broad range of issues. In particular, it is designed to deepen cooperation among participating states on foreign and security policy issues, as well as on matters related to justice and home affairs.

Turkey deserves one more specific comment. The Union has confirmed Turkey's eligibility for EU membership but has determined that the conditions are not now met to open accession negotiations. Macroeconomic instability is a source of concern, and major improvements in the political situation, in particular in the protection of human rights, need to be introduced. Good neighborly relations between Greece and Turkey should be established, and Turkey should contribute actively to a settlement of the Cyprus conflict. In the meantime, building on the positive results of the EU-Turkey customs union, cooperative relations should be further developed. Turkey has been invited to take part in the European conference.

Preparing the Accession

The Union has developed over the years a considerable body of policies, regulations, and actions, its so-called *acquis*. Moreover, it is made up of homogenous countries in terms of democratic practices and market economy. In order to align the applicant countries with the EU and member-states's acquis and standards as early as possible, the Luxembourg European Council has decided, given the Commission suggestion, to launch a reinforced pre-accession strategy. This strategy will be developed through a system of "accession partnerships" and a reinforced pre-accession aid program.

The accession partnerships to be negotiated by the Commission individually with the ten CEEC–and to be approved by qualified majority by the Council–will identify principles, priorities, intermediary aims, and conditions whereby applicant countries will progressively align themselves on the Union acquis. The accession partnerships will be regularly updated and priorities redefined. An element of "conditionality" will characterize them, that is, if an applicant country shows lack of determination in the adoption of the acquis or in the efforts to introduce democratic and economic reforms, the EU can decide to suspend the pre-accession assistance.

The implementation of the accession partnerships will be carried out through national programs for the adoption of the EU acquis. These programs will indicate the ways and the timetable for the applicant countries to translate into legislative measures the priorities set out in the accession partnerships. They will be the basis for the establishment of the annual financing memoranda to be signed by each country and the Commission. These memoranda will give precise indications on the financial assistance from the EU as regards sectors and projects planned by the country concerned. For instance, it is already agreed that for 1998 the priorities are institution building (30 percent of the overall allocation) and investment support (70 percent of the overall allocation). From the year 2000, pre-accession aid for all applicant CEEC will be substantially increased, concentrating in particular on agricultural and structural reforms. In the seven years from 2000 to 2006, the overall amount of pre-accession aid intended for the ten CEEC should rise to approximately $25 billion.

Negotiating the Accession

The Luxembourg European Council has followed the Commission recommendation concerning the launching of the accession negotiations with the individual CEEC. The Commission had assessed each application for membership according to the so-called accession criteria. These criteria relate to the stability of democratic institutions, to the functioning of the market economy, and to the ability to take on the obligations of membership. On the basis of a comprehensive and objective evaluation of the extent to which the ten applicant countries meet these criteria, the Commission had recommended that accession negotiations start with Hungary, Poland, Estonia, the Czech Republic, and Slovenia. It had considered that these countries could be in a position to satisfy all the conditions for membership in the medium term if they strongly sustain their preparation efforts. Moreover, it did accentuate the fact that the decision to open negotiations simultaneously with these countries did not necessarily imply that they would be concluded at the same time.

Notwithstanding this differentiation among applicants concerning the beginning of accession negotiations, enlargement is and will continue to be an overall process involving all applicants. Differentiation in no sense means discrimination. There will not be "ins and outs" but "ins and pre-ins," with the possibility for the latter to join the former as soon as the conditions are right. The first group of new member-countries is expected to join the EU formally, according to the informed players, around 2002.

The negotiations will define the terms and conditions on which each future EU member will accede. After accession some transitional periods may be needed for the new members to apply parts of the EU acquis, but the objective of the EU is that the new members apply the entire acquis upon accession. Therefore, the actual timetable for accession will depend on the progress made by individual countries in adopting, implementing, and enforcing the acquis. This explains the longer time frame needed for EU enlargement compared to that for NATO. Cyprus will join the five CEEC on the starting line for accession negotiations. The EU had already expressed itself positively on Cyprus membership and on an early start of negotiations. The division of the island, with the northern part being occupied by Turkish forces, raises problems, but the prospect of accession may provide a catalyst to bring about a lasting settlement. Such a settlement will permit a faster conclusion to accession negotiations. It will be facilitated if representatives of the Turkish Cypriot community are allowed to be involved in the accession process.

THE SECURITY CONTRIBUTION OF THE ENLARGED UNION

The enlarged Union is bound to increase its weight in external relations. Because of geography (from the Black to the Baltic Seas), population (around 500 million), resources, and economic potential, the new Union will in any case be a heavyweight on the international scene. It depends on the Union, however, whether these are going to be assets or liabilities. If it decides to make the best use of its increased power, it will be a major player. To this effect, all of its instruments–diplomatic, commercial, budgetary, humanitarian–should be mobilized under the efficient functioning of the new arrangements agreed in Amsterdam for the EU common foreign and security policy.

In the past four decades, the EU has developed into a genuine security community in which the use or even the threat of using force to resolve disputes has become unthinkable. EU enlargement is designed to export such security by promoting stability and eliminating "gray zones" in Central and Eastern Europe. In this context the EU has a vital interest in strengthening the multilateral system in all areas as well as in developing cooperative frameworks at the regional and subregional level. There is an obvious interrelation between security and well-functioning international institutions. For instance, as by far the largest trading group in the world, the enlarged EU will have a major interest in consolidating the new international trade structures. The Union should also seek to exploit its internal achievements such as the single market and, tomorrow, the monetary union to promote stability on the international scene.

In order to cope with the global challenges of the twenty-first century, the enlarged Union should play a more visible role in world affairs. At present it is by far the largest donor of assistance to the Middle East, to the Mediterranean countries, to Africa, to Russia, and to the CEEC. That this fact is often not recognized is mainly the fault of the Union itself. The enlargement will increase the EU's dominant role in providing global assistance, but its basic challenge is to achieve greater visibility in order to gain greater political influence and to win public support for the EU's actions.

EU and NATO are the most important Western structures. Their contribution to the European security architecture has been and is crucial. Ideally their respective enlargements should proceed together. In reality, the two organizations have taken different routes. The who, the when, and the how of enlargement differ substantially. The likelihood is that there will be, for some time, increasing divergence in their respective membership and no real parallelism in the enlargement processes. There are good reasons for this, largely related to the fact that rules and procedures for accession are different in the two organizations. Moreover, each of them has its own dynamic and agenda. The task ahead is to make sure that such differences do not become sources of tension and, in the final analysis, Western division. There are three main areas of concern in this respect:

- Some, especially on the American side of the Atlantic, wonder whether the long time frame of the EU enlargement is not evidence of a European incapacity to cope with the needs of the new Europe. It is true that accession to the EU will occur only in the next decade. But this must be appreciated in the light of its complexity and evolving nature. Joining NATO means essentially becoming a member of an alliance and integrating some armed forces. Joining the EU means to share the same political objectives and to integrate societies and economic systems within binding legal disciplines. The latter is most sensitive on the substance and much heavier on the procedures. Also, the EU must simultaneously embark on the difficult process of reforming itself in order to be able to integrate the newcomers. No wonder, then, that it takes time to achieve it. Accession to the EU is a long process, one that started in the early 1990s with a step-by-step insertion of candidates. Exchanges and trade have boomed; pre-accession assistance is steadily increasing; participation to joint institutions is developing. Candidates themselves seem to be satisfied about this progressive insertion since full membership will entail exposure to full competition and to all the obligations. All the above indicates that the EU, on its part, is fully contributing right now to the stable and cooperative architecture of the European continent.

- EU enlargement is in the short term a costly operation. It was mentioned earlier that the Commission proposes approximately $25 billion for the period 2000-2006 for assisting candidates in the preparation of their membership. On top of these budgetary costs, the opening of the markets will imply restructuring of productive sectors with considerable economic costs. The candidates themselves will have to open up to EU rules and competitions. In the years to come all this will add up to a substantial financial burden that, because EU enlargement contributes to their security, will be shouldered by the Europeans. The issue of NATO enlargement costs is the business of the alliance and of its members. Simply put, regarding the discussions in the appropriate fora on the amount of the costs and on its sharing, due account should be given to the overall European contribution—whether macroeconomic, budgetary, commercial, or other—to the security of the continent.

- The Amsterdam Treaty has given new impetus to the emergence of the Europe of Defense (European Security and Defense Identity [ESDI]). European members of NATO are unanimous in recognizing that Europe of Defense must be developed within the alliance. It should have some independent capabilities but mainly use NATO resources and infrastructures. ESDI should serve the European Union essentially in conflict prevention and management operations outside the alliance. ESDI would be developed, as it concerns defense aspects, within the WEU. Albania is a good example. The Union is heavily engaged in local crisis management, using humanitarian, budgetary, and diplomatic means of action. For the Albanian police reorganization, it has recourse to the WEU, which provides the specialized personnel and the related equipment. These developments should not be a source of apprehension in Washington. It is clear that Europeans do not want to build a new defense system of their own. They intend to build an effective defense capability, relieving when needed the United States from the burden of crisis management in low-scale local crisis. The respective role of this capability and of NATO and the modalities of their cooperation should be hence defined. The enlargement of the two organizations, with the increasingly different membership, adds to the importance of such a security dialogue.

And last, both organizations are committed to include Russia and Ukraine in the new European security architecture. The development of their relationship with Russia is a crucial element of their enlargement.

CONCLUSION

Central to the success of both enlargement processes is the transatlantic relationship. The expansion of NATO and of the EU is bound to accelerate change in the relationship between Europe and the United States. This change has been inevitable since the end of the Cold War. Enlargement is a major building block of the post–Cold War security architecture. It is in the interest of both sides of the Atlantic to proceed harmoniously. It offers the opportunity of translating into reality the grand design of the two-pillared alliance. The enlarged European Union and the North American nations should develop a full partnership between equals within the enlarged Atlantic Alliance. It is a historic chance not to be missed in the beginning of this new millennium.

BRITAIN, NATO, AND EUROPEAN UNION ENLARGEMENT: RELUCTANCE, DENIAL, AND CONFUSION?

Anthony Forster

The decision of the European Union (EU) at the Corfu European Council in June 1994 committed the Union to embark on the process of enlargement with Cyprus and Malta six months after the conclusion of the Amsterdam Treaty negotiations. Subsequent declarations reaffirmed the EU's commitment to the principle of enlargement, culminating in the Madrid European Council in December 1995 that endorsed a loose timetable for Central and Eastern European accession. In the North Atlantic Treaty Organization (NATO) at the Madrid summit in July 1997, the heads of state and government committed themselves to offer membership in the transatlantic alliance to the Czech Republic, Hungary, and Poland. In public fora the British government has gone out of its way to be supportive of the enlargement of both organizations and, yet, behind this stance, there is considerable confusion about the reconfiguration of multilateral organizations through which Britain has sought to exercise its influence. This study contends that despite public support for both processes, the British government has really only been fully supportive of the EU enlargement process, while a reluctant participant in NATO enlargement.

To explain the British policy stance, London's position must be understood in the context of three factors. First, British actions are shaped by key policy commitments based on long-term visions of how the EU and NATO should develop. Second, the British are acutely sensitive to American concern about the future evolution of NATO. Third, and finally, Britain's attitudes are premised on its insistence that NATO and EU enlargement are two separate and independent processes, and, consequently, London speaks publicly against any linkage between NATO and EU enlargement. Reluctance to embrace NATO enlargement, with the accompanying denial of the linkage between the two enlargement processes, has led to considerable confusion both in the presentation and pursuit of British policy.

BRITISH ATTITUDES TOWARD NATO AND EU ENLARGEMENT
NATO

The British government has been at the forefront of arguing that NATO rather than the EU was the preferred institution for handling the consequences of German unification. The Thatcher and Major governments were among the first to press both its West European allies and the United States for reform of the transatlantic alliance. Initially, Margaret Thatcher pressed for it by advocating an extension of NATO's mandate to operate out of area. Her successor, John Major, was at the forefront of those advocating that NATO adapt to the new strategic environment or face the prospect of withering away. The British government was instrumental in opposing French demands to develop an autonomous European security and defense identity (ESDI) outside NATO structures that might challenge the primacy of NATO. However, throughout the period between 1989-93, the British government did not evaluate NATO enlargement as a particularly useful way to adapt the alliance.

It preferred to emphasize reform of the alliance's strategic role and the possibility of changes to its military structure, though there was acceptance that at some stage in the future NATO might take in new members.

Certainly by the start of 1994, the British government and, in particular, the two lead departments, the Ministry of Defence (MD) and Foreign and Commonwealth Office (FCO), were relatively satisfied with how NATO had adapted to changed circumstances. The British view was that, while it was still necessary to be vigilant, the established relationship between security and economic frameworks had been maintained. NATO had been sufficiently reinvigorated to justify its position at the top of the hierarchy of European institutions, and Britain continued to play a central role in its military and political structures.

However, the British position changed first and foremost because, after several years of vacillation, the Clinton administration unambiguously committed itself to enlargement. Britain questioned the value of enlargement. London also feared that President Bill Clinton's newly found commitment to this issue was driven by American domestic pressures, particularly the Michigan Polish lobby and effective lobbying from Germany, rather than a hardheaded assessment of the security needs of potential applicants.[1] However, the U.S. lead on the issue was sufficiently forthright for British indifference to be subordinated to the need to keep the United States engaged in European security structures. As one British official in the Foreign and Commonwealth Office remarked, "Enlargement of NATO is not a policy of our choosing nor in circumstances that we would desire, but it's a policy the United States is committed to and a policy we can live with." Moreover, once the United States had posed the question of enlargement, London, faced with a stark choice, had to respond. It had either to embrace enlargement or run the risk that NATO might be perceived as unwilling to adapt itself to new challenges and the changed geography of Europe.[2] There was also a feeling, rarely articulated in public, that the transatlantic treaty emphasized shared values, a commitment to the principles of democracy and the rule of law, and that membership could not indefinitely be denied to states that met the criteria and indeed shared these values.

This did not lead to a complete alignment of American and British policy. A shift in the position was driven by the sense of inevitability, and London's commitment remained heavily qualified. Thus, officials projected pursuing a policy of "creative drag," arguing for a cautious approach to enlargement and for an expansion of the alliance that should not undermine the political and military solidarity of NATO.

There were a number of aspects to this approach. At the political level, the British were concerned that enlargement should not call into question the American commitment to the alliance. In particular, there was unease in London that the U.S. Senate debate over NATO enlargement might raise doubts about the alliance's long-term value. Rejection, or even a weak commitment to enlargement of NATO, might undermine or, at worst, destabilize the alliance. In particular, there was concern that potentially ill-informed American politicians might insist on linking developments in the security and economic frameworks and think that EU countries must take in Central and Eastern European countries as a consolation prize to compensate them for exclusion from NATO. A further worry was that ratification might unnecessarily entangle Senate ratification with domestic disagreements between a Republican Congress and a Democratic administration. Above all, the prism through which it viewed enlargement influenced British policy–that, however unilaterally the Americans might act, London would not fall out with Washington over this issue.

The overriding military concern, expressed by Prime Minister Tony Blair, was that "NATO is a military alliance, not a political club, and its collective defence obligations have to be taken with the utmost seriousness."[3] First, NATO's integrated military structure–seen by the British as the centerpiece of NATO–should not be undermined by enlargement. Second, there could be no second-class members of NATO, and, before accession, military planners had to be convinced that an applicant could be defended by conventional and, as a last resort, nuclear means.[4] One MD official remarked that "the only defence guarantee worth giving was one that would never be called into question." Finally, the British government remains concerned about how enlargement will be paid for.[5] London is already disillusioned with many existing European member-states "free riding" on higher levels of British defense expenditure. London has therefore insisted that any state joining the alliance has to be capable of offering its own effective defense and not presume to free ride on the defense expenditures or military capabilities of others.[6] London is at the forefront of arguing that any additional costs of enlargement should be negligible and that any subsequent command reform should be based on cost-effective streamlining and not just efficiency gains to pay for enlargement. Reported expense estimates of a Pentagon study that enlargement would cost existing members between $27-35 billion over thirteen years caused a flurry of concerns both in the MD and in the Treasury.[7] While the Foreign Office continued to argue that the costs would be negligible, the Congressional General Accounting Office endorsed the Pentagon figures and estimated the cost of enlargement to the British budget at $3.2-4.02 billion.[8]

For London, traditional British pragmatism characterized the issue of who might join the alliance, with three issues at the forefront of British considerations. First, there was the need to ensure that NATO's relationship with Moscow would not be undermined by enlargement. London's view held that NATO "cannot guarantee Europe's security without the full involvement of Europe's largest military power: Russia." In the vanguard of those arguing that institutional effort had to be directed toward securing Russian acquiescence to NATO enlargement, London pressed for a new and overarching relationship that would enable Moscow to be properly associated with decisions "which affect the security of Europe and enable her to contribute to the operations that may flow from those decisions."[9] While balking at clumsy Russian attempts to set the terms and conditions of NATO enlargement,[10] London perceived that the future of Russia remained the dominant issue for European security. Some Russian concerns were easily addressed, most notably transparency measures on infrastructure, dealt with in the Vienna Forum for Security Cooperation, and the issue of stationing of nuclear weapons and troops from existing NATO countries in new members, which was ruled out by NATO defense ministers in December 1996. The Founding Act between NATO and Russia, eventually signed in May 1997, was also considered to have gone a long way toward addressing Russian concerns and cleared the way for NATO enlargement.

Second, NATO should avoid issuing promissory notes charting a course on enlargement that might be too difficult and ambitious to sustain. The principal British concern here was to lend its support to "a manageable and limited enlargement"[11] that would not destabilize the alliance and would hold out the prospect of further enlargements on a case-by-case basis. Britain, therefore, joined the so-called "Viking Alliance" of Britain, Denmark, Iceland, and Norway in supporting the American preference for a limited enlargement of the Czech Republic, Hungary, and Poland.[12] A small shift was detectable with the incoming Labour government, when the new foreign secretary, Robin Cook, indicated some support for Slovenia (dropped in the face of American opposition) to provide a land bridge from existing NATO territory to Hungary,[13] but there was a feeling that, despite strong bilateral British military assistance to Romania, accession of a fourth country would simply be too much for NATO to assimilate in one round. In general terms, the policy of who should join NATO remained remarkably similar between the previous and current administrations.

Third, as a hesitant convert to NATO enlargement, Britain was acutely conscious of the sensitivities of candidates who would not be asked to begin negotiations and were keen to maintain "the incentive to pursue reform."[14] British preferences were for a sliding scale of announcements ranging from singling out specific countries for special mention through intensifying dialogue with aspiring members, to a general commitment to "those willing to take on the responsibilities of membership and whose inclusion would serve the interests of the Alliance and enhance overall European security."[15] Above all, the British government wanted NATO enlargement to be seen as an open-ended process. It was not, therefore, unhappy with the final decision to extend invitations to the Czech Republic, Hungary, and Poland, to encourage five other states with the possibility of further enlargements, and to arrange special bilateral agreements with Russia and Ukraine. Britain actually went further than most countries in arguing that Russia might one day join the alliance.

European Union

In contrast to NATO enlargement, the British government has long been an active supporter of the principle of EU enlargement. Indeed, it could be argued that it is one of the few consistently argued policies of the British government since it joined the European Community in 1973.[16] Margaret Thatcher stood in the vanguard of those calling for the enlargement of the European Community and, for example, in September 1988, some fourteen months before the fall of the Berlin Wall, proclaimed that Prague, Budapest, and Warsaw were also "great European cities."[17] Likewise in the run-up to the Maastricht European Council, John Major was the first to argue that the European Community should extend full membership to Eastern European and Baltic states "as soon as they are ready politically and economically" and did not explicitly rule out widening this offer to Soviet Republics.[18] Foreign Secretary Rifkind could argue with some truth "that no member of the European Union is more committed to extending membership of the European Union, and quickly, than Britain."[19] And the new Labour government has made equally strong commitments to EU enlargement by "playing a leading role in these negotiations."[20] However, distrust of British motivations undermined the credibility of this call, and many integrationist governments perceived this policy as "using an altruistic stance towards eastern Europe to undermine the goals of European federation."[21]

British strategy on EU enlargement is based upon five fundamental principles. First, there is a general commitment to form an EU as large and inclusive as possible. Second, as with NATO, London views the changes since 1989 as offering a historic opportunity to reintegrate Western and Eastern Europe and to build a European Union that embraces the whole of Europe, "a chance to put right many of the arbitrary injustices left over from the war . . . . if the tide is missed the opportunity may not reoccur."[22] Third, for both Conservative and Labour governments, EU expansion also presents an important market opportunity. The prospects for an expanded market of 500 million people provided underpinning for claims that "the EU must grasp this historic opportunity."[23] Indeed, for government ministers one of the most regularly quoted reasons for EU enlargement is trade liberalization and the need for open markets. British exports to Central and Eastern Europe rose by 20 percent in 1996, and exports exceeded imports by nearly one billion pounds. The "Open for Business in Central Europe" campaign, aimed at bringing one hundred new businesses to Central Europe by the end of 1998, is testament to the importance attached to the market issue and belated recognition that the response of British business lags well behind German and French commercial activity in this region. The path to EU membership (particularly through association agreements) and EU membership itself are therefore seen as an important means to promote political and economic change,[24] and, if the opportunity is missed, "the case for reform would be weakened; the willingness to take painful medicine reduced."[25]

Fourth and arguably most important of all, EU enlargement provides support for an alternative British vision of European integration. In September 1994, as the Conservative prime minister came under increasing pressure from a fractious right wing of his party, John Major pleaded with his counterparts in other European Union capitals for a more flexible framework of institutionalized cooperation and integration within an expanding EU.[26] London viewed flexibility as a means to reconcile the aspirations of those who want even closer integration and of those attached to existing patterns of cooperation, while also contributing to the preservation of the EU's cohesion.[27] Unsurprisingly, for London the core of the EU was the common market and common commercial policy that required European institutions and rules[28] and cooperation in other policy sectors with reinforced cooperation "open to all, agreed by all."[29] This was an alternative vision to the concept of a hard core of nations advocated in the Schauble-Lamers paper, which, by its exclusiveness, placed hard-core countries in a different category from their partners.[30] For the British, access to European institutions for those who wanted to deepen cooperation could only be acceptable if all member-states agreed.[31]

Enlargement of the European Union underlined Britain's vision of the future for a more flexible Union and the hope that it would act as a catalyst for change: A flexible European Union would be one "that is ready for enlargement."[32] Not all new member-states could or would be able to adhere to existing policy commitments of the EU. For example, not all countries could sign up for the single currency, and arrangements needed to be made for those member-states who could not or chose not to join it.[33] London perceived that the Amsterdam Treaty's recognized allowance for governments to integrate further outside the EU treaties (but with a national interest clause that allows a government to stop it being associated with the EU) as a start in introducing flexibility into the integration process.

Fifth, London was also at pains to point out to the more integrationist-minded EU member-states that the political commitment to enlargement needed to be met by practical internal reform. European Union enlargement is seen as more important than arguments over specific powers of EU institutions.[34] In the words of Malcolm Rifkind, the former foreign secretary, "it is not only the Central Europeans who need to change to allow enlargement to take place. The EU needs to put its own house in order."[35] Even Robin Cook, the new foreign secretary, has been at pains to emphasize that the EU "had to start to show that our rhetoric on this is matched by our willingness to face up to painful and difficult decisions."[36]

There are two specific aspects of reform highlighted by British ministers: reform of existing EU policies and institutional reform. At the policy level, London argued that the Common Agricultural Policy (CAP) would, with its present structure and price levels, need reform.[37] In part, this was so because of shifting consumption patterns and changing views on price supports, but, above all, because the next round of world trade negotiations would lead to further pressures for reform. Even a small enlargement would destabilize EU finances, with conventional wisdom warning that agricultural spending (currently 45 percent of the EU budget) would rise between 30-50 percent and increase overall EU spending by 15-25 percent.[38]

Structural and Cohesion Funds would have to be completely reformed, too. London was aware that inevitably this would lead to a reduction in the amount of money received by the British government, especially since the Structural Funds had been an important funnel for Britain to get back its money, and newcomers would have only a quarter of the purchasing power of the current EU states. If the system remained in place, this would require either a 60 percent increase in the budget or unpalatable reform, and, as Malcolm Rifkind highlighted, governments in more prosperous countries were already under pressure to meet the Maastricht convergence criteria for a single currency. The British had no appetite to contribute more, and, anyway, these programs were "designed to act as a catalyst for greater prosperity, not as a never ending system of handouts, encouraging dependency rather than enterprise."[39] However, claims for virtue were subsequently tempered by a warning that "Britain will insist that future arrangements should be fair," and that any reductions take "proper account of the UK's regional needs."[40]

Reform of the CAP and the Structural Funds was also intimately linked to the budgetary issue, with neither the Major nor Blair government willing to offer up the British rebate. This situation still left Britain the second net contributor to the EU but only the eleventh wealthiest member-state. The government therefore welcomed the Commission's recommendation, contained in its policy document "Agenda 2000," to limit the EC budget to 1.27 percent of Community GNP because of the pressure to implement policy reforms.[41]

At the institutional level, London maintained that some minor reform was necessary, but that it should aim at the minimum required to maintain the existing institutional balance.[42] In particular, the British government has for some time been dissatisfied with the existing underrepresentation of the larger member-states and desirous of reforms to reflect more accurately the difference between large and small states. The next enlargement would inevitably exacerbate this problem, with all potential applicants smaller than the UK, and particularly so with the accession of tiny states such as Cyprus and Malta. The partial agreement contained in the Amsterdam Treaty was a collective commitment to look at the issue of the Council's voting system, in order to offer Britain and other large member-states more votes at the time of the next enlargement. Those countries with two commissioners are prepared to lose one at the next enlargement, but only if the Council votes are reweighted to acknowledge the importance of the large member-states. However, the details of how any reweighting might work are likely to prove controversial, especially for the British government, which already indicated in 1994 the strength of its feelings over the issue.

In short, the British government views EU enlargement not only as highly desirable in its own right, to expand the EU to countries that had a historic right to join, but also because it provided the opportunity to increase pressure on governments for policy reform on a range of issues that had proved stubbornly resistant to change. However, other EU governments believed British calls for others to embrace policy reform, inevitably bringing with it painful change, were not accompanied by evidence that the British were themselves willing to face up to issues that might cause them discomfort. For instance, budget reform might threaten the British rebate, or another intergovernmental conference on issues most directly related to enlargement might pose further problems for London.[43]

In terms of the details of EU enlargement, the British government argued that it must be "successful, sustainable and affordable." There should be no "starry eyed idealism" and each candidate should be judged on its own merits.[44] If one or more applicants met the requirements of membership, it would be quite wrong for the EU to hold them back artificially.[45] Foreign Secretary Robin Cook welcomed the European Commission's recommendations on the candidates for enlargement and the opening of accession negotiations with Cyprus, Poland, Hungary, the Czech Republic, Slovenia, and Estonia.[46] London was also supportive of proposals (originally drawn up at the Essen European Council) for efforts to ensure that the less advanced applicants retain the incentive to continue reform. Under the British Presidency of the EU, extending from January to June 1998, the new government relished the prospect of playing a key "in moving away from introspection about our institutions to a new agenda based on the twin aims of enlargement and policy reform."[47]

THE LINKS BETWEEN THE TWO DEBATES

The standard British line is that there is no formal link between the enlargement of NATO and the EU. Unsurprisingly, there is therefore no official grand strategy for handling expansion of both institutions, despite the Labour government's claim that it is capable of working both to operate in terms of a five-year time frame and "to think strategically and plan for the next millennium."[48] Behind this position of pragmatism, that is, "a stated preference for practical politics over theology,"[49] there is considerable British satisfaction that NATO enlargement will take place prior to EU enlargement, thereby conveniently sorting out the security framework prior to economic integration. According to some commentators, through indecision Western European governments have allowed NATO to displace EU enlargement, and NATO, rather than the EU, will now define the structure and boundaries of a wider Europe.[50] For the British government this is neither unpalatable nor unwelcome.

There were, however, clearly practical overlaps between the two processes. With regard to the security framework, dual enlargement raised a number of important issues. First, NATO enlargement prior to that of the EU will profoundly affect the type of Common Foreign and Security Policy (CFSP) developed by the EU.[51] Two dimensions are apparent. First, the pragmatic position on the link between the security and economic frameworks is a convenient cover for the settled British preference for the status quo concerning the CFSP clauses of the EU, which remain heavily curtailed by the resilience and vitality of NATO. Despite changes to the CFSP clauses contained in the Amsterdam Treaty, foreign and security policy cooperation remains firmly intergovernmental, hampered by an unwillingness to match the heady rhetoric contained in the Maastricht Treaty on European Union with the procedural and institutional changes to make it effective.[52] The British continue to argue for member-state control of this issue area, with unanimity as the basic rule and the Council Secretariat answerable to national governments. The focus therefore remains on coordination of foreign policy with some spillover into soft security issues that do not challenge NATO.

At the level of defense cooperation, the British government has devoted a considerable amount of institutional effort toward taking the issue of Western European Union (WEU) more seriously as an alternative defense organization to the EU. The UK has always been lowest on the totem pole for supporting a purely European defense organization, but there is a view in both the FCO and MD that the WEU can provide a useful organization to head off the EU developing security responsibilities. To this end, London has been at the forefront of developing the operational side of WEU so that it can take on military tasks when the United States (and NATO) is unwilling or unable to carry out certain types of functions. Second, London has been at the forefront of strengthening the links between the WEU and NATO and, third, developing a patchwork of relationships that ensure that non-EU members of NATO (Iceland, Norway, and Turkey) are not further marginalized by the development of an ESDI. Clearly the latter cannot become full members of the WEU, but London has been very "protective" of and played a leading role in developing associate status and ensuring that it provides a means to take their interests into account. It also reduces the chance of "WEU requests being treated as alien when they come to NATO."[53] As a corollary of this, London has also opposed allowing non-NATO members of the EU to join the WEU in order to prevent NATO from providing an indirect defense guarantee to these countries. In particular, London has opposed strengthening the role of neutral countries in the WEU through the development of "Observer Status," a level whereby these countries gain the privileges of WEU membership without undertaking a binding treaty commitment to collective defense in NATO or the WEU.

London applauded NATO's September 1995 Enlargement Study that NATO and full WEU membership should be kept in line, but the British saw real value in different NATO and EU memberships. In part, this is because formalism and symmetry between all three institutions would raise too many difficulties, and, with NATO at the top of the British hierarchy of security institutions, the current status quo preserves British interests. An additional reason for supporting a pragmatic approach is that it ensures that importance of national coordination to ensure synchronization of policies–something the British consider themselves to be good at, and something which again is perceived as working to the British advantage. The British are therefore keen to encourage a cosmopolitan approach to enlargement, rejecting demands made by German foreign minister Klaus Kinkel and others for NATO and the EU to have a small and identical enlargement that leaves the militarily difficult and economically weak to one side. London is also sensitive toward the "double rejects," those states invited to join neither NATO nor the EU, especially the Baltic states (and in a different category than Russia and Ukraine). London has worked hard to develop WEU associate partner status and "constructive engagement" as an answer to this problem.

While the British do not link the two enlargement processes, there is concern that others do. Specifically, there are genuine fears that the ratification process in the United States might lead its politicians and policymakers to link security and economic issues. In January 1994, President Clinton supported the idea of ESDI as a means of sharing the financial burden of European defense and appeared more supportive of an independent ESDI than President George Bush,[54] but significantly, in Britain, the only acceptable form of ESDI is through the development of WEU as the European pillar of NATO and not through the further strengthening of WEU with the EU.[55]

There is more than military and financial burdensharing, which already raises concerns. There is also British anxiety that the Europeans might be expected to follow the U.S. lead and support American policies outside NATO in return for continued American underwriting of the alliance. Policy differences over Cuba, epitomized by the Helms-Burton Act and, nearer to home, over the American lifting of the arms embargo on Bosnia in 1994 and over the pursuit of war criminals in Bosnia, has led to tensions in the Anglo-American relationship concerning the quality of American leadership and the nature of European followership–and a British fear that this might paralyze NATO.

There is additional concern that some politicians and policymakers, notably Paul Nitze, might expect the EU or indeed WEU membership to act as a sort of consolation prize for those countries not invited to join NATO in the first enlargement round. Even though EU (rather than NATO) membership might be more acceptable to Russia, this form of linkage is not acceptable to the British. Not only would it undermine the clearly distinct conditions for EU and WEU membership, but in the case of WEU, it would lead to a dangerous misalignment of membership with that of NATO.

Concerns also exist over Greek-Turkish problems and the "running sore" of the Cyprus question. This issue has the potential to provoke a Turkish veto in NATO enlargement over the handling of the accession negotiations of Cyprus in the EU. The British have been at the forefront of those arguing that the EU should keep the door open to Turkish membership. The importance attached to the Greek-Turkish problem and the potential repercussions for the enlargement of both the EU and NATO is evidenced by the appointment in January 1998 of Sir Brian Hannay as Britain's special envoy to Turkey. Hannay also serves as the EU's envoy to Cyprus, and hopes are high that this issue can be brought to a satisfactory conclusion.

CONCLUSION

At first glance there is a striking contrast between the two enlargement debates. London has invested considerable political energy into ensuring enlargement of the EU, but the British government has been more hesitant concerning the need of, or value in, enlarging NATO. In the EU, the British government has been a leading advocate of reform in a number of what it deems as unpalatable policies, yet in NATO London has favored the status quo–but the differences are less marked than they might initially appear. In both NATO and the EU, the British government has denied the need for any fundamental change in the internal institutional structure and balance and has been keen to preserve existing procedures and practices. Whether Conservative or Labour, the British government considers that enlargement should proceed at a pace that does not change the essential character of these organizations.

The most remarkable aspect of the British debate on the dual enlargements taking place in NATO and the EU is how little British foreign policy has changed since the end of the Cold War: The whole debate on the nature and shape of institutional structures in Europe has revealed marked continuity with British policy during the Cold War. First, there is a continuing assumption that, in defense and security matters, the United States is Britain's preferred partner and NATO the key defense organization. Britain's emphasis on the longevity of the alliance and on the need to retain a privileged role within NATO dominates London's approach to the process. In the EU, enlargement is seen as the antidote to supranationalism and has been the preferred policy of all British governments since joining the European Community in 1973.

Second, inside each organization London views the issues through the prism of great power politics: in NATO, Britain values the use of the United States to counterbalance the influence of Germany and France and nurtures continued concerns about a revanchist Russia; in the EU, London is keen to use enlargement to satisfy British aspirations for a more flexible Europe and appreciates the need for Germany to have a secure political and economic region on its eastern border. A preference for handling dual enlargement through bilateral relations with the major European powers and the United States has also dominated the British reaction. London's response has been filtered through its relations with the United States in NATO and Germany in the EU, more than in any direct initiatives toward Russia or the Central and East European countries.

Characteristic of Britain's foreign policy self-image as "pragmatic," there has been no intellectual contribution by Britain to the debates about the type, shape, and role of international organizations. Indeed, the government has avoided any systematic reflection on the implications for British foreign policy.[56] In the absence of any intellectual reappraisal, the British government has been pulled along by other governments, notably the United States and Germany. Above all, incremental adaptation and a preoccupation with how enlargement might affect British interests in these organizations appear to have been the predominant British response.

This approach has been accompanied by no significant domestic debate on these issues, either inside or outside Parliament. There has only been a handful of adjournment debates brought by backbenchers late at night and provoking little interest. Neither will parliamentary select committees exercise influence on anything like the scale of the debates in House and Senate committees. The British foreign and defense select committees have limited input into the policy-making process, for they were created to scrutinize how policy had worked and to provide a forum for expert opinion, rather than an alternative source for planning.[57] Since all select committees are dominated by the ruling party, a bias exists toward adopting positions that generally avoid directly confronting government policy.

British newspapers rarely carry the issue on their pages, and one needs to read the international, rather than British, press to get a flavor of the key issues involved. Neither will a ratification debate occur comparable with that in the United States. Formally, the head of state or a representative will sign the respective treaties, which, unless contested, will come into effect without the necessity for a parliamentary debate. The size of the new Labour government's majority will ensure that, since even if Conservatives choose to bring the issue to the floor of the House of Commons for tactical partisan reasons, the size of the government's majority will ensure no mishap arises.

Clear contradictions in the British approach to the transformation of Cold War institutions has been the hallmark of Britain's reaction to dual enlargement. A major reshaping of these key organizations will thus be passed off as yet another simple incremental adjustment raising little if any public debate. Few outside a small circle of key policymakers understand how closely the NATO and EU debates are linked and the implications of expansion for each organization. But even if there are no direct British interests engaged in this dual eastern enlargement, clearly, what is at stake is the future shape of these organizations and Britain's role in the new European order.

ENDNOTES

1. "Fateful Error: A Sage Speaks on NATO Expansion–Americans Should Listen," *Times* (London), 7 February 1997, 19.

2. "'Enlarging NATO: Why Big Is Better' Madeleine Albright by Invitation," *Economist*, 15 February 1997.

3. Tony Blair, "NATO Summit Madrid," statement by the prime minister, House of Commons, London, 9 July 1997, 1.

4. Charles Bobinski and Andrew Robinson, "Cosmopolitan Comrade," *Financial Times*, 23 October 1996; P. Wise, "NATO: Divisions Emerge over New Member States," *Financial Times*, 30 May 1997.

5. Philip Gordon, "Will Anyone Pay to Enlarge NATO–and If So Who?" *International Herald Tribune*, 30 April 1997.

6. Wise, "NATO: Divisions Emerge."

7. The study suggested that it would cost $27-35 billion over thirteen years: one-third of direct costs of extending NATO's infrastructure, pipelines, and air defense; one-third of the indirect cost of new members improving their forces; and one-third of indirect costs of existing members putting together rapid reaction forces to defend new members. The United States would contribute 15 percent of direct costs ($150-200 million per annum) but none of the indirect costs. "A Bigger NATO: Europe Changes Shape," *Economist*, 12 July 1997, 21. A RAND study placed the cost slightly higher, at $42 billion over ten years. Bobinski and Robinson, "Cosmopolitan Comrade."

8. General Accounting Office, "NATO Enlargement: Cost Estimates Developed to Date Are Notional," *Report to Congressional Requesters*, GAO/NSIAD-97-209, August 1997.

9. Malcolm Rifkind, "Reuniting Our Continent: Britain's Approach to EU and NATO Enlargement," speech by the foreign secretary to the Council on Foreign Relations, New York, 27 September 1996, 2.

10. Charles Goldsmith, "Russia Indicates Terms to Accept Larger NATO," *Wall Street Journal* (Europe), 13 March 1995.

11. Blair, "NATO Summit Madrid."

12. "A Bigger NATO: Europe Changes Shape," *Economist*, 21.

13. Wise, "NATO: Divisions Emerge."

14. Douglas Henderson, "Britain and the New Europe," speech by minister for Europe at the Future of Europe Trust Conference, Lancaster House, London, 11 June 1997, 4.

15. Blair, "NATO Summit Madrid."

16. Helen Wallace, "Britain out on a Limb?" *Political Quarterly* 166, no. 1 (1995): 46-58.

17. Lawrence Freedman, ed., *Europe Transformed: Documents on the End of the Cold War* (London: Triservice Press, 1990), 267-74.

18. Ian Davidson and Ivo Dawnay, "Major Urges EC to Admit East European States," *Financial Times*, 13 September 1991; Rifkind, "Reuniting Our Continent," 3.

19. Malcolm Rifkind, "Europe's Future Security," speech by the foreign secretary at the Carnegie Endowment for International Peace, Washington, DC, 10 March 1997, 6.

20. Tony Blair, "European Council, Amsterdam, 16-17 June," statement by the prime minister, House of Commons, 18 June 1997, 2.

21. Davidson and Dawnay, "Major Urges EC."

22. Rifkind, "Reuniting Our Continent," 1; idem, "Britain's Modern Vision of Europe," speech by the foreign secretary to the French Chamber of Commerce, Dorchester Hotel, London, 23 January 1995, 6.

23. Robin Cook, "Statement by the Foreign Secretary: European Commission Agenda 2000," 16 July 1997 (London: Foreign and Commonwealth Office Press Release).

24. Henderson, "Britain and the New Europe," 2.

25. Rifkind, "Reuniting Our Continent," 2.

26. John Major, "Europe: A Future That Works; The 2nd William and Mary Lecture," Leiden, the Netherlands, 7 September 1994 (London: Foreign and Commonwealth Service: Verbatim Service).

27. Malcolm Rifkind, "Europe: Where Do the Limits of Integration Lie?" speech by the foreign secretary to the Swedish Institute of International Affairs, Stockholm, 3 February 1997, 6.

28. Douglas Hurd, "1996 and Beyond: Preparing for an Expanded European Union," speech by the foreign secretary to Institut Français des relations Internationales, Paris, 12 January 1995, 2.

29. Rifkind, "Britain's Modern Vision of Europe," 6.

30. Hurd, "1996 and Beyond," 4; Malcolm Rifkind, "Queen's Speech: Foreign Affairs Debate," extracts from a speech by the foreign secretary, House of Commons, 24 October 1996, 3.

31. Rifkind, "Queen's Speech," 4.

32. Rifkind, "Britain's Modern Vision of Europe," 6.

33. Quentin Peel, "Rifkind Revives Churchillian Vision," *Financial Times*, 18 September 1996.

34. Rifkind, "Reuniting Our Continent," 3; idem, "Queen's Speech," 4.

35. Rifkind, "Reuniting Our Continent," 4.

36. Andrew Gowers and Philip Stephens, "Amsterdam Summit: Cook Urges EU to Set Its Sights on New Goals," *Financial Times*, 16 June 1997.

37. Hurd, "1996 and Beyond," 2.

38. William Wallace, *Opening the Door: The Entanglement of NATO and the European Union* (London: Centre for European Reform, 1996), 20.

39. Rifkind, "Reuniting Our Continent," 5.

40. Cook, "Statement by the Foreign Secretary."

41. Commission of the European Communities, "Agenda 2000: For a Stronger and Wider Union," *Bulletin of the European Union*, Supplement 5/97 (Luxembourg: Office of Official Publications, 1997).

42. John Major, "The Challenges of the 21st Century," speech by the prime minister at the Lord Mayor's Banquet, the Guildhall, London, 20 November 1995, 4; Tony Blair, "European Council, Amsterdam, 16-17 June."

43. Robert Preston, "Blair's Line: Win Friends and Influence Results," *Financial Times*, 18 June 1997.

44. Rifkind, "Europe: Where Do the Limits of Integration Lie?" 2; idem, "Reuniting Our Continent," 1.

45. Rifkind, "Reuniting Our Continent," 3.

46. Commission of the European Communities, "Agenda 2000."

47. Cook, "Statement by the Foreign Secretary."

48. Henderson, "Britain and the New Europe," 3.

49. Gowers and Stephens, "Amsterdam Summit."

50. Wallace, *Opening the Door*.

51. Anthony Forster, "The Ratchet of European Defence: Britain and the Reactivation of WEU 1984-91," in *European Security, Defence and Integration: Western European Union 1954-96*, ed. Ann Deighton (Reading: European Interdependence Research Unit, St. Antony's College, Oxford, 1997), 39.

52. William Wallace and Anthony Forster, "British Approaches to Rethinking European Order since 1989," in *Rethinking European Order: West European Responses, 1989-1997*, ed. Robin Niblett and William Wallace (Oxford: Oxford University Press, 1998).

53. Alyson Bailes, "Western European Union and Contemporary European Security: A British Perspective," in *European Security, Defence and Integration*, 52, 49.

54. John Peterson, "Europe and America in the Clinton Era," *Journal of Common Market Studies* 32, no. 3 (September 1994): 422.

55. Forster, "The Ratchet of European Defence," 27-46.

56. Wallace and Forster, "British Approaches to Rethinking European Order."

57. Anthony Forster, "The United Kingdom," in *Disconcerted Europe: The Search for a New Security Architecture*, ed. Charles Anstis and Alexander Moens (Oxford: Westview Press, 1994), 139.

GERMANY'S STANCE ON NATO-EUROPEAN UNION POLICY DIRECTIONS: SQUARING CIRCLES

Peter Schmidt

In the years after the breakdown of the Communist systems in Europe, Germany's foreign and security policy moved through two, albeit overlapping, phases. The first extended from the collapse of the German Democratic Republic (GDR) in 1989-90 to the end of 1993, when the Treaty on European Union (Maastricht Treaty) came into force. The predominant question during this interval was how this bigger Germany could be integrated into the European system of states without causing new intra-European struggles and power games. From this perspective, the Maastricht Treaty, and especially the fixed time frame for the European Monetary Union, must be viewed as a belatedly realized precondition for the unification of Germany.[1] All earlier German theorizing on possible unification since the 1950s had come to the conclusion that unification should (and could), if ever, only happen within a pre-established, tight, political European framework. The European Community (EC) and NATO were expected to be the dominant frameworks within which this should happen. It represented an axiom of German political thinking that a real European Union should presuppose German unification and that a strong Atlantic link should be maintained. Certainly, there is agreement that the Maastricht Treaty did not bring about a real political union, although significant steps toward integration and intensified cooperation have been taken, especially with regard to the Monetary Union. The resulting deepening of European integration was a vital element of German *Ordnungspolitik* as well as the avoidance of any major disturbances between European integration and further development of the NATO framework. These considerations aimed at limiting the conceivably adverse effects of German unification on the European political order.

The second phase brought a different German interest to the fore: the stabilization of Central and Southeastern Europe. Whereas the reaction to the paramount problem of the initial period was an attempt to deepen the EU and to accommodate NATO to the new security situation, the major foreign and security policy goal during the second phase was the extension of the area of Western European stability through an eastward enlargement of EU and of NATO. The policy imperative of the first and the second period are, however, at odds with each other. Any deepening of the EU makes it more difficult to enlarge quickly. Enlargement, however, supported a tendency toward a community without strong political personality. A similar tradeoff exists with regard to NATO. Nevertheless, on the path from the first to the second period, the question of how and where the deepening of the European Union and reform of NATO challenged the goal of extending both organizations was not carefully reviewed. The German government basically combined the politico-strategic imperatives of both periods: Simultaneity of "intensification/deepening" and "enlargement/extension" of the two major European institutions became the leitmotif of German security policy. The strategy for overcoming this problem pointed to

111

deepening the EU before enlargement occurred. Germany followed a similar approach with regard to NATO.

In political practice, however, this tack could not solve the problem. Enlargement of the EU demands not only substantial institutional reform, in order to make the EU capable of absorbing new members without losing its cohesion and capacity to act; but also it urges the EU to revise a number of cost-intensive and well-established policies regarded by many member-states and European institutions as belonging to the sacred area of the so-called *acquis communitaire* of the European Union. The EU just cannot afford to extend these cost-intensive policies to the new member countries that represent "natural targets" for these funds.

A similar picture emerged with regard to the Atlantic Alliance. The retention of a robust NATO had to be brought into accord with a stronger European component, the European Security and Defense Identity (ESDI), as a consequence of the envisaged broadening of the EU's scope into security policy, and also with enlargement to new member-states. By nature, however, enlargement of the alliance raises questions of cohesion and effectiveness. In addition, it was increasingly realized that possible countermeasures by Russia against the admission of new members to NATO raised hard questions, one of which was how Russian opposition to NATO's enlargement could be appeased. And indeed, the new NATO-Russian and subsequent NATO-Ukrainian Councils, along with the Euro-Atlantic Partnership Council, have created an institutional complexity that makes NATO's administration only more difficult. All this indicates that an analysis of the German position on EU and NATO policy directions requires a close look at the problems of the dual postulate of deepening or retention and enlargement of EU and NATO.

SQUARING THE CIRCLE I: EU's DEEPENING AND ENLARGEMENT

The German government did not view the enlargement of the EU as simply a major instrument to enlarge the area of political and economic stability. Further goals were to place the burdens of the policy of stabilization on more shoulders and to prevent the perception of a German hegemonic position that may have surfaced if Germany would have developed special bilateral relations with the new bordering countries. Germany, therefore, was the major driving force behind the political pressure toward enlargement. There were reservations and opposition within the EU, but Germany finally did manage to convince its EU partners that enlargement was unavoidable and necessary. Now the EU has decided to open up negotiations with Hungary, the Czech Republic, Poland, Slovenia, Estonia, and Cyprus. Nevertheless, it was and still is difficult to eliminate the existing strain between deepening and enlarging the EU. In order to avoid this tension, Germany applied a strategy of "deepening first." But the Intergovernmental Conference, which led to a revision of the Maastricht Treaty, did not succeed in initiating the necessary institutional reforms that would enable the EU to manage a substantial number of new member-states.[2] There are, therefore, good reasons to assume that both goals will remain in conflict in the years to come. Whether the introduction of the euro will develop a great integrative pull overcoming these disintegrative tendencies, although it is very much hoped for, remains an open question, particularly since all new members will certainly not be able to join the euro club within a short time.

Beyond the euro question, five reasons point toward a contentious situation:

(a) The enlargement of the EU is beneficial for Germany insofar as it is an appropriate means of allaying foreign fears of a German "national sphere of influence." Concurrently, however, EU partner countries view themselves only to a limited extent as members of a "strategic community" with a common set of interests and priorities and a willingness to share the burdens in a fair way. Up to now, Germany has shouldered the main burden of stabilization support for eastern Central Europe.[3] Germany has also been the main host country for refugees, particularly those from the former Yugoslavia. In addition, the continued high standard of social security attracts people from other EU regions.[4] However, the financial situation has deteriorated because of the high costs of unification. The debt figure of Germany between 1989 and 1995 increased by more than 110 percent, whereas it had only increased by 38.7 percent between 1983 and 1989.[5] All these indicators contribute to constant German criticism and to a diminished willingness to maintain Germany's role as the primary net contributor to the EU's budget.

(b) The EU is still an economically heterogeneous community with extreme disparities in basic economic structure, efficiency, importance of the primary sector, growth rates, and GNP. The consequence is that poorer (mostly southern) member-states have a strong interest in financial transfers from the EU in their behalf. This situation is not completely against the interests of the richer states, which have acknowledged the importance of balancing the economic situation within the EU area. Otherwise, the Single Market with its free exchange of goods, services, and capital could lead to social and political conflicts within the EU. Nevertheless, the richer countries have to legitimize these transfers before their constituencies and want, therefore, to exert strict control over this policy. This constellation of interests indicates that the poorer EU states want at least to maintain the previous level of financial transfers to their region. Because enlargement will cost much money and decisions on concrete conditions of accession have to be made unanimously, these countries have a strong voice in the process. A certain clash of interests will be unavoidable and is already taking place.

(c) An additional factor impeding unconditional enlargement is the current economic situation. A reconciliation of the outlined clash of interests through the distribution of budget increases based on substantial economic growth rates is improbable in the near future. Even more, serious adjustment problems to the new international order in some of the richer EU countries, including Germany, do exist, and there is general agreement that the introduction of the euro will aggravate these problems, at least for the initial transition period. There will be much pressure to increase the amount of money for unemployment programs to downplay possible social conflicts, making it difficult for them to open up fully to countries that would increase the pressure on politically sensitive economic sectors such as agriculture.

(d) It is generally argued that Germany's economic gains in the Single Market markedly exceed the financial burdens of EU membership. In the meantime, however, Germany's net transfer to the EU has reached a level that has not only triggered public discussion but also prompted the government to demand corrective moves in the year 1999, when new decisions are to be taken on the EU's financial system. Sweden, the Netherlands and Austria, three other major net contributors to the EU budget, have joined the German camp regarding this question, which worsens the situation.[6] The argument of costs is often countered by claiming that German benefits from the EU's Single Market are to a large extent due to its high export rate. However, this position does not hold water. Most member-states carry out a much larger part of their trade with EU partners than Germany. Consequently, Germany is not only exposed to a larger burden brought on by unification and financial transfers to Central and Eastern Europe, but it also makes particularly large contributions to the EU (in net terms) in comparison with other member-states. It is to be expected, therefore, that Germany will be in a difficult position to bear the financial consequences of enlargement despite its favorable backing of the EU's extension.

(e) Agricultural policy costs still absorb almost 50 percent of the EU's budget, a general level that will not be sustainable because the agricultural sector in accession countries is far too large to be financed similarly. Requisite reforms will cause substantial conflicts, especially in France and certain German regions. Although the percentage of people working in agriculture is decreasing in Germany, the agricultural sector represents a decisive section of the electorate in certain regions of the country. Dealing with these challenges requires political prudence and will slow down the reform process and full integration of the accession countries into the EU.

This situation does not rule out intermediate steps and interim solutions in the form of long-term transition arrangements and gradual enlargement. However, the integration of new states into the EU will be a complex process and will cause major difficulties among current member countries.

SQUARING THE CIRCLE II:
NATO'S ENLARGEMENT AND NATO REFORM

Another cornerstone of German foreign and security policy is the transatlantic link embodied in the Atlantic Alliance. The EU dynamic should not contradict the maintenance of a strong European-American link in the framework of NATO. Within the EU, however, Germany is linked with France, a country that does not view European security policy as complementary to Atlantic relations but as some sort of a rival enterprise. Although France has changed its position on NATO incrementally since 1990, it still resists a complete integration in NATO's military structure. In opposition to this general French position, maintaining the substance of European-American relations and developing it as far as possible in a complementary role to European integration is a constitutive aspect of German foreign policy. Although the operative European military potential should open up an option for independent military action, it should not separate this from the alliance. French policy, however, urges extensive autonomy of the Common Foreign and Security Policy/Western European Union (WEU) vis-à-vis NATO. There is, therefore, an ongoing struggle involving how French military staff can and should be linked to this enterprise. Additional subjects of conflict are: the Combined Joint Task Forces (CJTF) of

NATO, by which Europeans are to be enabled to carry out independent operations with the support of NATO and the United States if necessary; the extent of NATO's enlargement process, whereby France argues very much in favor of further enlargement, especially to Romania; and the extension of NATO's reach toward regional conflicts beyond the NATO area. In many of these sensitive disputes, Germany seeks to be an intermediary between French and American positions.

Against this background, NATO's session in spring 1999, where the major decisions on the new strategic concept will have to be taken, will certainly raise serious questions of cohesion among NATO members.

COORDINATING ENLARGEMENT PROCESSES

EU and NATO enlargements offer a dual problem for Germany. In both instances, Germany succeeded in receiving the approval for these processes. Nevertheless, the logic and political basis of NATO enlargement are different from the EU's extension. NATO governments agreed to negotiate with Hungary, the Czech Republic, and Poland in a first round, while the EU opened up negotiations for its next enlargement with these countries plus Slovenia and Estonia. A certain tension results between the two processes for two reasons.

First, there has always been the demand for the position that the EU should develop, as well for security and defense issues, into a "single actor" and that new member countries would have to join the WEU as the EU's defense arm. But this did not happen during the previous round of enlargement with Austria, Finland, and Sweden. Nevertheless, according to the guidelines of the Amsterdam Treaty that the European CFSP "shall include all questions relating to the security of the Union, including the progressive framing of a common defence policy,"[7] there will be pressure on new member-states to join the WEU.

Second, a clear American position maintains that, in order to avoid backdoor commitments, there should not be any WEU member that is not simultaneously part of NATO. It is, however, quite improbable that Estonia, due to vehement Russian opposition, will become a member of NATO in the near future. This will lead to a situation in which either the European Union has to put the one-actor idea further into the background or the United States has to give up the position of avoiding backdoor commitments.

CONCLUSION

Germany's foreign and security policy in Europe has a primarily institutional orientation. The stabilization of Europe as a whole is to be achieved above all by deepening and enlargement of existing security institutions in the EU and NATO (or sustaining and developing them further). This policy, however, does have its major difficulties, and not only because it arouses expectations among eastern Central European states that probably can only be fulfilled in the long run. This policy is also problematic because of the fact that Germany, along with other member-states of the EU and NATO, is confronted with difficult decisions inside the traditional security frameworks that Germany is keen to maintain and develop further.

Thus, it can be confirmed that the approach so far has triggered positive side effects among countries seeking accession: They are making great efforts to become "accessionable." But the promise to enlarge the EU and NATO soon will bring into question the internal cohesion of both organizations. For a number of reasons, these tensions are more serious in the EU's case. The major point is that the EU has a much broader sphere of competence than NATO, thereby raising great questions of the future cohesion and character of the EU as a political actor on the world scene. The major question will be whether the introduction of the euro will have integrative or disintegrative effects on the EU.

Additionally, there are complications in coordinating both enlargement processes. For all these reasons, Germany's stance on the policy directions of the EU and NATO is very much a policy of "as-well-as." This is certainly a rational choice in these times of big and quick changes. The avoidance of a clear choice helps only to buy some time, but the underlying conflicts cannot be solved by this policy. Nevertheless, with the passing of time new political constellations and positions are likely to evolve that may help to overcome current contradictions and dilemmas.

ENDNOTES

1. There is much evidence that France urged Germany to give up the deutsch mark in the framework of the Maastricht Treaty as a prerequisite for France's stance toward German unification. See "Dunkelste Stunden. Der Kanzler öffnet die Akten über die deutsche Einheit. Die Dokumente zeigen: Frankreich hat das schnelle Ende der Mark erzwungen," *Der Spiegel* 18 (1998): 108-12.

2. This is especially the case with regard to the question of qualified majority decisions in Common Foreign and Security Policy (CFSP) and the inclusion of the Western European Union into the EU's scope. In both cases, Germany failed to include these positions into the Amsterdam Treaty.

3. From 1989 to the end of 1996 Germany has supported the economic development of the Commonwealth of Independent States (including guarantees for credits) by 125.7 billion DM. This is more than 50 percent of all bilateral assistance programs.

4. On 22 April 1998, the German government refused to accept a proposal by the EU Commission that aimed to open up the German welfare system to EU citizens.

5. *Statistiches Jahrbuch 1997 für die Bundesrepublik Deutschland* (Wiesbaden, 1997), 521; "Verschiedene Fragen zur Finanzierung der Deutschen Einheit," *Wissenschaftlicher Dienst des Deutschen Bundestages* (November 1993), 8.

6. The German finance minister, Theo Waigel, clearly indicated during an informal EU meeting in York that Germany is not willing to accept a strategy of reforming the agricultural, structural, and budget policy of the EU without a substantial reduction of Germany's net contribution to the budget. "Waigel schlägt gemeinsame Erklärung der EU-Finanzminister zum Euro vor," *Frankfurter Allgemeine Zeitung*, 23 March 1998, 1.

7. Article J.7, 1.

RUSSIA, NATO, AND EUROPE

Igor F. Maximytchev

In the next century, the harsh realities of international competition will require additional stability and cohesion in the existing or emerging centers of strength (the "innovation centers"). This factor determines the growing tendency of an organic integration (full or partial) of the states belonging to particular regions or groupings of countries. Even the United States, an incontestable world leader, has formed around itself a North American Free Trade Association (NAFTA). Europe, which has been experiencing a latent internal crisis for a long time, is experiencing this trend in a particularly acute way. The beginning of the post-confrontation period–with the signing on 21 November 1990 of the Charter of Paris for a New Europe under the auspices of the Conference for Security and Cooperation in Europe–has laid the theoretical and practical foundations for the unification of the European continent in its entirety, thus enabling the creation of a "Great Europe," a "Europe from Dublin to Vladivostok."

However, this new chapter of European history, opened by the end of the apocalyptic East-West confrontation, has failed to create new "tools" for regulating the continent's affairs. Europeans have nothing but the instruments inherited from the Cold War period, stigmatized by their origin and only capable of reproducing turbulence in a world that is vastly changed. Attempts to modernize these tools so far have not brought any major success. Moreover, the decision to enlarge NATO threatens to revive a certain degree of confrontation. It appears that the inability to reflect on the existing realities and the revision of major organizational structures is now the central European issue.

While addressing the problems of the Continent's unification, Europeans have to rely on the capacities of NATO, the European Union (EU), the Council of Europe, the Organization for Security and Cooperation in Europe (OSCE), and a few smaller and less important organizations. Only the least potent of all the above organizations, the OSCE, includes all European states plus the United States and Canada. The hardly more efficient Council of Europe embraces all the European countries without the United States. The powerful NATO and European Union do not include half of Europe, precisely the half that, until 1990, stood in confrontation with the rest of the Continent. Therefore, it is logical that further developments will be determined by the transformation and modus operandi of the two latter organizations and, most important, by their relations with the countries of Europe that lost their supranational connections with the end of the Warsaw Treaty and the Council for Mutual Economic Assistance (COMECON).

This situation brings to the forefront the issue of NATO enlargement, often labeled as a means of ensuring an all-European security, which, in turn, could provide the potential base for the unification of the entire continent. The answer to one question may clarify the justification of this affirmation: "Will it ever be possible for Russia to join NATO?" The only obvious answer is "no."

118

There is no place and there will never be one for Russia in NATO. Even if today one hears from time to time comforting assurances that Russia's membership in NATO is possible "after a certain probationary period," strong opposition exists within the bloc itself. The West often claims that NATO is already an "open community," and that, after it completes its reconstruction, no country belonging to the North Atlantic region and desiring to join it will be prevented from doing so. This appears to be a willful or unintentional distortion of the facts designed to facilitate a smooth admission into the bloc of the first three new applicants. Further expansion will follow the tested track. As long as Russia remains an independent state capable and willing to pursue its own interests in Europe and in the rest of the world, even those who claim that there is nothing anti-Russian in NATO enlargement will assert that Russia's accession would divest NATO of its mission. The unwillingness to let Russia in is sometimes justified by apprehension that a Russia in NATO's ranks will have the potential to negate common action as it already can in the OSCE and the United Nations. This situation is something that Western politicians, conscious of their responsibility for maintaining global law and order, believe they cannot let happen.

It appears that no matter what statements and declarations are made by the alliance, the one and only raison d'être of NATO has been the deterrence of the Soviet Union in the past and now of Russia. If it were not true, the enlargement of the bloc should have commenced with a formal or informal proposal for Russia to consider joining it. This approach would have enabled the alliance to acquire a genuinely all-European stature. Many pro-West Russian politicians and parliamentarians have indicated the desirability of such a step from the very first days of the debate over NATO expansion and even at the height of pre-Madrid polemics. But nothing of the sort happened, and the alliance leaders merely made a few nebulous hints about some distant future. At the working level, it was made clear that nobody was going to invite the Russians anywhere: "Let them submit the application, and we will consider it." But this is totally unacceptable for Russia.

Morally and psychologically, the submission of an application by Russia would amount to public recognition of its "defeat" in the Cold War. It is clear to everybody in Russia that the country could not lose a war it has never waged. Such an interpretation of European realities would never be acceptable to the Russian public that initiated the normalization of relations with the West on equal terms and not on the conditions of "voluntary capitulation." An application for NATO membership would be viewed as an unconditional surrender, opening the way to the winner's diktat. There are no illusions as to the character of such a diktat: The double standards of the West in its approach to the situation in the states of the former Soviet Union are jeopardizing Russian interests.

On the other hand, for Russia an application for NATO membership would be a hopelessly useless humiliation because its rejection is simply inevitable. First, there are forces within the alliance that would never agree to let Russia inside for the same reasons they are enlarging NATO now. Second, Russia's accession to NATO, apart from political problems, would create formidable organizational complications.

Membership of such a potentially powerful state as Russia would make NATO managers wrack their brains over the necessity to accommodate this great country in the alliance's command structures without violating the rights and hurting the feelings of old (and not so old) members of the organization. This situation has been illustrated by a sometimes extremely heated debate over the redistribution of posts among the founding members that took place in Madrid. No solution was found. The dispute was left unsettled. Naturally, Poland, the Czech Republic, and Hungary will have to accept whatever they are offered. Such treatment of Russia would be possible only if it accepted a weakened status and position. But who will need Russia this way?

Furthermore, even if the unbelievable happens, the accession of Russia to NATO would immediately undermine the security of Russia's Asian borders. The mere request to admit Russia to the alliance (not the admission itself) would complicate Russia's relations with its numerous southern neighbors. A military alliance is always anti-somebody. The attempts of NATO theoreticians to prove that the "new NATO" is based on a broader concept of security that does not need an enemy and is only concerned with universal security fail to answer a simple question: Why conserve and expand NATO as a military alliance instead of embarking immediately on the creation of a continentwide system of security? Our Asian neighbors may become suspicious about the target of such an impressive military grouping (American-led, naturally) comprising the entire Northern Hemisphere. Should NATO and Russia then invite Iran and China to join the band too? Theoretically, it is not inconceivable, if one gives a flexible enough interpretation of the terms of the Treaty of Washington, for even Turkey is in NATO. But even if one disregards the intentions and preferences of these countries, the question remains: How far can NATO go without actually substituting itself for the United Nations? Iran and China, in turn, have their own neighbors capable of becoming suspicious. In any case, the only result of any enlargement of NATO may be new dividing lines, new antagonisms, and new dangers.

NATO is the only international organization functioning in Europe that is and will always be closed for Russia as an equal partner. East-West "peaceful coexistence" was possible as long as NATO limited itself to the role prescribed to it by the military strength of the Soviet Union—that of maintaining stability in Western Europe. The NATO decision to embark on the military integration of the continent without (i.e., against) Russia made future antagonism between them inevitable. NATO's strategy of "deterring Russia" necessitates Russia's response in the form of "deterring NATO." Since Russia is far weaker and much more vulnerable than the former Soviet Union, this would be substantially more difficult. But Russia would be compelled to do just that if no reasonable compromise could be found to limit NATO expansion. Even President Boris Yeltsin, a known friend of the West and particularly the United States, warned in late 1997 that such a development was unavoidable if alliance leaders continued to lend a deaf ear to Russia's apprehensions.

The Russia-NATO Founding Act, signed in Paris on 27 May 1997, has a polyvalent character. It may offer new opportunities for convergence and cooperation of the parties or for their divergence. What will really count is the interpretation of its ambiguous provisions. The only definite thing so far is the beginning of NATO enlargement. Before the signing of the act, there were still certain doubts as to the readiness of the parliaments of some NATO members to sanction a direct conflict with Russia over the advancement of NATO's military structures eastward toward Russian borders. After Moscow's partial consent to such a step, all doubts vanished. With the passing of some time, the possible argument may be used that if you press hard enough, Russia will drop its objections about the accession to the bloc of the other Central and Eastern European states, including former Soviet republics. But this would signal a real confrontation.

All the other provisions of the Founding Act are extremely vague. The price Russia had to pay for the West's promise to be more attentive to its interests in the future was high, especially if one takes into account the fact that this promise is in no way binding for the West. The emphasis that U.S. Secretary of State Madeleine Albright puts on the political character of the commitments arising from the document (instead of legal commitments demanded by Russia) really means that the West may very well forget them if, suppose, the situation in Europe changes or new governments come to power in the states/parties to the act. Ultimately, everything will depend upon the goodwill of the parties vis-à-vis the interpretation of the agreements.

What is definitely unacceptable to Russia are the attempts to present the Founding Act as a "peace treaty" that has allegedly put an end to the Cold War. It is important to understand and respect that Russia has never been in a state of war with the West, be it "cold" or "hot," and is therefore not going to make peace when it has never been violated. The agreements to end the confrontation between NATO and the Warsaw Pact, and the West and the former Soviet Union were signed (and, as appropriate, ratified) in 1990 with all the required formalities. It happened after Europe opted for common all-European solutions to the existing problems. The truth is that the West evaded the commitments it assumed then and decided to enlarge the NATO bloc, thus endangering, once again, the integrity of the continent. NATO members would like to make everybody believe that Europe and the world are starting from a tabula rasa situation. But the tabula is not that rasa. It has certain Western debts inscribed on it, and sooner or later the West will have to think of paying them, if it wants to maintain its reputation as a reliable partner.

There is not much in the text of the Founding Act that would support the West's claim that it is the first step to a future all-European system of collective security. In principle, the Permanent Joint Russia-NATO Council could carry out such a function, but its competence is not precise. Endless Western assertions that no state will have the right to veto NATO decisions only confirms the conclusion that the West is not prepared to deal with Russia on equal terms in security matters. A system of collective security can be based only on the principle of consensus that makes the voice of each country an absolute value. The negation of the "right of veto" is, in fact, a mere disguise for the refusal to deal with Russia on the basis of consensus. Consequently, the creation of an all-European security system and a new order based on it that would replace the Yalta-Potsdam system still remains a very distant goal.

Unprecedented military activity of NATO on territories bordering Russia has furthermore created a growing concern in the Russian public. On 26 September

1997 the Russian Parliament (State Duma) adopted a special appeal on this subject which, *inter alia,* states: "There is no doubt that under the cover of the declarations on the peace-keeping nature of such manoeuvres the military of the United States of America are exploring new theatres in direct proximity of the borders of the Russian Federation. One cannot exclude that in the course of such super-distant landing operations the capability of US troops to land in the territory of the Russian Federation itself is being tested."

The signing of the Founding Act cannot, therefore, be viewed as a conclusion or as a beginning of some new post-confrontational period of international relations. It will not limit the enlargement of NATO, which seriously endangers European unity, but at the same time, it may provide new opportunities for a constructive dialogue between Russia and all alliance members. One can only regret that the crisis in Russia-NATO relations is not settled but merely postponed. Russia seeks ways to use the opportunities provided by this respite to avoid the threat of isolation.

Today's situation in Europe is developing in a totally different direction from that envisaged by the majority of Europeans at the time of the Cold War's end in 1989-90. Then, the general direction of the continent's progress was determined by the Charter of Paris for a New Europe unanimously adopted by the meeting of heads of state and government of the member-states of the Conference on Security and Cooperation in Europe (CSCE) on 21 November 1990. This document comprises clearly formulated collective commitments of the Europeans for the coming decades. The second sentence of the charter's text contains a most important provision expressing the very essence of the new period of European history: "The era of confrontation and division of Europe has ended." When a "new era is dawning in Europe," the parties to the charter assumed the obligation to "expand and strengthen friendly relations and co-operation among the States of Europe, the United States of America and Canada, and to promote friendship among our peoples." They further declared: "With the ending of the division of Europe, we will strive for a new quality in our security relations" and "help to overcome the mistrust of decades, to increase stability and to build a united Europe." They emphasized that "Europe whole and free is calling for a new beginning."

The charter pointed out: "The establishment of the national unity of Germany is an important contribution to a just and lasting order of peace for a united, democratic Europe aware of its responsibility for stability, peace and co-operation." And, "We recognise the essential contribution of our common European culture and our shared values in overcoming the division of the continent." The 10 July 1992 CSCE follow-up summit meeting in Helsinki on "Challenges of the Times of Change" stated that "The Charter of Paris for a New Europe outlined the guiding principles of the establishment of a community of free and democratic states from Vancouver to Vladivostok."

However, further developments in the continent thereafter took another path. The concept of an "evil empire" was revived, this time associated with Russia. In practice, this resulted in the demand to take "preventive action" against the eastern giant and to establish some sort of quarantine for it. For the purpose of propaganda, the necessity to discriminate against Russia is often justified by speculations about the alleged similarity of Hitlerism and "real socialism" in its Soviet version. To justify the enlargement of NATO, the following line of reasoning is being elaborated. Thus, the aggressive policy of Nazi Germany generated a great fear of Germans, who, after 1945 had to go through a rather lengthy process of democratic reeducation, limited sovereignty, and unequal integration in alliances of democratic states. Similarly, the aggressive policy of the Soviet Union generated a fear of Russians, and, therefore, they too will have to go through a long period of democratic reeducation under the supervision and guidance of Western teachers before being admitted to Western communities. In doing so, an important detail is deliberately being ignored. For the liberation from Nazi barbarism, humankind paid an incredibly high price, with more than fifty-five million lives lost in World War II unleashed by Germany and its allies, cities lying in ruins across Europe and Asia, and an unprecedented destruction of industries and productive forces. In the case of Russia, it did away with its totalitarian regime by itself, without any war or destruction, on its own initiative and with its own will. Is there any similarity, even if we leave aside the substantive difference between fascism and communism?

For the purpose of proving Russia's international "inadequacy," Russia is being accused of alleged "remilitarization" of its policy (with the Russian army experiencing its last gasp), "rerussification" of its national minorities (with the impotency of the federal government to tackle aggressive chauvinism, as in Chechnya), and "neo-imperialism" of Moscow in the Commonwealth of Independent States (with Moscow unable even to implement the union with Belarus). There are many who wish to see Russia within a hairbreadth of disintegration, hardly breathing and happy to eat the leftovers from the master's table. They will not let Russia crumble because it would be too expensive to feed endless flows of refugees, but it is consistently and systematically prevented from restoring its forces. No one is interested in strengthening a rival and competitor, no matter what the global market economy "idealists" say.

The urgent task of the OSCE members is to remove the flagrant contradiction between their obligations under the Charter of Paris and an unlimited enlargement of NATO that is seen by some of them as high political wisdom. The range of future possibilities goes beyond the one posed by NATO, that of an unchecked expansion of NATO or a disorganized region of Central and Eastern Europe. The most farsighted realize that the fundamental difference between the profound integration of Western Europe and the amorphous state of the rest of the continent cannot last forever, and they therefore should begin looking for a solution. In 1992, Poland's president Lech Walesa forwarded the idea of the establishment of a "NATO-bis" and an "EU-bis" in Eastern Europe that would serve as the second pillar (with Russia and the Commonwealth of Independent States [CIS] as the third one) of an all-European structure uniting the entire continent without any exceptions. This constructive idea of Walesa did not find any support either in Central and Eastern Europe, or, more importantly, in Russia, and therefore vanished. The reaction of the West was equally negative, and the policy of NATO enlargement replaced the Walesa plan. But one cannot exclude the emergence of other proposals. This is one more reason why one should not hurry with the threatening advancement of NATO toward Russian borders.

The projected NATO enlargement should not stress the division of the continent but focus on the development of constructive NATO-Russia relations. To this end, from the very start, the full potential of the Permanent Joint Council established in Paris should be used to develop an ambitious program of its activities ultimately aimed at laying the foundations of an all-European system of collective security.

In a reference to the OSCE that is still suffering from obvious impotency, the Founding Act states: "The OSCE, as the only pan-European security organisation, has a key role in European peace and stability. In strengthening the OSCE, Russia and NATO will co-operate to prevent any possibility of returning to a Europe of division and confrontation, or the isolation of any state." This solemn formula should find an adequate reflection in practical deeds of European states and the United States. It is necessary to embark quickly on a process of finding answers to the problems of collective security on the basis of a structure embracing the entire continent–be it a reformed OSCE, a transformed NATO including all European states, the Russia-NATO Permanent Joint Council, or something totally new.

Because there are apprehensions in Europe regarding possible interference in its affairs from outside (as alleged by NATO enlargement protagonists), the Russia-NATO Council could be assigned a very concrete mission, that is, to elaborate and adopt a universally acceptable definition of interference and to develop a set of preventive measures obligatory for everyone. Since one of the motives for joining the alliance is said to be the fear of a possible unexpected attack, the council could be asked to implement a pan-European early-warning system. The combination of such concrete measures would result in the desired all-European effect.

The Permanent Joint Council should also accommodate German, French, and British influences in order to prevent negative effects of the NATO enlargement process for Russia and the rest of Europe. Of key importance will be the position of Germany. As the first Western country to demand an accelerated eastward expansion of the alliance and as one of the most consistent advocates of this process, it has assumed a huge responsibility for the destiny of the continent. Now, the time has come to show that it is up to this responsibility.

It is also necessary to consider the role of the EU and European integration in the restructuring of Europe. Russia's involvement in the process of European integration through a gradual association with the European Union is becoming a priority of Moscow's foreign policy. Such involvement would require an inevitable transformation of both partners. In the long-term perspective, the transformation of the "little-European integration" (even after the admission of selected countries from Central and Eastern Europe, the EU will still constitute a "Little Europe") into a truly all-European entity will not only neutralize the most harmful divisive effects of NATO enlargement but also open new horizons for Russian foreign policy as well. An application for EU membership would strengthen the international status of Russia. As a potential member of the EU, one of the most powerful global centers of power, Russia would acquire a totally different basis for dialogue with the United

States, Japan, China, and the new Asian and Pacific region players. This approach, of course, should not be viewed in isolation from Russia's CIS and U.S. policies, just as European integration cannot be isolated from Russian bilateral relations with the major players of the European scene–Germany, France, and Great Britain. These aspects remain closely interrelated, and the organizers of Russian foreign policy should constantly keep them in mind, taking into account the limitations of Russian foreign policy potential and its need to restore urgently internal equilibrium.

It is in this spirit that Foreign Minister Yevgeny Primakov put forward the proposal to elaborate a Charter of European Security based on the Helsinki Final Act and the decisions of the OSCE summits in Paris, Helsinki, Budapest, and Lisbon, which would give Europe a code of principles of conduct oriented to the twenty-first century. Regional security remains the most important sphere of collaboration of all Europeans, and the time has come to refine details of this architecture. In doing so, any competition among peacekeepers should be excluded. Only a true partnership in peacekeeping based on close coordination, as in Bosnia, may pave the way to all-European solutions. The key role in this situation has been played by the Contact Group (France, Germany, Great Britain, Russia, and the United States) engaged in the search for concrete solutions in Bosnia.

The positive potential of such cooperation exists in the OSCE Minsk group on Karabakh (France, United States, and Russia), which made substantial progress in establishing the collaboration of its three co-chairs. They have elaborated the platform of settlement submitted to the consideration of parties concerned that hopefully will bring beneficial results. Russia has also made real efforts to improve coordination with the United States, which is a cosponsor of the Madrid peace process in the Middle East, and with the European Union in pursuing an Arab-Israeli settlement.

International terrorism and organized crime require international consolidation of efforts to combat them. The scale and gravity of these problems are directly related to the rise of political and religious extremism and the growing number of unsettled regional and local conflicts undermining the basis of law and order in many states. Unfortunately, the liberalization of border-crossing regimes, which is a great achievement of the post-confrontation period, contributes to the internationalization of these threats. All of the above necessitate the strengthening of integration and consolidation of efforts, not bloc-based division. This is the only way for Europe and the world to ensure the fundamental right of all peoples to equal protection from old and new threats to their security.

The initial period of the post-confrontation era was characterised by the parallel existence of a well-organized and integrated Western Europe and, to the east, a region that had returned to an amorphous condition with nothing comparable to the secure Western European structures. The dissolution of the Warsaw Pact and COMECON was not followed by anything similar, a situation aggravated further by the disintegration of the Soviet Union. This contradiction in developments in the East and West, however, should not jeopardize the creation of a Great Europe in the future. The basic feature of the situation is the diversity, not the opposition. The greatest danger of the next period, which is beginning now, consists in the emerging conflict between NATO and non-NATO that threatens to make the post-confrontation peri-od very short. Both the governing authorities and the public in Russia basically view very favorably the concept of the construction of a Great Europe with Russia's full participation. The necessity of integrating Russian foreign policy into an all-European framework is being debated at this very moment.

The time has come for Russia to apply for membership in the European Union, which is the only real and possible nucleus of a future united Europe. After a long period of estrangement, both the European Union and Russia find much to dis-like about each other, which is quite natural, given the differences of their initial start-ing positions. The period of mutual adaptation is, therefore, expected to be lengthy. But this should not be considered a a serious obstacle for an accelerated beginning of convergence. For Russia, it is important that further East-West contacts are not viewed from the perspective of future confrontation but in the context of defining mutually acceptable policy. What distinguishes the European Union from NATO is that the former has influential forces desiring to involve Russia in the closest possible cooperation for a powerful and independent Europe in the twenty-first century. Thus, the prospect of full-fledged Russian participation in European integration is quite realistic. It does not matter how long it may take, because what counts for his-tory is the durability of the result. It is important to give an incentive to organize rou-tine work aimed at bringing the partners closer.

A clear European perspective of Russia (and it will become reality right after the submission of the Russian application for EU membership) will contain NATO's activities to isolate the East European giant. A new division of the Continent will be very difficult, if at all possible, once the general outline of a Great Europe is clarified. This will contribute to the formation of a political environment on the Continent that would enable the Permanent Joint Russia-NATO Council to work successfully and productively.

Basically a European state belonging to European civilization, Russia has three perspectives in geographic, political, and strategic terms. These points of view look respectively westward (to the rest of Europe and to the Atlantic), eastward (to East Asia and the Pacific), and southward (to the Near and the Middle East). In mod-ern history, the western direction presented Russia with by far the most formidable security challenges. It is probable that the future dangers for Russia will be coming from the east and/or the south. Russian policy is preparing itself for such prospects. But it is essential to eliminate, at first, even the possibility of conflict with the West. The end of the Cold War provides a historic opportunity to demilitarize effectively and securely Russia's relationship with the Euro-Atlantic world and to make the use of force as unthinkable as it is now between France and Germany. The achievement of this goal is realistic, if it is assured that Russia's damaging isolation from the rest of Europe is ended, once and for all. Security and prosperity in Europe can never be assured unless both these opportunities are vigorously seized upon.

Russia's vision of Europe's security architecture is not limited to an alliance that excludes her. Moscow has proposed creating an effective collective security system built around an institutionalised CSCE, complete with a security council of its own, with the North Atlantic Cooperation Council acting as its security arm par excellence, and NATO, WEU, and the CIS as its associated bodies. These suggestions were rejected. NATO is beginning its expansion.

The aim of Russia is to belong to a formal group of decisionmakers competent in all major issues of European security, and, thus, to be anchored firmly in Europe. The Russia-NATO Permanent Joint Council can be the solution of the problem provided that both sides try to attain this objective. The emerging triangle of Jacques Chirac, Helmut Kohl, and Boris Yeltsin could be an excellent support for this mechanism. If the process of rapprochement between Russia and the European Union could be strengthened parallel to this kind of progress in the security field, the emergence of a basis for a Great Europe would become a greater possibility.

THE BALKANS AND THE POST-DAYTON ENVIRONMENT: RESTRUCTURING OR INSTABILITY?

Vladimir Veres

The Dayton Peace Agreement (21 November 1995) for Bosnia and Herzegovina marked a turning point in the Yugoslav crisis and the region's war. The terms of the agreement essentially defined and set the course for normalizing the situation in the entire area of the former Yugoslavia as well as for the development of international relations in this region, primarily among Bosnia and Herzegovina, Croatia, and the Federal Republic of Yugoslavia (i.e., Serbia and Montenegro). These three main contracting parties have undertaken obligations: to end the war and establish peace in Bosnia and Herzegovina, including its legal institutions; to normalize their mutual relations; to respect international law and human rights as embodied in the principles of the United Nations; to eliminate the grave consequences of war; and to establish a military balance at a lower level, both bilaterally and subregionally. The system of Dayton obligations, in effect, incorporates the crux of important conditions for the international political rehabilitation of the Federal Republic of Yugoslavia (FRY), whose strategy for reincorporation into the world community requires their full and consistent fulfilment.

Several concurrent processes condition the present political situation in the Balkans. On the global level, the disintegration of the Soviet Union, the Warsaw Pact, and the Council for Mutual Economic Assistance (COMECON) marked the breakdown of bipolarism that characterized international relations in the decades following World War II. At the regional level, the former Yugoslavia fell apart with war on part of its territory. Finally, on the national levels, radical internal changes occurred in the states that used to belong to the so-called "socialist bloc." The Balkan peninsula, which has long borne–often due to the involvement of outside forces and great powers–the reputation of a "powder keg," has again become a zone of instability, of real or potential conflicts.

One can argue that, after several decades of relative stability, we are again witnessing, at least partially, the resumption of a process of "balkanization,"defined as a "constant conflict among the Balkan nations over territories and a chain-line atomisation of the Balkan region."[1] The disappearance of intrabloc restrictions and of the one-party monopoly of power created a vacuum primarily filled by nationalism with its accompanying territorial claims and national pretensions. Nationalism was understood and used as the most efficient instrument for both the preservation or gaining of power and for maintaining the old or newly formed states. The former Yugoslavia provided the prime setting for these currents. Indeed, the history of the Balkans is a history of conflicting nationalisms, but never before has nationalism been highlighted in such contrasting terms with democratic and integrative processes in Europe, as well as with the true interests of the Balkan peoples.

Historically speaking, as Serguey Russev argues, "this new militant nationalism is fundamentally different from the historically rooted concept of national identity as a precondition for the establishment of civil society."[2] Recent events, especially in the former Yugoslavia, threatened to discredit significantly the key positive elements of processes in Eastern Europe at the end of the 1980s, such as the breakdown of the structure for bloc confrontation, the drastic reduction of the nuclear threat, the acquisition of a real independence by the former Soviet allies, and the internal democratization and affirmation of market economy based on dismantling the historically obsolete model of "real socialism." "But while we greeted the appearance of the old flags and symbols as signs of liberation after decades of oppression in Riga, Moscow or Bucharest, we more often than not failed to see the magnitude of the dangers this represented in the ethnic mosaic of South-Eastern Europe."[3] Objective problems of transition, common for all of Eastern Europe, were supplemented in the Balkans by the renovation and reemergence of past conflicts. Since "for historical reasons, the Balkan societies lack a democratic legacy and a tradition of civil society," they are now facing a task of "the emergence of civil society and containing of ethnic nationalism."[4] Along with the escalation of nationalism on the territory of the former Yugoslavia, national tension rose in other Balkan states as well, aggravating border or minority issues. Fortunately, if one can speak about any positive effects emanating from the Yugoslav experience, it may be considered to be the traumatic influence of these events on other Balkan peoples to behave with more restraint and rationality in solving international problems.

We are now clearly witnessing the process of "restructuring" the Balkans in the realm of international security. The most important issue here is the balancing of two parallel currents: first, the disintegration of the Eastern bloc and liquidation of the bipolar confrontation in the region where three Warsaw Pact countries (Hungary, Romania, Bulgaria) used to face two NATO members (Greece, Turkey), with one nonaligned state (Yugoslavia) and one semi-isolationist (Albania) also present; second, the emergence of newly independent states on the territory of the former Yugoslavia. Both processes are conditioned by the internal transformation of the former communist countries and the acceptance and realization of the main principles of parliamentary democracy, multiparty political systems, a market economy, and the observance of human rights. Domestic changes are a priority.

Domestic forces–social, political and economic–influence foreign policy in these countries, perhaps to a greater degree than ever. It is especially visible in the case of the former Yugoslavia. The breakdown of this country and the war that followed, which has had the most tragic consequences in Bosnia and Herzegovina, resulted primarily from internal political dynamics. As for the external factor, the international community and major powers failed to react in time and did not move expeditiously to prevent the slippage into military conflict.

The contention that the primary responsibility for the resulting disaster lies with the international community and great powers mostly serves the diversionary function of avoiding discussion about the real responsibility of domestic political factors in the former Yugoslavia. In Belgrade, one can often hear accusations that the outside world contributed greatly to the breakdown of the country out of bias against Serbia and Montenegro; in Zagreb, arguments maintain that international opinion lined up against independence for Croatia; and in Sarajevo, sentiment prevails that the international community did not do enough to preserve the independence and unity of Bosnia and Herzegovina. All these contentions contributed to the feelings of distrust toward the outside world that are hard to surmount and that hinder participation of all these states in international security structures. Besides, it is apparent that these countries could not pretend to participate seriously in the processes of European integration without solving basic problems between themselves, such as formal diplomatic recognition and establishment of relations, the renewing of transport links, the dismantling of trade barriers, and the repatriation of the refugees.

Although it is clear enough that antagonism and hatred cannot be easily overcome, it should also be apparent that these countries and peoples cannot simply leave the region: They are destined to live, coexist, and cooperate with each other. Thus far, all major issues are being resolved with the heavy involvement of the international factor, primarily that of the United States. There is no short-term military exit strategy possible for the international Stabilization Force (SFOR) without a consequent and substantial political collapse.[5] At this moment, pressure is an indispensable element for settling existing problems. In the long run, however, such pressure will not be effective if a climate of at least minimal mutual confidence is not created that stresses the common interests of all these countries, first on the economic and finally on the security level.

A NEW REGIONAL SECURITY STRUCTURE

Participation of international organizations and institutions in shaping a new political and security structure in the Balkans is of key importance for many reasons. According to Dimitrios Triantaphyllou, "Since ex-communist Balkan states have no collective arrangement and little money to spend on defense, they must look to be integrated into the Western European stability network via various European and Transatlantic institutions such as NATO, EU [European Union] and WEU [Western European Union]."[6] The crucial factor in reducing tensions in the Balkans still does not originate from bilateral or multilateral arrangements between Balkan states, but instead either from belonging to the same military and political alliance (e.g., Greece and Turkey) or from the intention of all countries to join the European economic and integrated security structure. Such an orientation requires restraint and reduction of tensions in border, minority, and other questions. In this context, Yugoslav analyst Ranko Petkovic claims that "in the entire history of the Balkans after liberation from Turkish rule there was no record of the Balkan countries striving towards the same goal, as is nowadays the case: joining the European institutions and organizations."[7] This seems to be the key positive element these days in the Balkans.

Historically, the Balkan countries were often members of different alliances, possessed different ideologies and political systems, and relied upon various outside powers. Unfortunately, such traditions still have a serious impact on the relations between Balkan countries and peoples. However, gradual stabilization in post-Cold War Europe, adaptation to the absence of bipolar division and confrontation, settlement of the Yugoslav crisis, and appeasement in Bosnia and Herzegovina on the basis of the Dayton Agreement will enable Balkan states to face squarely the fact that join-

ing the European integration process requires solutions for inherited or newly created problems. If all the Balkan states accept the prevailing European framework, it
means that basically all of them must opt for the same model of political and economic development, regardless of the ideological identification of their leading political forces or parties. Such acceptance requires meeting the obligations and standards
determined by European organizations. As a ready example, one can point to the decisive role played by their European orientations in contributing to the significant
reduction of tensions between Hungary and Romania. A regional approach by the EU
seems to provide a viable solution for the Balkans. Improved and increased mutual
relations among the Balkan states will obviously be made a condition for their closer
ties with Europe, since European organizations seek a guarantee that the Balkan
states, while joining European institutions, will not bring in their own unsolved problems. It is a false premise that any country can develop its relations with European
centers without first settling issues with its own neighbors. European priorities must
prevail in the Balkans, meaning that social and economic development should be given
primary emphasis. Before reaching this critical threshold, it will be necessary to rede-
fine all previous Balkan concepts of international security, not only in the current
political but also in a historical and philosophical sense.

Security in the Balkans has traditionally been understood in the narrow
geopolitical sense–that is, in categories of borders, sovereignty, alliances, and blocs.
Most recently, some of these elements gained strength. The basic European trend,
however, is quite opposite, and security in the Balkans clearly defies patterns to the
west: borders must not be made a fetish of and turned into national myth; sovereignty in the contemporary world is relative and necessarily limited by accepted international obligations and standards; economic development, human rights and living
standards, rather than military might and power of the state, become more and more
the fundamental criteria for the international position of a particular country. The
very conception that regional relations in the Balkans involve competition between
states and peoples over borders, territories, and influence must be altered. European
institutions and practices must work to eliminate the very underpinnings of international relations in the Balkans with roots in past centuries and conflicts and often with
the interference of the great powers that turned the region into their playground. In
spite of all these problems, the Balkans are gradually entering a period when social and
economic dimensions of security must prevail over geostrategic and military orientations.

These observations provide a political and philosophical basis for the new
system of international relations in the Balkans. More concretely, the main issue is the
organizational and institutional framework of security in the region. Notwithstanding the obvious importance of mutual relations between the Balkan states, stability in
the Balkans, and especially in the former Yugoslavia, is closely connected with wider
and more universal organizations and alliances. Very important in this regard is a role
played by NATO. Indeed, the Yugoslav crisis very much contributed to shaping the
profile of NATO in the post-Cold War era after the dissolution of its main adversary,
the USSR and the Warsaw Pact. Also, the crisis not only pointed to the increased

prominence of the United States but also to the problems and limitations Washington faces, particularly in relations with Western European allies and Russia. As Stephen Larrabee emphasizes, "if anything, the crisis has reinforced the importance of the United States–and NATO–for the resolution of European security problems. At the same time, it has prompted a significant shift in the American perception of NATO's role, especially in out-of-area conflicts. These conflicts, once regarded as beyond NATO's responsibility, are now seen as legitimate NATO concerns."[8] Consequently, NATO now faces three tasks: defining precisely its "out-of-area" role; restructuring the alliance since many existing nonmembers aspire to join it; and redefining NATO's raison d'être in the absence of older threats and the emergence of new hot spots and sources of instability.

The Balkans did to a certain degree lose their strategic importance for the West due to the collapse of the USSR, but the Yugoslav crisis has reminded NATO leaders of the risk in considering any problem in the Balkans a "local" one and of underestimating the degree to which a crisis in the region and its fallout effect can threaten the new post-Cold War security order in Europe.[9] NATO is now directly present in the Balkans, with Greece and Turkey as members, with troops in Bosnia and Herzegovina, and with the membership of former communist states in the Partnership for Peace and the North Atlantic Cooperation Council (NACC). Although there are different opinions among political forces in Balkan countries about NATO's future role, it is obvious that in contemporary Europe NATO and the EU are the only real and efficient frameworks for creating a system of security that would also include the Balkans. However, for this to happen, it is necessary that NATO redefines itself and adopts a new order of priorities: Its main role will not be opposing a specific adversary, such as the USSR, during the Cold War, but preventing and settling conflicts in the post-Cold War era, whose nature differs from conflicts in the earlier period.

There will also be an increased role for NATO, not as a primarily military alliance with the mission of collective defense but as an alliance of states that share common values, such as democracy, a market economy, and human rights. Accordingly, membership or some form of association with NATO will mean not only–or even primarily–common defense but also a commitment to the strengthening of democratic values and institutions. Such an orientation will lead to a certain relativization of military factors and emphasis on political and economic components in NATO's development. Certainly, the military aspects will remain important, especially in the instance of unpredictable events or the emergence of crisis areas, but political and economic considerations will obviously gain importance for the internal difficulties that confront states in Eastern and Southeastern Europe. The enlargement of NATO and its general opening toward these countries will have a greater value if it is to be accompanied with such a redefinition of the alliance's role.

Needless to say, in such a context special importance must be attached to NATO's relations with Russia. The termination of the Cold War gradually reveals the existence of some (more or less legitimate) interests that had been hidden by layers of ideology and bloc-antagonism. These interests could be partly conflicting, differing, or simply not always fully overlapping. That is why a transition period–and obviously a rather difficult one–is necessary. The interests of Russia and its key partners (United States, European Union, China, and Japan) should be identified and defined under new circumstances in order to establish which interests have become closer or even overlapped due to the Cold War's end, and which are still differing or even conflicting. It is a sort of crystallization of interests in their natural and objective form, without ideological and Cold War layers. With certain oscillations, the new Russian policy is searching for a "middle road," one without ruinous confrontation and without absolute harmony, which is impossible. Overcoming long-lasting confrontation is a reality, but the presence of certain differences is also inevitable. Such differences should be accepted as normal and legitimate and should be solved realistically and reasonably, avoiding moves that could serve in favor of extremists and the confrontation-minded on the other side. At this point, the political wisdom of Russia, as well as of its leading Western partners, is experiencing a very serious test. Russia should, with all its existing problems, evaluate realistically its position, especially its internal needs, and work to contain or limit all temptations that could lead to serious confrontation with key partners or even to a possible new policy of isolation, since this would mostly damage Russia itself, particularly its population. For their part, the United States, Western Europe, and Japan should take into account not only legitimate Russian interests but also the very sensitive position of this country and the oscillations of Russian public opinion. A possible intention to weaken the international position of Russia, which might, intentionally or not, be conjectured from some Western moves, could backfire and hit primarily Western interests. The isolation of Russia and possible internal disturbances would threaten the basic structure of contemporary international relations.

The room for maneuver and compromise between Moscow and the West clearly exists. But more tactfulness and flexibility on both sides is required. The West must understand the complexity and delicacy of the situation in Russia and its wish not to feel isolated or challenged by NATO's enlargement. On its part, Russia must accept the fact that tension with the West, particularly in the manifestation of neo-imperial tendencies toward its neighbors, could primarily aggravate its position. Moscow should also appreciate the concern of Eastern European states about instability in Russia. These same countries must be mindful of the importance of Russia as their essential and unavoidable partner.

Still, the key for all problems lies in the internal situation in Russia. It seems that the world depends more on developments in Russia than vice versa. For this reason, any analysis of the Russia-NATO relationship bears the stamp of relativity, since it will be easier to formulate policy for NATO enlargement and for the institutionalization of its relations with Moscow than to predict future developments in Russia itself.

NEW YUGOSLAVIA AND NEW ENVIRONMENT

The disintegration of the USSR and of the Warsaw Pact fundamentally changed the international position of Yugoslavia. The country lost its place as a "buffer zone" between two military and political alliances. During the Cold War each side–East and West–was primarily concerned that Yugoslavia remained nonaligned and that Belgrade would deny access to its territory or military facilities for the other alliance. Providing it with important room for maneuver, Belgrade skillfully manipulated nonalignment to its advantage. Indeed, the former Yugoslavia played a more significant role in international relations than would have been expected by its size or population. Consequently, the disappearance of the Cold War division contributed to Yugoslavia's disintegration, since in the "old" constellation the dissolution of the country would have probably been prevented by the superpowers. However, this is not to say that the breakup of the USSR and the Warsaw Pact dissolved Yugoslavia. The changes in the international constellation made the disintegration possible only under the condition that there already existed internal forces and circumstances that led to the crisis and, finally, dissolution. Rather, international changes served as a necessary, but not sufficient, source of Yugoslavia's fall. In fact, Yugoslavia disintegrated before the Soviet Union did.

As already mentioned, the prime fault of the international community was its initial underestimation and then inadequate response to the developing Yugoslav crisis, which led to the absence of preventive measures. It is a generally shared opinion among analysts that in the period from 1989 to 1991 the former Yugoslavia had a better starting position for economic and political reforms than other East or Southeast European countries. Its political and economic system, even with all of its faults, was more democratic, flexible, and adaptable than institutions and practices in the former Warsaw Pact. Since 1991, however, the situation dramatically shifted in favor of countries such as Poland, the Czech Republic, Slovakia, and Hungary. As a result, Yugoslavia has had to adapt not only to the new neighborhood but also to a profoundly different role and diminished influence in the international community when compared to its predecessor. Such a reorientation requires not only political and economic measures and reforms but also a sort of psychological identification with the smaller size of the country and the more modest international role. Yugoslavia now confronts the task of coping with problems that most East European countries started to solve back in 1989, although not with equal success. Unfortunately, for Yugoslavia, its starting position now is much weaker and the circumstances more unfavorable. Belgrade's foreign policy will have to respond to a new international role and neighborhood, and to the limited political and economic capabilities of the country.

There is also one additional change from conditions confronting its predecessor: The Yugoslav crisis became an important international issue and its settlement an international responsibility. It appeared that a seemingly internal or local conflict, particularly in such a volatile area as the Balkans, could have far worse repercussions for the international community than was understood at the very onset. The problems of former Yugoslavia will certainly continue to be a burden on the international community's shoulders. As a consequence, the political choices for former Yugoslav republics, including Serbia-Montenegro, will be limited and marked by international demands and requests.

The Dayton Agreement comprises a combination of obligations, demands, and pressures. Belgrade additionally faces certain conditions for reestablishing ties with the United Nations, the Organization for Security and Cooperation in Europe (OSCE), and international monetary and financial organizations. These conditions are connected with the regulation of remaining sensitive issues with former Yugoslav republics and certain internal issues in Yugoslavia, including minority issues and Kosovo.

According to Willy de Clercq, chairman of the Committee on External Economic Relations of the European Parliament, the EU believes that the development of a good relationship with Yugoslavia and its position within the international community are dependent on a constructive approach by Belgrade on the following points:

> a) the respect for and full and correct application of the Dayton and Paris Peace Agreements, the precondition and the very base of the European Commission's approach, including respect of The Hague Peace Tribunal;
> b) the development of regional cooperation between the countries of former Yugoslavia based on mutual recognition among all the states;
> c) a constructive approach toward agreements among all the states of the former Yugoslavia on succession issues;
> d) the principle of democratization, including the solution of the Kosovo problem.[10]

Closer commercial links within the region and the reestablishment of trade with traditional partners are of great importance for Yugoslavia. The state of the national economy is the most serious problem facing Belgrade now and, obviously, closely interrelated with the problems of democratization and stability. If Yugoslavia is to cooperate effectively with its neighbors, the EU, and other partners, it will have to undergo a substantial internal transformation, particularly a significant privatization of the public sector and a restructuring of the commercial banking sector. There is simply no way out of the economic crisis without access to foreign capital and foreign investment. With a GNP of only about $10 billion, Yugoslavia's foreign debt amounts to approximately $9 billion that is accompanied by a constantly expanding trade deficit. Moreover, the debt to citizens that lost their life savings in foreign currency in domestic banks stands at roughly $5 billion. Pension funds are in serious trouble, and the foreign currency reserve is poor. Financial institutions lack credibility for the public.[11]

In no uncertain terms, the country desperately needs the net inflow of foreign capital. But the precondition for such aid is the normalization of relations with the international economic and monetary institutions, such as the International Monetary Fund (IMF), World Trade Organization, World Bank, and the London and Paris clubs of creditors. Normalization presumes compliance with the clauses of the Dayton Agreement, which means that solution of major political issues is closely connected to the prospects for the economic recovery of Yugoslavia. Whatever the importance of the foreign policy and relationship with the international environment, the decisive factor will be Yugoslavia's ability to undertake serious internal political and economic reforms in order to achieve stability and economic recovery. A very important precondition for all changes is a containment of nationalism, isolationism, and xenophobia–phenomena that have taken roots in the country during the last decade's dramatic events. It is not possible to have democratic changes in the country if the population displays a mindset characterized by a siege mentality and the tendency to see world relations in the alleged terms of inevitable conflicts and divisions, alliances of one against the other, and constant conspiracies.

What Yugoslavia requires is a realistic and rational policy without creating an artificial atmosphere of threat and siege. In this context, emphasis should be placed on regional initiatives for security and cooperation that can be, geographically and politically, divided into the following categories:

> a) *Cooperation between Balkan countries.* It should include a gradual solution of outstanding   political issues. Although there is always a temptation to avoid political questions because of their sensitivity and to limit cooperation to economy, transport, etc., it is extremely important that gradually, under appropriate conditions, all these problems are approached and solved;

> b) *Balkan-Danube cooperation.* It can serve as an efficient means to connect Southeastern Europe, and especially Serbia, with Central and Western Europe;

> c) *Balkan-Mediterranean cooperation.* If the Danube is Yugoslavia's link with Europe, the Mediterranean is a link with the entire world;

> d) *Balkan-Black Sea cooperation.* It is the expedient route to establishing closer relations with Turkey, Russia, and Ukraine.

There are political and economic initiatives that can be taken by the Balkan countries themselves, such as organizing ministerial meetings, parliamentary cooperation, a free trade zone in the Balkans, and a "Balkan OSCE," a controversial proposal. Additionally, EU initiatives can contribute, for example, by fostering cooperation between countries and encouraging the reestablishment of links between the former Yugoslav republics. Finally, there exists the American-sponsored Southeastern European Cooperation Initiative (SECI), whose core is an examination and financing of infrastructure projects to stimulate private investment and surmount administrative barriers. Differences notwithstanding, the general idea behind the European and American initiatives is clear: to stimulate all the Southeastern European countries to solve existing problems and to achieve stability and economic recovery through cooperation and gradual integration.

Of course, these efforts primarily apply to the countries of former Yugoslavia and former communist states. The war in former Yugoslavia and the turmoil in Albania have clearly demonstrated the dangers of civil and intranational conflicts that can easily cross borders of countries or regions. Accordingly, the international community is very interested in finding appropriate formulas for containing nationalism with its role in fueling territorial or border disputes. Because the policy of prevention failed–or was not exercised in full strength–two instruments now appear at the international community's disposal: First, political and military measures in place, as the implementation of the Dayton Agreement, can secure that conflicts do not resume; second, economies must be stimulated and democratic institutions reinforced in the expectation that a more stable and prosperous environment will deprive the nationalists of their steam and strengthen moderate and liberal political forces. Moreover, this formula contains the very useful element that access to European integrative processes and institutions will be denied to those states that fail to resolve their local problems. Although there will be no lack of politicians ready to label such an approach as pressure or even blackmail, it seems that the policy could be productive in bringing former conflicting groups closer to establishing normal relations, at least in the economic field. Outside pressure is likely to remain an important stimulant and contribute to stabilization in the whole region.

The Yugoslav crisis also demonstrated that nationalists are quite ready to sacrifice economic prosperity for their own territorial and other goals. Still, after all the suffering, the populations in the former Yugoslav republics are much less likely to welcome another round of conflict and are more prone to respond positively to prospects of economic betterment. Yet no form of foreign assistance can be effective without fundamental internal reform. Such is the crossroads point where Yugoslavia stands now.

Doubtless, the top priority for Yugoslavia is improved relations with its neighbors, particularly the former Yugoslav republics. It is vitally important to solve problems caused by war and the disintegration of the former common state, such as the issue of succession; to ensure conditions for a free and safe return of refugees and exiles; and to regulate their civil status and property issues. This approach would truly end the war and tension on the territory of the former Yugoslavia, constituting an essential condition for lifting the "outer wall" of sanctions. In view of all the circumstances related to the Serbo-Croatian relationship and the complexity of disputable issues, normalization, and cooperation between Yugoslavia and Croatia are of foremost bilateral importance and vital to harmony and stability in the region, including the peace process in Bosnia and Herzegovina. A mutual and long-term interest of both countries is to expand the prospects for cooperation, allow for free movement, solve the refugee issues, and renew normal communications and economic links.

The relationship with Bosnia and Herzegovina should be marked by full implementation of the Dayton accords, including the commitment to and realization of the territorial integrity of Bosnia and Herzegovina, securing the return of refugees, cooperation with The Hague Tribunal, and establishment of full diplomatic relations.

Yugoslavia has a long history of relations with most of the "old neighbors," yet these relations have also suffered from the Yugoslav crisis and war. This situation should be adjusted now for the new realities. Since some past grievances and limitations have been mostly overcome, Yugoslavia can gradually rejoin the international community and enter an era of stability with both its immediate and more distant neighbors, such as Greece, Austria, Italy, and Turkey.

The second circle of priorities for Yugoslavia consists of the EU countries and countries of the Commonwealth of Independent States (CIS), such as Russia and Ukraine. The EU is the most important source of economic and financial support. The absence of cooperation with the EU has drastically affected the overall political and economic position of Yugoslavia. Positive interaction with the EU remains, therefore, a vital objective and the only means to prevent further stagnation and to secure access to capital, technology, know-how, and a developed market. The crisis drove Yugoslavia away from the integration path and left it in a sui generis position toward the EU and European organizations, with the EU prescribing concrete conditions for cooperation: a democratic parliamentary order, market economy, and civil state.

Relations and cooperation with the European Union can no longer be reduced solely to the economic sphere, despite its obvious primary importance. Full account must be taken of the EU's role as one of the key actors in the broader area of European policy and, additionally, with its increasing activity, in the military-security sphere. The approach to the normalization and promotion of relations and cooperation with the European Union must, therefore, start from its prominent role in all aspects of intra-European relations as a whole.

Although Russia has a largely altered global geostrategic role stemming from its problems of internal transformation, it is still one of the key actors in international politics and plays an important role in the Balkans. In view of the numerous historical, traditional, and cultural ties, Yugoslavia can develop its relations with Moscow, as well as with other former Soviet republics, without the political burden characteristic of the period when the USSR existed. Especially important for Belgrade are economic links with Russia and CIS countries. Their development, however, requires adaptation to the entirely new circumstances of free market and competition.

Relations with the United States require the greatest attention. In addition to the undoubtedly decisive influence it has on Yugoslavia's access to international political and economic institutions, the United States is increasingly reinforcing its position in Europe. Over the past few years, the United States has exercised a growing influence in the former Eastern bloc countries and, more importantly for Yugoslavia, in Southeastern Europe by using both its diplomatic leverage and military presence independently or within NATO. The Dayton Agreement and the American engagement in Eastern Slavonia ensure for America a long-term role in the territories of Bosnia and Herzegovina, Croatia, and Serbia, and the American-inspired Southeast European Cooperation Initiative (SECI) makes this engagement still broader and more ambitious. Yugoslavia's relations with the United States should therefore be given special attention in Belgrade's foreign policy, since the degree of trust and the nature of contacts and cooperation with America will determine numerous other important interests for Yugoslavia. The normalization of relations with the United States—a difficult, delicate, and exceptionally important issue–is indispensable for Yugoslavia's future.

Yugoslavia is, at the moment, the only state in the Balkans without any kind of arrangement with NATO. The official position of Belgrade toward the Partnership for Peace, NATO enlargement, and the alliance's future role in the Balkans has not been defined yet, which is at least partly understandable. Political forces in Yugoslavia express different and often indefinite attitudes, and public opinion would be rather divided if this issue surfaced in open debate. Besides, Yugoslavia now faces more urgent and immediate tasks: implementation of the Dayton Agreement and definite and full return into the international community with its organizations and institutions (e.g., United Nations, OSCE, IMF), and regional organizations such as the

Central European initiative and the Council of Europe. Since Yugoslavia is gradually emerging from isolation, the country is more ready to solve these immediate problems than to define its long-term foreign policy. However, for Yugoslavia to strengthen its international position, in addition to full implementation of Dayton, Belgrade must consider two important facts. First, all of Yugoslavia's neighbors and all Balkan states have certain arrangements and links with NATO in various forms. It will be a political and geostrategic risk for Yugoslavia to be the only country to stay outside these arrangements. Today Belgrade can hardly exercise the policy of nonalignment that existed for the former Yugoslavia. Second, the development of a civil society with economic reforms and fulfilment of the criteria for international financial organizations is hardly possible without associations with the European integration process, including military and security aspects. Clearly, strategic decision making concerning possible arrangements with NATO depends primarily on the domestic situation and coordination of political forces in Yugoslavia. However, any realistic and rational policy will have to consider very seriously the issue of joining European security structures, whose core, evidently, will be NATO, and finally to make a long-term decision in this regard. Although it is too early to predict all possible conditions of such a relationship, it would clearly require serious internal changes and adaptation to European criteria and standards.

ENDNOTES

1. Ranko Petkovic, "Effects of the Yugoslav Crisis upon the Balkan Situation," *CSS Survey* 3 (March 1996): 5.

2. Serguey Russev, "Instability factors in Southeastern Europe," *CSS Survey* 10 (October 1996): 5.

3. Karl Bildt, "Europe and Bosnia: Lessons of the Past and Paths for the Future," *CSS Survey* 17 (May 1997): 2.

4. George Politikis and Charalambos Tsardanidis, "Balkans: The Political and Economic Process of Transformation," *The Southeast European Yearbook, 1994-95* (Athens: Hellenic Foundation for European and Foreign Policy, 1995), 556.

5. Bildt, "Europe and Bosnia," 6.

6. Dimitrios Triantaphyllou, "An Appraisal of the Evolving European Security Structure and Its Impact on the Ex-Communist States of the Balkans," *The Southeast European Yearbook, 1994-95* (Athens: Hellenic Foundation for European and Foreign Policy, 1995), 581.

7. Petkovic, "Effects of the Yugoslav Crisis," 3.

8. F. Stephen Larrabee, "Implications for Transatlantic Relations," in *The Implications of the Yugoslav Crisis for Western Europe's Foreign Relations* (Chaillot Papers) (Paris: Institute for Strategic Studies–Western European Union, 1994), 3.

9. Ibid., 18.

10. Willy de Clercq, "Benefits of European Integration and Yugoslavia," *CSS Survey* 15 (March 1997): 3-4.

11. See Stojan Babic, "Comments on the Program of Radical Economic Reforms Elaborated by Group of 17," *CSS Survey* 15 (March 1997): 11.

INTRA-ALLIANCE DISPUTE:
THE CASE OF GREECE AND TURKEY
Thanos Veremis

The most important foreign policy and security considerations of Greece since 1974, when Turkey invaded Cyprus, center on relations with Turkey. In addition to the occupation of Cyprus, Greek-Turkish tensions in the 1970s and 1980s revolved mainly around the delimitation of the continental shelf in the Aegean Sea, which brought the two countries close to war in 1976 and 1987. Subsequent efforts by Greek prime minister Andreas Papandreou and Turkish president Turgut Ozal to discover a modus vivendi based on a peaceful resolution of differences in 1988 foundered on the European Community's negative reply to the Turkish application for membership a year later. Deprived from a vital incentive to pursue a Greco-Turkish détente, subsequent Turkish governments have been less willing to revive the Papandreou-Ozal initiative.[1]

In March 1995, Greece lifted its objections to Turkey's entry into a European Union (EU) Customs Union agreement, with the understanding that the application of Cyprus for EU membership would enter the "accession talks" stage in Brussels following the completion of the Intergovernmental Conference in 1997. This important gesture elicited no positive response from Tansu Ciller's government. A series of incidents between the two states that began in 1994 over Greece's right to extend its territorial waters from six to twelve miles, reached a high point on 8 June 1995 when the Turkish parliament granted Ciller's government license to take whatever measures necessary, including military action, if Greece proceeded to extend its territorial sea.

Then, in January 1996 a team of Turkish journalists removed a Greek flag from the barren islet of Imia in the Dodecanese complex and hoisted a Turkish one. Greek soldiers replaced the Greek flag, and Foreign Minister Theodore Pangalos considered the affair closed until Ciller placed an official claim on that and many other Greek islets and commenced a confrontation that almost led to war. American mediation defused the crisis but yet another item, this time a territorial claim, was added to the overburdened agenda of Greek-Turkish problems.

Besides the United States, NATO became involved in an effort to mediate between its two member-states. Secretary General Javier Solana proposed confidence-building measures to avoid crises from breaking out. In July 1996 the EU Council of Ministers issued a declaration stating that relations between Turkey and the EU should be guided by respect for international law, international agreements, and the sovereignty and territorial integrity of the EU member-states.[2]

In April 1997 Greece and Turkey agreed with the proposal of the Dutch presidency of the EU to establish a committee of experts to study bilateral problems. In his letter of 16 May to Dutch minister of foreign affairs Hans Van Mierlo, Pangalos pointed out that the exchange of views between the experts was "neither a political dialogue nor an arbitration." It was presumably an exercise to promote détente.

Of the two Turkish experts, former ambassador to Washington Sukru Elekdag had authored an article, "2 1/2 War Strategy," one year before assuming his new position. Elekdag believes that Greece and Syria together, "with their claims on

Turkey's vital interests," prevent his country from enjoying the peace dividend. Unlike other officials who attribute the Turkish military buildup to eastern and northern threats, the former ambassador promotes the novel view that Turkey must always be in a state of readiness to wage two and one-half wars (against Greece, Syria, and the Kurds). Allegations of Greek support of the PKK (Kurdish Workers Party) and a Greek "strategic control belt" around Turkey, with Cyprus as its cornerstone, abound in his text. That the Turkish government has chosen Elekdag to contribute to Greek-Turkish détente is hardly encouraging for the prospects of the exercise.[3]

The Necmettin Erbakan-Ciller coalition government of July 1996 was too preoccupied with opposition from the Turkish military and Western criticism to resume pressures on Greece, but it did reiterate the allegation that there are "gray zones" in the Aegean that have not been defined by treaties.

Western journalists, who on other occasions had refrained from voicing their views on questions of principle, raised their objections against the Ciller-Erbakan alliance. The *Washington Post*'s Jim Hoagland accused Ciller of striking a "cynical" deal to save herself from legal prosecution and for turning a blind eye to the brutalities of the military. "The military has in fact been throwing its weight around in this time of domestic uncertainty, stroking the fires of nationalism by aggressively courting confrontation with Greece and smacking around Turkey's own citizens and guerrillas in Iraq and Iran."[4] The *Wall Street Journal*, on the other hand, with its "Get Serious about Turkey" editorial made no bones about its view of democracy. "While the West waits for the seemingly inevitable collapse of this [i.e., Erbakan's] government, its strategy should be to reaffirm its commitment to a Western-oriented Turkey without conferring undue legitimacy on its titular head. That includes affirming in every way possible Western commitment to Turkey's military, which strongly values its relations to NATO."[5] This shortsighted pragmatism may or may not serve American priorities in the region, but it helps to sustain the anomaly of an institutionalized military presence in Turkish politics.

The coalition's removal from power allowed a new Greek-Turkish rapprochement to materialize, engineered by U.S. secretary of state Madeleine Albright in the Madrid NATO summit meeting of July 1997. An agreement signed by Greek prime minister Costas Simitis and Turkish president Suleyman Demirel provided that the two sides would abstain from coercion and other initiatives that would affect each other's legitimate vital interests and would respect the provisions of international agreements.[6]

Throughout the Greek-Turkish disputes, Greece has proposed that the continental shelf issue, and, since 1996, the Imia islet's regime, be referred to the International Court of Justice for adjudication. Such an option would exclude confrontational attitudes and would spare politicians on both sides from domestic embarrassment. Turkey, however, insists that all differences between the two states be discussed on a bilateral political basis. Although such talks did occur in the past (1977-81), they failed to produce results. Furthermore, Greece believes that Turkey is constantly burdening the agenda with new claims so that, if bilateral negotiations occur, they will take place only on a Turkish-made agenda.[7]

The Simitis government that won the elections of October 1996 has quietly disavowed the Papandreou tradition in domestic and foreign affairs. The new leader of the Panhellenic Socialist Movement (PASOK) is in every sense the antithesis of his charismatic and populist predecessor. His main priority, to which he subordinated all other considerations, has been to achieve convergence with EU criteria in order to join the Economic and Monetary Union (EMU). Foreign Minister Theodore Pangalos's affirmations that Turkey can rightly belong in Europe surprised his EU colleagues and, when linked with the Madrid agreement, point to a policy that seeks to protect Greece's foremost pursuit of EMU membership from being sidetracked by unforeseen external crises. Although Simitis secured a popular mandate that extends well into the constituency of the New Democracy opposition, he has still to deal with a number of vocal PASOK deputies who oppose his policies and criticize his "modernizing" supporters in parliament.

Governing Greek-Turkish relations are perceptions that each side nurtures for the other. In terms of the Aegean, Turkey believes that Greece wants to transform it into a "Greek lake," while Greece believes that Turkey aspires to make inroads in the area at the expense of Greek sovereignty in the eastern Aegean islands. On the whole, Greece's policy is centered on defending the territorial status quo, while Turkey appears to be challenging certain legal features that have remained unchallenged for a long time.

With Cyprus, attitudes vis-à-vis the status quo are reversed. The Turkish Cypriots and Turkey are not entirely unhappy with the status quo, while the Greek Cypriots would very much like to see a reunited Cyprus. Security considerations weigh heavily in each side's willingness to find a solution. The Turkish Cypriots feel secure with 35,000 Turkish troops in the north while the Greek Cypriots are insecure for the same reason. The prospect of EU membership has raised Greek Cypriot hopes that this may inhibit Turkey's willingness to use force in the future and that membership may facilitate a reunification of the divided island. The Turkish Cypriots and Turkey believe that such a development would remove Cyprus from Turkey's strategic control and will enhance the position of the Greek majority.

Cyprus and Aegean issues are not officially linked in Greece's current policy toward Turkey, but, in fact, the former constitutes a major catalyst in Greek-Turkish relations. The island has remained divided since Turkey occupied the northern third in 1974, in the immediate aftermath of the coup organized by the Greek military dictatorship against the island's president, Archbishop Makarios. The Turkish forces displaced the Greek Cypriot element and established the entire 18 percent Turkish Cypriot community in a self-proclaimed state in the north. Repeated resolutions of the United Nations urging a withdrawal of foreign troops from Cyprus and intercommunal talks to reconstitute the divided island have been fruitless.

The round of talks between Turkish Cypriot leader Rauf Denktash and Cyprus president Glafcos Clerides began in New York in July 1997 and continued in Glion, Switzerland, under UN mediator and special Cyprus envoy Diego Cordovez. The objective of reuniting the island under a bizonal, bicommunal federation was overtaken by the prospect of accession discussions between the government of

Cyprus and the European Union in 1998. Turkey maintains Cyprus cannot join the EU without the consent of the Turkish Cypriots, or before Turkey itself is admitted. This attitude is rejected by the EU Council of Ministers and the European Commission, which hold that the accession of Cyprus to the trading bloc would assist the effort of a settlement of its problems. Even before the round of intercommunal discussions commenced, a threatening agreement concluded for the closer integration of the Turkish Cypriot breakaway state with Turkey, indicating the latter's reluctance to improve possibilities of Cyprus's accession by facilitating the reconciliation of the two communities.

Glion was predictably a failure. In a press conference after the breakdown of the discussions, Rauf Denktash declared: "I made no secret of the fact that we would not talk if the EU starts negotiating with Cyprus." Sir David Hannay, the special British envoy on Cyprus who was present, told the Associated Press: "The Turkish side can say anything it likes, but it is not in its right to tell the EU, of which it is not a member, how its going to handle its affairs. The EU is going to do one thing, and one thing only, which is the opening of negotiations with Cyprus. . . . I do not believe that that will be changed."[8]

German and British officials advised the government of Cyprus to consider reconciliation with the Turkish Cypriot community, practically as a prerequisite for membership to the EU. After developments in Glion it became increasingly obvious that the opposition of the Turkish Cypriot leadership to accession is a policy dictated by Turkey and will not change, even if the two communities agreed to a reunified Cyprus. Denktash is in line with Turkey's position when he threatens to integrate the north of the island with Turkey if accession talks between Cyprus and the EU are not abandoned. It is, therefore, becoming clear to EU members that denying Cyprus membership if it does not concede to an understanding with Turkey, which excludes accession talks, is an exercise in futility.

Throughout the summer of 1997 the spirit of Madrid was severely tried. Americans persisted in their attempt to reconcile the two sides, in spite of indications that neither was prepared to make concessions–Greece, because the opposition within PASOK precluded conciliatory gestures beyond Madrid, and Turkey, because the expected ban on Erbakan's Islamic Refah had sent most parties scrambling for position in the competition for its hard-line political constituency.

In the Luxembourg EU summit meeting of 12-14 December 1997, Turkey failed to make the list of candidates for accession due to its poor human rights record, highly strained relations with Greece, and its negative position on Cyprus. The EU's fifteen leaders, however, invited Ankara to attend the European Conference to be held in Britain in 1998. The official Turkish reaction combined bitterness for the rebuff, with an attitude that dismissed the importance of EU membership for Turkey. On 16 December, Turkish foreign minister Ismail Cem threatened that Ankara would proceed with the annexation of northern Cyprus if the EU began admission talks with the Cypriot government in March 1998. These developments will most certainly have a negative impact on Greek-Turkish relations in the coming months. Turkish violations of Greek airspace have been stepped up, and Cypriot officials fear military action on the island.[9]

At the end of December 1997, Ankara announced its decision to conduct military exercises in the Aegean throughout January 1998. The maneuvers were planned in areas where Turkey disputes Greek sovereignty, including the Kalogiri islets in the middle of the Aegean and the artillery range of the island of Andros. This protracted exercise threatened to impede civil aviation flights between the Greek mainland and the islands and obliged the Greek armed forces to remain in a state of alert for a month. The United States has through its ambassador to Athens, Nicholas Burns, exercised its restraining influence on both sides. It declared its support of Greece's position on the islets but reiterated that it recognizes only six (not ten) miles as Greece's sovereign airspace.[10]

The Russian S-300 missiles order by Cyprus, which elicited strong Turkish reaction, came at the end of a protracted upgrading of Turkey's military systems (including orders of advanced tactical missile systems [ATACMs] and air refueling capability) and the continuous violation of the Republic's airspace by Turkish fighters. The configuration of forces on Cyprus, the strategic advantage of the Turkish side on the green line dividing the island in two, and finally the proximity of Turkey and the remoteness of Greece make it exceedingly obvious that a military solution could not favor the Greek Cypriots. The S-300 missiles can only make sense as a ground-to-air weapon of anti-aircraft defense. Given Turkey's reluctance to accept a no-fly zone over Cyprus and the vulnerability of Cypriot airspace and its constant violation, the S-300 missiles constitute a minor correction in the republic's vast military disadvantage vis-à-vis Turkey or a bargaining chip to be exchanged for the demilitarization of the island, repeatedly proposed by President Clerides.[11]

The decision of Turkey's constitutional court on 16 January 1998 to ban the Islamic National Salvation Party and the exclusion of its leader, Necmettin Erbakan, from parliamentary politics for five years has created a setback in the country's democratic process. There is little doubt that the leadership of the armed forces provided the force behind this decision. The Turkish military, as the ultimate guarantors of Kemal Ataturk's secular doctrine, has thus succeeded in excluding a significant segment of society from being represented in parliament. The list widens. The Kurds, the Alevis, the nonnationalist left-wingers and now the adherents of the Refah Party constitute more than half of Turkey's population. Instead of coopting them into the system, the military has chosen the exclusion of ethnic, religious, and social groups that do not fit the Kemalist ideology.

As Shireen Hunter put it in her influential *Turkey at the Crossroads: Islamic Past or European Future?* "Kemalism has failed to engender a strong sense of common national identity and solidarity in Turkey because, despite its assimilationist and homogenizing tendencies, it has not succeeded in blunting ethnic and linguistic differences. . . . Kemalism has also at best only partially succeeded in supplanting Islam as the spiritual foundation of Turkish society. Nor has Ataturkian secularism won the acceptance and approval of all Turks."[12]

The present paradox in Turkish politics is that the military runs the state via Mesut Yilmaz, a politician of the non-Kemalist tradition. A coalition, or better still, a merger of his Motherland Party (ANAP) and the True Path Party (another non-Kemalist force) still under Ciller, has become the army's best hope for countering

Islam in Turkey. If the officers had allowed politics to take their course, the two centrist parties with their Islamic wings could have attracted in time disillusioned voters from Erbakan's camp, had he been allowed to complete his term in office. If the constituency of Refah now rallies around the new Islamist party and does not split into moderates and hard-liners, then the military will have failed even in terms of tactics.

Greek observers of developments in Turkey are worried about what the military will choose to do next. If the outcry against the Islamic exclusion widens, the time-honored prescription of picking a war with a neighbor to divert attention and rally the Turks around the flag might be applied.

In March 1998, an EU program of support to environmental improvements in certain Greek islands elicited a Turkish official statement that reiterated the gray area principle. Four inhabited islands of the eastern Aegean–Fourni, Agathonisi, Pharmakonisi, and Pserimos–were deemed of dubious Greek sovereignty by the Turks. The Greek Ministry of Foreign Affairs disclosed the allegation on 28 April with a predictable impact on public opinion.

The likelihood of war, although not imminent, cannot be overruled if at least one of the two sides considers it seriously as an instrument of policy. There is little doubt that war would alter the present parameters in Greek-Turkish relations and indeed of those determining the status quo in the Eastern Mediterranean.

NATO will be the first casualty from such a war, and its credibility will suffer irreparably. The most likely battlefield would develop around some Greek islands. If the Turkish forces take advantage of the surprise factor and manage to capture one or more islands, then it would be reasonable to assume that a militarization of Greece will take place throughout the following decade and a continuation of hostilities will ensue for the foreseeable future. Obviously, this would mean the end of Turkey's prospects in the EU, its decline as a crossroad for energy transfers from East to West, and Russia's ascent as the main regulator of the traffic of oil and gas to Europe. If a Turkish military operation against the islands fails, this would have serious domestic repercussions in Turkey. Failure would damage the credibility of the Turkish military, whose mettle has not been tried in full-scale warfare since World War I, and would unleash anti-Kemalist sentiments that may usher in a transformation of the state. Greece's economy would suffer badly, but, depending upon the outcome, parliamentary democracy might survive the hardships of the war.

If rational choice prevails in decisions of war and peace, it is almost certain that the present crisis, protracted as it may be, will one day make way for the blooming of common endeavor. Discovering opportunities of mutual interest between Greece and Turkey appear slim at this particular juncture. Yet during the better days of the 1988 Davos talks, the Committee of Economic Cooperation, set up to record possible common undertakings, suggested an impressive number of propositions such as Greek-Turkish joint ventures, cooperation in tourism and communications, and the founding of a common chamber of commerce, among other projects.[13] Under conditions of détente Greece will be able to pursue its convergence policy and its stabilization role in the Balkans, while Turkey can realize its aspiration to become the junction of energy transfers between east and west.

The most imminent crisis that may offer Turkey an opportunity to wage a limited war in Cyprus and ensure the Finlandization of the island is the S-300 issue. Although the government of Cyprus has attempted to connect the deferment of the missiles' delivery with the establishment of a no-fly zone over the island, the Turks overrule any concession that will question their military control of the entire region, north and south. The United States and the EU in pressing Clerides to withdraw the S-300 factor without a tradeoff are not only violating the principle of the right to self-defense of a dwarf (Cyprus) at the mercy of a giant (Turkey), but unwittingly confirming Turkey's policy of establishing its unquestioned military presence in the region.

Besides the current differences between Greece and Turkey, there is a more lasting cleavage between the two states that blocks any effort to solve their problems. They are set apart by their level of democratic rule, political stability, distribution of income, role of the military in decision making, human rights record, and overall standard of living. Such divergence influences each side's strategy toward the other. Greece would prefer the tools of the community of states to which it belongs: law, international organizations, and the mediation of the European Union. It aspires to draw Turkey into an integration process that would encourage it to play by the European rules. Turkey, however, would like to establish its own pecking order in the region, determined by size, military power, and geostrategic significance and relying on bilateralism in its relations with Greece.

Greece's best hope is that Turkey's economic development may eventually bridge the gap in perceptions so that military power will cease to be viewed as a major instrument of foreign policy. That the Turkish military will relinquish its role in politics by its own free will, however, appears highly unlikely. It is therefore predictable that Turkey's policy in the foreseeable future will be limited to the economic sphere.

ENDNOTES

1. T. Veremis, "Greek-Turkish Relations and the Balkans," *The Southeast European Yearbook 1991* (Athens: ELIAMEP, 1992), 238.

2. Carol Migdalovitz, "Greece and Turkey: Aegean Issues–Background and Recent Developments," *CRS Report from Congress*, 21 August 1997 (Washington, DC: Congressional Research Service, 1997), 4-5.

3. Sukru Elekdag, "2 1/2 War Strategy," *Perceptions: Journal of International Affairs* 1, no. 1 (March-May 1996): 33-57.

4. Jim Hoagland, "Political Con Game in Turkey," *Washington Post*, 11 July 1996, A25.

5. *Wall Street Journal*, 16 August 1996.

6. Migdalovitz, "Greece and Turkey," 7-8.

7. Yannis Valinakis, *Greece's Security in the Post-Cold War Era* (Ebenhausen: Stiftung Wissenschaft und Politik, 1994), 27-34.

8. *War Report*, no. 54 (September 1997), 16-34.

9. "Turkey Loses Its Balance," *Washington Post*, 18 December 1997.

10. Kostas Iordanidis, "Oi vrachonisides kai i Tourkia" (The Islets and Turkey), *Kathimerini*, 11 January 1998.

11. Yannis Valinakis, *Me orama kai programma* (With Vision and Program) (Athens: ELIAMEP, 1997), 91-100.

12. Shireen T. Hunter, *Turkey at the Crossroads: Islamic Past or European Future?* CEPS Paper no. 63 (Brussels, 1995), 122-23.

13. Panos Kazakos and Panos Liargovas, *I Ellinotourkiki economiki synergasia* (The Greco-Turkish Economic Cooperation) (Athens: ELIAMEP-Papazisis, 1997). This work contains a full menu of fields on which the two states could develop their cooperation.

THREATS FACING HUMANKIND
AND THE SEARCH FOR AN ADEQUATE RESPONSE
Theodore Couloumbis

Can the international system, with its substandard regulatory institutions, survive the multiple challenges it is facing? To ask an even more basic question, can the human race itself survive without drastically changing its global and regional institutional structures?

The way we respond to these and similar questions depends heavily on our assumptions regarding the processes that characteristically attend the genesis, growth, maintenance, and even death of political and social institutions, such as governments, political parties, pressure groups, international organizations, and multinational corporations. Are social and political institutions spontaneous and even accidental phenomena, or are they conscious human inventions aimed to serve concrete human needs and to facilitate collective living? Our view is that social and political institutions reflect, for the most part, conscious efforts of individuals and groups to provide collective security and needs satisfaction and to facilitate, through various regulatory mechanisms, the challenge of collective living.

The oldest enemies of humankind have been hunger, war, and disease. In this century–and primarily as a result of technological growth–we have added new and purely human-produced challenges to our existence. Collective dangers from environmental pollution, high noise levels, climate alterations, opinion control, and nuclear holocaust are twentieth-century phenomena. Scientists are warning us against destabilizing important equilibriums in the biosphere that might expose our planet to acute if not ultimate dangers. The limits of finite resources of food, energy, and production are within sight. And population growth, if unchecked, is certain to aggravate all of these challenges.

Following the decolonization of large portions of the earth, the nation-state became clearly the predominant form of political organization on the international scene. By and large, national governments have sought to redistribute income through taxation and public expenditures; to provide for public needs, such as roads, canals, dams, and fortifications; to regulate transportation and communications; to stimulate and finance education; to ensure that crime is controlled; and, in general, to see that public order is kept. Above all, national governments have assumed the responsibility for defense against external threats.

Regardless of the relative effectiveness of governments in combatting purely national problems, one thing remains clear: National governments are not institutionally equipped to face a number of challenges that transcend national boundaries. Environmental pollution, natural-resource exhaustion, multinational corporate growth, international terrorism, transnational crime and narcotics syndicates, and mass population movements are the types of problems that lend themselves to international and supranational regulatory practices. The international institutions that have been developed so far do not have the authority and capacity to legislate and enforce the necessary regulatory measures for combatting such problems. Eventually, if past practices offer any guidance, the people of this earth will be forced to develop complementary supranational, national, transnational, and subnational institutions to ensure at least the minimum goal of global survival. The international system, as we know it today, is likely to change, and traditional concepts, such as national sovereignty, nonintervention, and noninterference in domestic affairs, are likely to be watered down considerably, if not eventually abandoned.

In the evolving post-Cold War architecture of global politics, the European Union together with North America, Japan, and the remaining advanced states belonging to the Organization for Economic Cooperation and Development (OECD) comprise a regional platform of political stability and economic interdependence. Unfortunately, vast regions of what we used to call the Third World, as well as parts of the post-Communist Balkans and the former Soviet Union, are still in a state of real or potential fluidity and instability.

With the passage of time, the gap in economic levels of wealth and development is growing rather than shrinking. The countries of the planet's North tend to be importers of raw materials (especially oil), and they process and export finished goods. The countries in the South are raw-material and agricultural-product exporters, and they import (maintaining a sizable trade imbalance) manufactured goods. In the North the economies are capital-intensive and the cost of labor is high, while in the South the economies are labor-intensive and labor is cheap. Both in the North and the South there are high rates of unemployment, but the advanced and industrialized states of the North afford safety-net mechanisms and social welfare institutions that tend to cushion the shocks, tempering attendant challenges to political stability.

The Human Development Report 1996, published by the United Nations Development Program (UNDP), documents the new "bipolarity" that is now defining the post-Cold War structure of the international system. The world is cleanly divided between the rich and the poor, and the gap is growing rather than shrinking. For example, of the $23 trillion global GDP in 1993, the developing countries, comprising 80 percent of the planet's population, accounted for only $5 trillion. The poorest 20 percent of the world's population experienced a sharp decline in their share of global income from 2.3 to 1.4 percent. Not surprisingly, the share of the richest 20 percent rose from 70 to 85 percent during the same period. Today the ratio of the shares of the global pie between the rich and the poor is 61 to 1, up from 30 to 1 in 1960. Further, the gap in per capita income, between the industrial and developing worlds, tripled from $5,700 in 1960 to $15,400 in 1993. The UNDP report gloomily reminds us that "the assets of the world's 358 billionaires exceed the combined annual incomes of countries with 45 percent of the world's people."[1]

Other figures indicative of comparative quality of life unequivocally demonstrate that there is abundance in the North and abject poverty in the South. Whether we are talking about indicators such as nutrition, housing, health care, literacy, and environmental protection, the gap is huge–and growing.[2]

On another very sensitive statistical indicator–income distribution–one could talk about societies of four-fifths in the comfortable (middle class) category in the North versus the privileged one-tenth in the less egalitarian South, where overwhelming majorities live well below the level of poverty feeding the fires of revolutionary movements (mostly of the anti-Western, fundamentalist variety) that could be likened to a bomb with a short fuse.

Appropriately, the end of the Cold War has been greeted with relief by the people of Western industrialized countries. The specter of nuclear holocaust that had haunted the generations of the Cold War has been nearly eliminated. NATO countries have substituted the word "threat" (stemming from an expansionist and Soviet-controlled Warsaw Pact) with the word "risk" with all the attendant implications for Western defense and security doctrines. Normal "risk-lists" preoccupying NATO strategists today include nuclear-chemical-missile proliferation, international terrorism, narcotics and other transnational criminal organizations, and the specter of political and economic refugees fleeing from regions of famine, pestilence, and war (civil and international) in the global South.

It is the thesis of this paper that all of the so-called risks above are epiphenomena of the growing structural inequality dividing the planet's rich from the planet's poor. A close reading of current patterns unequivocally illustrates that conflicts (and their induced refugee waves) predominantly take place in the world's poor regions where population growth is high, literacy low, infant mortality high, and life expectancy low, all of which facilitate the rise of populist politicians that exploit ethnic, religious, linguistic, and other differences to secure and retain power.

If we accept this thesis, the central question that remains is what, if anything, can be done (especially by the well-to-do in the North, who have the capabilities) to defuse the global time bomb ticking at the foundations of our planet.

European history (and, by extension, global history seen from a Eurocentric perspective) has been divided into three long cycles of relative stability and peace interrupted by two (if World Wars I and II are lumped together) shorter but intense periods of near total warfare. The periods 1648-1789 and 1815-1914 were times of relative structural stability, at least from the vantage point of major European powers. Wars during those two periods were frequently fought but they normally involved marginal territorial rearrangements and were designed to result in limited political and economic gains for each of the belligerents. The drastic reordering of political and territorial structures only took place in major peace conferences such as Vienna (1815), Versailles (1919), and Yalta/Potsdam (1945). These conferences followed on the heels of great and destructive wars that had been fought to the bitter end.

During the first two long periods, peace and stability, always in relative terms, were the products of ideologically compatible regimes functioning in concert as an informal directorate of great powers. Together, they found it to their mutual advantage to manage conflict well below a threshold that could endanger a favorable/tolerable order. Great (unlimited) wars exploded when the leaders of one or more of the great powers (e.g., Napoleon in the nineteenth century and Hitler in the twentieth), whatever their ultimate objectives, sought to achieve world hegemony and thus to alter drastically the preexisting oligopolar balance of the power system.

The post-World War II order (let us call it "the order of Yalta") contained initially all the basic ingredients of global instability, given the total ideological incompatibility of the Eastern and Western camps. The Cold War, however, which was a symbol and an incarnation of extreme intersuperpower hostility, never crossed the hot war threshold. Most analysts seem to credit, with mixed emotions, the nuclear balance of terror for the gradual stabilization of bipolarity.

In the early 1950s, the interbloc relationship began alternating between subcycles of "managed tension" (not crossing a ceiling leading to nuclear war) and "managed détente" (not allowing relaxation to "deteriorate" to total harmony, a condition that would have seriously threatened the orienting logic and the resultant institutions of East-West bipolarity).

Following 1985 and the assumption of power in the former Soviet Union by Mikhail Gorbachev, a large-scale phenomenon, without parallel in post-Westphalian history, began unfolding. The world witnessed drastic revolutionary changes taking place without resort to major internal violence in the regions of the former Soviet Union and the former Warsaw Pact. More importantly, for our purposes here, the world began witnessing the forging of a drastic global power redistribution without resort to war, the midwife of change in days past. No one would have dared assume during the Cold War years that the reunification of Germany, which was at the core of the Yalta order, would have taken place with such remarkable speed and a minimum of turbulence, and that what had been the mighty Soviet Union would have broken up into fifteen parts, each facing deep economic problems and considerable ethnic, autonomist pressures while struggling to forge democracy with a market economy under the most uncertain circumstances.

The historic events of 1989-91 have fundamentally altered the very core of the international system. The relatively bloodless "revolutions" in the former Soviet Union and in most countries of Eastern Europe, the peaceful reunification of Germany, the process of voluntary dissolution of the Warsaw Pact and the Council of Mutual Economic Assistance (CMEA), the significant progress made in nuclear and conventional arms control, the Gulf War (as a response to Iraq's regional aggression) under the United Nations Security Council's legitimizing umbrella, and the civil/constitutional conflict in former Yugoslavia all are clear indications that the Cold War and bipolarity are conditions of the past.

Most analysts/commentators have accepted the notion that our planet has crossed the threshold of the post-Cold War era. But what kind of profile will this successor era assume? Is our planet on the way to developing a new "world order" based on premises of respect for the territorial integrity of states, enhancement and consolidation of democratic institutions, the protection of the human rights of all the citizens of all states, and institutionalization of structures and processes for the peaceful settlement of international and intrastate disputes? Or are we moving toward a period of disorder, disorientation, fluidity, ethnic separatism, and escalating economic protectionism, all resulting in higher frequency and intensity of local conflicts? Will the so-called "limited wars," which have been taking place in the troubled South of our planet, with the Middle East (and sub-Saharan Africa) occupying the apex of a pyramid of global conflict, continue to plague much of humankind?

In a world where a number of states still possess awesome military capabilities (including weapons of nuclear mass destruction), there is no rational substitute for a system of global order, enjoying the backing of major centers of military and economic power, which can provide for adequate institutional mechanisms for the peaceful and tolerably just settlement of disputes. The destabilizing vacuum that is being temporarily created by the rapid disintegration of Cold War bipolarity must not be allowed to drift into global anarchy and chaos. After all, there was, despite its dangers, an inherent stability to a bipolar system that was premised on the mutually deterring balance of nuclear terror. The new architecture of global security should, therefore, be based on an implicit, if not explicit, consensus on fundamental premises shared by the world's major centers of power. Needless to say, a great-power consensus on the rules of the international game cannot survive unless it is shared by a considerable number of small and intermediate (in terms of power) states.

If we were to assume the perpetuation of what appears to be a global great power consensus, a series of interlocking international institutions of economic and political cooperation can be further developed and sustained. At the very apex of the new global order it is likely that the North Atlantic Treaty Organization (NATO) will be maintained and politically strengthened. However, this great postwar regional security organization will have to reorient seriously its purposes in order to survive and prosper. Its central function will no longer be to contain Soviet communism but rather to maintain and manage the historic partnership between a North American and a European pillar on each side of the Atlantic. NATO can and will progressively shift to the status of a grand organizational experiment whose main function will be to prevent the gradual drifting apart of its two strong pillars and to protect conditions of Euro-American interdependence based on premises of equality and partnership, thus forming a stable core around which global security can be structured for generations to come.

Following the logic of institutional complementarity (concentric, overlapping, adjacent), NATO, as a security producing structure, is likely to be enhanced by the projected speeding up of the process of integration taking place within the European Union. This union of fifteen European states, most of which are also members of NATO, will invariably emerge as a complex but unified entity not only in the economic but also in the political and security dimensions. The European Union, whether it eventually absorbs existing institutions or develops new structures for EU-wide planning and implementation of common security policies, will most probably have a substantively integrated character by the end of this century.

With two powerful and equal defense pillars that operate on assumptions of partnership, interdependence, mutuality of interests, and common cultural and economic values, NATO will be able to serve as a stable global platform contributing systematically to spill-over integrative processes in other parts of the planet that can be modeled upon tried, tested, and successful institutional experiments that have created nearly unbreakable bonds among the states of the Atlantic Community.

It must be clearly understood, however, that a solitary global island of stability (a two-pillared Atlantic Community) surrounded by a sea of disorder will be doomed to a sorry fate, ultimately sliding to a global in scale confrontation between "haves" and "have-nots" employing (following overt and covert patterns of nuclear proliferation) weapons of mass destruction. Today, therefore, the crucial challenge facing humankind rests on the need to establish a set of complementary and overlapping security structures in areas of potential conflict such as Eastern Europe (including the Balkans), the former Soviet Union, East and Southeast Asia, the Middle East and Mediterranean, Africa, and Central and Latin America.

The institutional vacuum that has been created by the disestablishment of East European international organizations is more than likely going to be filled, at least partially, by parallel sets of association agreements between the countries of Eastern and Southeastern Europe and the European Union. However, with democratization proceeding at various rates of speed and effectiveness in the erstwhile socialist camp, there are a number of new problems (chief among them, the challenge of ethnic autonomist movements) that could easily cross the threshold of armed conflict. The Organization on Security and Cooperation in Europe (OSCE) appears to be slated for a role beyond standard-setting and confidence-building to include conflict prevention, peacekeeping, and peacemaking. It will also become necessary with the passage of time to develop additional subregional economic cooperation and security organizations in Central and Eastern Europe that will mirror and complement the successful institutional models of NATO and the European Union.

The Gulf War has sharpened the sensitivities of global, Middle Eastern, and Mediterranean powers regarding the need to develop ad hoc as well as long-lived institutional mechanisms for the settlement of unresolved disputes, such as the Arab-Israeli and the Palestinian, as well as long-simmering crises of states threatened by partitionist movements throughout the planet. The institutional patterns of the North (especially OSCE) can hopefully be modified for application to regional settings such as the Mediterranean, the Middle East, South Asia, East Asia, Africa, and Central and South America. The disappointing record of conflict management in the Yugoslav civil/constitutional conflagration has been a harsh reminder of the unpreparedness of global and regional institutions to control/prevent complicated intrastate and interethnic conflicts.

Further, in this cursory review of the post-Cold War international system, we must not lose sight of the great potential for peacekeeping available to the United Nations (through the reinforced role of the Security Council and the Secretariat) now that the Security Council's permanent members (with veto privileges) appear to be converging on fundamental questions involving North-North, North-South, and South-South relations. Once again, we must point out the remarkable cohesiveness and staying power demonstrated by a coalition of diverse powers operating under the legitimizing umbrella of the United Nations Security Council, which was brought to bear in order to reverse a clear-cut case of aggression-occupation-annexation perpetrated in 1990 by Saddam Hussein's Iraq.

It has been argued that the most plausible strategy for conflict management in the global South must be premised on assumptions of a functioning "global concert of powers," operating through UN authorized mechanisms for peacekeeping and peace-implementation. But this "firefighter" approach does not tackle the underlying causes of structural inequality that feed the fires of crisis and conflict. What is needed, therefore, beyond firefighting, is a feasible and adequate fire-prevention strategy.

The fundamental question, which we must answer from a normative perspective, is whether the differences and distances in the global setting (North, South, East, and West) make it likely, difficult, or impossible to generate lasting regimes of peaceful and cooperative global coexistence. Without a response to this question, any attempt to devise a feasible global strategy for "fire prevention" will be doomed to failure.

From the enlightened perspective of the economically advanced democracies, there is every incentive to widen and solidify patterns of peace and interdependence across the North-South divide. If the world's rich and powerful fail to contribute substantively and in a timely fashion to the process of economic development of the global South, then they will be undermining the very foundations of peace, stability, and prosperity in their own societies. Economic development in the South will contribute to political stability, lower unemployment and birthrates, and reduce the tension in the current zones of high-conflict quotients. Ultimately, it will reduce the creation of mass refugee waves that so preoccupy the North.

A global "fire-prevention" strategy must be multidimensional. In the cultural dimension, we must cultivate a spirit of mutual understanding and appreciation that will gradually transform the planet into a single space of peaceful and cooperative projects that take advantage of the long and rich religious and secular traditions of Christianity, Islam, Judaism, Hinduism, Buddhism, Confucianism, and other cultures and religions.

In the economic dimension, cooperation should not be considered "philanthropy" by those in the privileged North. The North's investments in labor-intensive enterprises will invigorate the economies of the South and reduce unemployment and resultant pressures for legal and illegal immigration. The removal by the North of protectionist measures targeting the products of the South will permit the growth of exports from South to North and simultaneously will reduce governmental methods that have been perpetuating state monopolies and inefficient public-owned enterprises in the South. Simultaneously, a variety of regional credit, investment, and cooperation programs will gradually reverse current trends in the so-called brain-drain and will permit the citizens of developing states to resist the siren songs of populism, nationalist fanaticism, and fundamentalist exclusivism.

In the political dimension, the institutionalization of bilateral, subregional, regional, and multilateral mechanisms for tension-reduction, dispute resolution, and, in cases of conflict, peacekeeping, peace-building, and humanitarian operations should be at the top of the North's priorities list. But major powers should resist the temptation of becoming participants rather than intermediaries in potential conflict situations.

It appears that after two global confrontations, fought mainly on European soil between 1914-45, West Europeans and North Americans have hit upon a constructive synthesis of realism and idealism in materializing David Mitrany's and Jean Monnet's functionalist dreams. The "end," a political union transcending old and bitter nationalist divisions, has clearly been idealistic. The "means," however, involving discrete, partial, gradual, voluntaristic, functional steps, could be unequivocally termed pragmatic and realistic. The "spillover" effects from the functional into the political sphere defy classification as realist or idealist and represent a masterful amalgam of the products of a timeless debate. Indeed, the challenge for the southern part of our planet, as well as the regions of the former Warsaw Pact, is to emulate this great transnational experiment.

ENDNOTES

1. United Nations Development Program, *Human Development Report 1996* (New York: Oxford University Press, 1996), 2.

2. Ibid., 20-21.